Brasília, Plan and Reality

Brasília, Plan and Reality

A Study of
Planned and Spontaneous
Urban Development

David G. Epstein

University of California Press

Berkeley • Los Angeles • London

UNIVERSITY OF CALIFORNIA PRESS
BERKELEY AND LOS ANGELES, CALIFORNIA

UNIVERSITY OF CALIFORNIA PRESS, LTD.
LONDON, ENGLAND

COPYRIGHT © 1973 BY THE REGENTS OF THE UNIVERSITY OF CALIFORNIA
ISBN: 0-520-02203-3
LIBRARY OF CONGRESS CATALOG CARD NUMBER: 72-186103
DESIGNED BY BOB ODELL
PRINTED IN THE UNITED STATES OF AMERICA

Aos trabalhadores de Brasília, que construíram a nova capital;
Aos trabalhadores de Brasil, que pagaram.

To the workers of Brasília, who built the new capital;
To the workers of Brazil, who paid for it.

Preface

This book is a considerably revised version of my doctoral dissertation. I wanted it to deal with ongoing social trends instead of the merely exotic or the archaic, so often pursued by anthropologists. I also wanted to contribute to knowledge of the differential distribution of wealth and power and the means by which it is maintained, rather than to explore the esoteric calculi of cognition or the intricacies of cross-cousin marriage rules (cf. Sanjek 1969). Research is scarce. To allocate it to the irrelevant is a political act which reduces our opportunity to understand and to act for or against the prevailing arrangement of the political economy. Claims of political neutrality in social science can almost invariably be proven false, and the felony is compounded by airs of ingenuousness about the latent biases that the stances of objectivity, neutrality, and value-freedom usually attempt to obscure. From this viewpoint there follows, of course, no denial of the importance of the highest standards of accuracy in scientific reportage, nor any advocacy of the substitution of propaganda for honest inquiry.

Brasília seemed a good place for me to undertake research along these lines. I had first been there in 1962 and in 1964 lived there for several months while engaged in studies unconnected with the present research. I was struck both by the "feel" of Brasília, quite different from other regions of Brazil I had experienced, and by the contrast between the "planned" area of apartment houses and the squatter settlements and satellite towns—almost a caricature of the social structure of Brazil as a whole. The dramatic experiment of a planned city and its unanticipated results seemed a natural topic for more detailed investigation.

The Foreign Area Fellowship Foundation agreed to support my work, and I am grateful not only for its support but for the fact that the foundation made no effort to control my methods or conclusions. In Brazil, I enjoyed the moral support of the Latin American Social Science Research Center. The research was carried out in Rio de Janeiro and Brasília from late 1966 through the end of 1967.

Professor Marvin Harris, my thesis adviser, is the person who has had the greatest influence on my outlook on anthropology. His friendship, support, and encouragement were vital to this enterprise. To the degree that this effort meets high standards of reportage and analysis, it is because of Professor Harris's influence; in the many ways it falls short of such standards, the fault is mine.

Among the other persons in the United States who have helped me with ideas and comments are Lambros Comitas, Sid Greenfield, Dan Gross, Tony Leeds, Paul Mandell, Nan Pendrell, John Turner, and Charles Wagley.

I am deeply grateful for the help extended to me by many Brazilians of all classes and persuasions. My gratitude is no less by virtue of the fact that prudence suggests that I not mention them by name.

I am especially indebted to my aunt, Sophie Silver, for her devoted assistance in typing the manuscript of this work in dissertation form, and to Beatrice Gould of the Central Stenographic Bureau at the University of California, Los Angeles, for her work on the final version. Esther Beaton redrew the maps.

Many others also provided valuable information and other favors, especially my friends and neighbors in the Social Security Invasion, to whom even a far better account than this one would be but partial repayment. And whatever our differences may have been later, the help extended by my former wife Dilene was generous and well-nigh indispensable.

D. G. E.

Contents

Acronyms

Acronym	Portuguese in full	English translation
BNH	Banco Nacional de Habitação	National Housing Bank
CB	Correio Braziliense	Brasília Courier (daily newspaper)
CEMIG	Centrais Elétricas de Minas Gerais	Minas Gerais Electrical Stations
CODEBRAS	Coordenação de Desenvolvimento de Brasília	Brasília Development Coordination
COHAB	Companhia Habitacional	Housing Company
DCN	Diário do Congresso Nacional	National Congressional Daily
DNOCS	Departamento Nacional de Obras Contra as Sêcas	National Anti-Drought Works Department
DOU	Diário Oficial da União	Official Daily of the Union
FSS	Fundação do Serviço Social	Social Service Foundation
GTB	Grupo de Trabalho de Brasília	Brasília Working Group
IAPB	Instituto de Aposentadoria e Pensões dos Bancários	Bank Employees' Social Security Institute
IAPC	Instituto de Aposentadoria e Pensões does Comerciários	Commercial Employees' Social Security Institute
IAPETEC	Instituto de Aposentadoria e Pensões dos Empregados em Transporte e Cargas	Transport Workers' Social Security Institute
IAPI	Instituto de Aposentadoria e Pensões dos Industriários	Industrial Workers' Social Security Institute

IAPM	Instituto de Aposentadoria e Pensões dos Marítimos	Merchant Marine Social Security Institute
IBGE	Instituto Brasileiro de Geografia e Estatística	Brazilian Geographical and Statistical Institute
IBRA	Instituto Brasileiro de Reforma Agraria	Brazilian Institute of Agrarian Reform
INIC	Instituto Nacional de Imigração e Colonização	National Immigration and Colonization Institute
INPS	Instituto Nacional de Previdência Social	National Social Security Institute
IPASE	Instituto de Previdência e Aposentadoria dos Servidores do Estado	Government Employees' Social Security Institute
JK	Juscelino Kubitschek de Oliveira	Juscelino Kubitschek de Oliveira [President]
NOVACAP	Companhia Urbanizadora da Nova Capital do Brazil	Company to Urbanize the New Capital of Brazil
PDF	Prefeitura do Distrito Federal	Prefecture of the Federal District
PDF-SEC	PDF—Secretaria de da Previdência Social	PDF—Education and Culture Secretariat
PETROBRAS	Petróleo Brasileiro, S.A.	Brazilian Petroleum, Inc.
PSD	Partido Social Democrático	Social Democratic Party
PTB	Partido Trabalhista Brasileiro	Brazilian Labor Party
SAB	Sociedade de Abastecimento de Brasília	Brazilian Supply Company
SAPS	Serviço de Alimentação da Previdência Social	Social Security Food Service
SCS	Setor Comerical Sul	South Commercial Sector
SERFHAU	Serviço Federal de Habitação e Urbanismo	Federal Housing and City Planning Service
SHEB	Sociedade de Habitações Economicas de Brasília	Brasília Economical Housing Company
SHIGS	Setor de Habitaçoes Individuais Geminadas Sul	South Sector of Individual Row Housing

SHIS	Sociedade de Habitacoes de Interêsse Social	Company for Housing of Social Interest
SIA	Setor de Indústria e Abastecimento	Industrial and Supply Sector
SQN	Super Quadra Norte	North [Wing] Superblock
SQS	Super Quadra Sul	South [Wing] Superblock
SUDENE	Superintendéncia de Desenvolvimento do Nordeste	Northeast Development Superintendency
TCB	Transportes Coletivos de Brasília Ltda.	Collective Transport of Brasília, Ltd.
UDN	Uniao Democrática Nacional	National Democratic Union [political party]
USAID	[translation] Agência de Desenvolvimento Internacional dos Estados Unidos	United States Agency for International Development
ZBM	Zona de Baixo Meretrício	Zone of Low Prostitution (slang)

Introduction

This book is about Brasília, and the empirical material it contains deals only with that new capital. Yet the logic of my argument and the process of intellectual formation in which this book is a way station both suggest that some considerations about Brazil as a whole should be presented. The relationship between national-level and local systems is a vexed one, in anthropology as elsewhere, and part of my present work is concerned with this question. Nevertheless it seems to me essential to present my views on this subject as they affected the research presented here.

Dualism is a theme of much of the literature on Brazil (Lambert 1959) and on other underdeveloped countries, not only in discussions of urbanization, but in treatments of regional characteristics, minority and ethnic relations, and economic development.[1] They are supported by evident contrasts in living standards and, in certain cases, life-styles that are the hallmark of underdevelopment in the capitalist world: contrasts between more or less industrialized areas, between more or less prosperous regions, between city and country, between the well-to-do neighborhoods and the squatments and central-city slums. The central error of the dualist approach is to look at the social segments which manifest these contrasts as if they were isolated from one another.

The dualist picture of contemporary national societies is often projected into an image of history that is a contemporary version of nineteenth-century evolutionism—what Hoetink (1965) refers to as the "new evolutionism" of the unilinear variety. While making some allowances for differences between individual countries and regions, this unilinear school describes contemporary world history as the progression of each country from underdeveloped or traditional to developed and modern, and postulates a series of two or sometimes more stages through which all countries are alleged sooner or later to pass. Thus the more "traditional" of the dual

1. For example, see Boeke (1953), Higgins (1961), Ellsworth (1962), Elkan (1963), Dasgupta (1964), and Watanabe (1965).

1

segments is seen as historically more archaic or less advanced, and it can see in the less traditional of the two segments the image of its own future.

Rostow, perhaps the most well known of these unilinear theorists, postulates five states: (*a*) traditional society, (*b*) the preconditions for takeoff, (*c*) takeoff, (*d*) the drive for maturity, and (*e*) high mass consumption (1960: 4–12). Cyril E. Black is more sensitive to the differences between countries, listing seven patterns of modernization, but he nevertheless suggests that all societies (nation-states) do pass through four stages: (*a*) traditional society challenged by modernity, (*b*) the consolidation of modernizing leadership, (*c*) economic and social transformation, and (*d*) the integration of ("modern") society (Black 1966: 67–68).

Influenced by dualist theories of this kind, one could easily enough ascribe most forms of social or economic inferiority to lag on the single path of modernization and development. Writers of this school deny, or more frequently neglect, the possibility that the causes of underdevelopment lie outside the individual society and have to do with the distribution of power and other facets of the *global* society. They prefer to prescribe a strategy for development based heavily on the transformation of the dominant values of the underdeveloped societies, accompanied by prophylactic methods against such "diseases of the transition" as communism, to which societies at this stage of development are said to be particularly vulnerable (Rostow 1960: 162–164). Hence the frequent connection of dualist theory with "liberal-conservative" strategies—community development and education, for instance—for dealing with problems such as those posed by the economic and social conditions of squatters. Such strategies generally seek a smoothing over and acceleration of the transition of the more "backward" national society (or segment of a region or city) to resemble the more "advanced."

Many writers, including Stavenhagen (1968: 14–18), Frank (1967*a*: 143–278; 1967*b*: 45–63), and Prado, Jr. (1966: 43–75), have attacked the unilinear view as applied to Brazilian society as a whole. As we have already indicated, the dualist model is not applicable to the squatter settlements of Brasília: it is inadequate to explain—in fact, even to describe—the relation of the Pilot Plan to the other settlements in the new capital. Just as the dualist viewpoint is connected to a conception of modern history and a theory of development, so the alternative analysis of Brasília's urban expansion, which we shall propose, is connected to a different interpretation of Brazilian society in the context of recent world history.

Andre Gunder Frank has offered a comprehensive model of Brazilian political economy based on relations of dependency. The world "metropolis" or dominant center at the present time is the United States, which has the southern United States as an internal satellite or dependent region[2] and the São Paulo region of Brazil as one of its many international satellites. São Paulo in turn dominates regional centers in Brazil such as Belo Horizonte and Recife, and similar chains of dependence and dominance link these regional centers with smaller units, down to and including the most impoverished and apparently isolated peasant. This is a single, integrated system; the impoverishment and backwardness of each dependent unit relative to its dominating center is accounted for as a product of the dynamics of the system as a whole. Frank lists four major features of this model:

(1) Close economic, political, social and cultural ties between each metropolis and its satellites, which results in the total integration of the farthest outpost and peasant into the system as a whole. This contrasts with the supposed isolation and non-incorporation of large parts of the society according to the dualist model. (2) Monopolistic structure of the whole system, in which each metropolis holds monopoly power over its satellites; the source or form of this monopoly varies from one case to another, but the existence of this monopoly is universal throughout the system. (3) As occurs in any monopolistic system, misuse and misdirection of available resources throughout the whole system and metropolis-satellite cain. (4) As part of this misuse, the expropriation and appropriation of a large part or even all of and more than the economic surplus or surplus value of the satellite by its local, regional, national, or international metropolis (1967a: 146–147).

In historical terms, Latin American underdevelopment is seen to have been produced by European expansion and the development of capitalism. Underdevelopment at one pole of the system is a consequence of development at the other end, not the result of Latin America's failure to make or delay in making the transition from traditional to modern, or feudal to capitalist. Frank is never explicit as to whether he is referring to geographic regions as whole as the upper-level units in his model, or to classes and other stratified groups located within such geographical units. In the case of Brasília this distinction is not crucial, since the classes are largely geographically segregated.

Frank's model provides a framework which explicates the basis for many phenomena of Brazilian society observed by anthropologists, such as several analyses which have been made of patronage and clientage. Wagley, in a brief description of traditional Brazil, for instance, mentions

---

2. Or had. Some analysts believe the "cowboy" or Southern and Western economic interests have taken over from the "Yankee" or Eastern Establishment (Oglesby 1968). This writer endorses most of Frank's views on Brazil, but has no definitive views at this point on the real position of the Southern United States.

the dependence of lower-class people, both rural and urban, on the *patrão* (boss), as a pervasive feature of Brazilian society:

> Essentially, the *patrão*-worker relationship was an economic one, between employer and employee. It was also highly exploitative . . . Yet, the *patrão*-worker relationship was something more than economic. It involved a sense of *noblesse oblige* and paternalism on the part of the employer toward the worker . . . On the part of the worker, it involved a sense of loyalty to the *patrão* (1960: 183).

By extension, the term *patrão* also applies in cases of dependence based on debt rather than employment, and of political loyalty to the local *coronel* (literally, colonel, but also political boss).

In a discussion of the lifeways of rural-urban migrants in Rio de Janeiro, Andrew Pearse suggests that what he calls *populism* is one of the more recent substitutes for the *patrão*-client relationship. Populism is a pattern of political behavior characteristic of emerging urban Brazil, according to Pearse. For the upper classes it represents the maintenance of traditional positions "and authority in the face of the institutions of constitutional democracy" (1961: 201–202). From the viewpoint of the populist politicians it concerns the struggle for political office and is "supported by structures based on clientage in which benefits are handed down in return for votes and personal loyalties" (202). Benefits to the masses include labor legislation and access to services "through the intervention of populist leaders at various levels" (202). Pearse suggests that the system mediates between traditional dependence on the *patrão* for multiple forms of protection and the isolation of the urban industrial worker linked to the centers of power only through his job.

Leeds (1964) offers a model of Brazilian society in which there is a fundamental division between the "classes" and the "masses"; the latter are also referred to (using a term from Anísio Teixeira) as "internally colonized." The upper group is made up of a series of interconnected vertically parallel "oligarchies." Within this field operate informal units: the *panelinha* (little pot) composed of people on the same level, and the *igrejinha* (little church) made up of a leader and a number of his lower-level dependents. Each of these groups is devoted to the exchange of favors among its members. *Panelinha* participants exchange favors by each member drawing on his special area of competence—banking, the customs, law, politics, journalism, and so forth. In the *igrejinha* the leader uses his power to protect and favor the "congregation," while the followers offer the leader support, for example in the form of publicity. *Panelinhas* are also linked vertically with higher and lower units of the same kind: there are federal-level, state-level, and local-level *panelinhas* (1964: 1939).

Greenfield (1966) suggests that in addition to the formal bureaucratic structure of Brazilian society there is an informal structure whose fundamental unit is the *patronage network* which is made up of dyadic patron-client relationships. These are characterized by what Greenfield, citing Foster (1961: 1117), calls "assymetrical reciprocity" (Greenfield 1966: 2): the client offers more to the patron than he receives, but both parties do receive something. The principal commodities supplied by the lowest-level clients are labor service and votes. Votes are exchanged for goods and services controlled by the state—a very large proportion of the total goods and services produced in Brazil. Between the voters and public officeholders a number of intermediaries funnel votes upward and services down.

From the point of view of the underclass, of course, every viable system of classes involves an unequal bargain. The "assymetrical reciprocity" of Greenfield's patronage networks is just one instance of the extreme inequality and exploitation pervading the entire Brazilian and international stratification system.

Each of these four concepts—*patrão*-worker relationships, populism, a series of oligarchies bound together by *igrejinhas* and *panelinhas* on different levels, and patronage networks—is consistent with the more general model offered by Frank. Wagley clearly connects the *patrão* to the export commodities whose production has been the mainstay of the Brazilian economy: he cites coffee and natural rubber, and could have cited sugar, cacao, sisal, and Brazil nuts (*castanha-do-pará*) as well. In the regions dominated directly by such products[3] the local *patrão* was linked to the regional exporting center through ties to the major exporting houses (della Cava 1966: 108), and through them to the overseas metropolis. Pearse explicitly states that the role of populism is to preserve the traditional class relations in an urban setting, where the dependent individuals are workers, and the formal political system one of constitutional democracy. Leeds's discussion of the Brazilian "oligarchies" or specialized hierarchies is confined to the limits of the nation-state, but his description of individual careers as passing "ideally, through a hierarchy of *panelinhas,* mainly identified with the *município,* state and federal political levels" (1964: 1339) jibes with the lower reaches of Frank's model. Greenfield's networks are very similar to the structures associated with Pearse's populism,

3. Even the arid *sertão* of the Northeast was at certain periods devoted to meat production for use in the export commodity-producing coastal regions, and thus in a somewhat indirect fashion was also linked to the export trade (Furtado 1963: 61–66). With the decadence of that trade the entire region remained dependent but followed the pattern of "passive involution" (Frank 1967a: 1966). It has continued to export people (see Chapter V, section I), as well as some minor products such as sisal (Gross 1969).

and show an historical continuity with the *coronelismo* (political bossism) mentioned by Wagley as one form of power exercised by a *patrão*. Greenfield differs from Pearse by casting doubt upon the exclusively urban character of the phenomenon, found by him to exist "throughout the land" (1966: 11) and "within each municipality" (12).

From the point of view of Frank's general model, each of the discussions dealt with above treats a form of dependency which is subsidiary to the general client or satellite status of Brazil vis-à-vis the United States, and formerly, Great Britain. Frank himself suggests a connection between international metropolis-satellite relations, in particular the decline of such traditional exports as sugar and precious minerals, and the persistence of clientelism in the regions affected by the decline. In these "passively involuted" regions clientelism exists, but not simply as a consequence of isolation: "Rather, the clientelism and political opportunism are widely taken advantage of by the national and international metropolis through the chain of metropolises and satellites which reaches to the most supposedly isolated village and farm" (1967a: 167).

This view of Brazilian society as being composed of metropolises and satellites integrated in a vast network of dominance and dependence is applicable to both rural and urban areas. Specifically, it is useful in dealing with the phenomenon of squatting, and thus in explaining the developing urban settlement pattern of Brasília.

The relationship between each metropolis and its satellites, each patron and his clients, is part of the vast social system sketched above. Foster (1961), in dealing with such relations among individuals, refers to the "dyadic contract." Each such connection has special features which should be understood. (1) The relationship is *reciprocal*; each party derives some benefit from it in terms of power or wealth. (2) At the same time, the distribution of benefits is *assymetrical*. The more powerful member systematically derives a larger share of these benefits than the less powerful. (3) While founded on economics, the system of links is *integrated* and includes political-bureaucratic, cultural, and ideological dependency as well; the hegemony of the metropolis is general, though its different aspects may be at times expressed through specialized institutions (which are nevertheless connected and consistent with one another, rather than conflicting).

Over the system as a whole, at each level there are fewer metropolises or dominant units than satellites or dependent units. Thus the system resembles a pyramid with the metropolis at its head and the furthest satellites at its broad base. At least under some conditions, links are formed horizontally as well (alliances of peasants against landlords, underdeveloped against developed nations, and so forth).

The three features above apply to the relationship between the squatment and the city around it as discussed by Leeds, who argues:

From an external point of view, the most important resource of the slum locality [read "squatment"] is, of course, masses of people: in a place like Rio, where perhaps 30% of the city's population lives in "unsightly" *favelas* [squatments], they constitute significant parts of the electorate and of the potencial [*sic*] labor force. They also comprise potencially [*sic*] large forces of riot and rebellion (1966: 13).

Official and upper-class treatment of the squatters consists in the mobilization of their electoral and labor power, and repression of their potential for disorder. On the other hand, the state and the political parties "are brought into the position of doing favors for, carrying out public works in, providing public welfare and relief to" the squatment. These people also derive income from the outside economy. Leeds also points out that some sanctions are available to the locality residents: "riot, disorder, voting non-cooperation or even direct opposition, legal representation, and so on" (1966: 13). Thus the relationship of the locality to the supralocal powers-that-be involves mutual benefit and tacit bargaining—it is reciprocal. It is also assymetrical, for the squatters get far less in services and income than do many other city dwellers.

These three features—reciprocity, assymetry, and integration—also characterize the relation of Brasília's lower-class squatment residents to the government and outside economic institutions. They run through the development of the urban settlement pattern of the new capital from the inception of its construction.

Building Brasília required large numbers of workers and they came from the poorest sections of Brazil, the Northeast (including Bahia) and the Center-West (see Chapter V, section I).

Just as the main strategic resource supplied by Africa in the slavery period was labor, today many underdeveloped regional poles of economies such as Brazil's have as a principal function the exportation of cheap labor. In Brazil this function is fulfilled by the Northeast and to a lesser extent by some other rural areas, as in Minas Gerais. The Northeast regularly disgorges migratory streams in accordance with the exigencies of the economy—to the Amazon if the revival of the rubber trade becomes necessary, to the industries of São Paulo, to Brasília when a new capital is abuilding. Minas Gerais, a secondary source of such migrants, is also a case of "passive involution" (Frank 1967a: 156–159). To the extent that the conditions which underlie this exportation of human beings thereby serve the needs of the extant economic and political elites, serious doubts must arise as to the prospects for success of programs administered by these same elites with the declared intention of combating regional underdevelopment.

Additional connections between the national level social structure and the evolution of Brasília's settlement plan are manifested in the process of planning, the symbolic content of the Lúcio Costa plan, and the public works complex which characterized the work of the Kubitschek administration in building the city. All of these matters are dealt with in subsequent chapters.

CHAPTER I

The Problem of Brasília:
Duality or Dependence?

I. The Problem

Building Brasília, Brazil's new national capital in the interior, was perhaps the largest single coordinated city-building effort in modern times. It was a major experiment in city planning, for the entire city was to have been built according to a plan submitted by Brazilian architect Lúcio Costa (1957), incorporating modern city planning doctrines which had never before been applied on so large a scale. From the standpoint of economic growth, Brasília's construction required the allocation over a period of years of a large part of Brazil's potential economic surplus (Baran 1957) to an investment project of a kind not usually thought central to economic development, by a government whose leading slogan was "developmentism" (*desenvolvimentismo*). Yet there has been little scientific study of the Brasília experience, an omission which this work attempts to remedy. Besides the voluminous esthetic literature, there have been two geographical studies (Ludwig 1966; Mandell in preparation) and two broad sample surveys, one on migration (Pastore 1968, 1969) and the other on communications (Samaniego 1967).

In the years before work on the new city was started, Brazilian cities had begun to suffer more and more from problems of transportation, housing, public utilities, and distribution, which were sources of frustration to all but the most wealthy residents of the national metropolises of Rio de Janeiro and São Paulo and of the regional centers such as Belo Horizonte and Recife. Brasília, a new, planned capital, seemed to offer hope of relieving population pressures on existing cities and providing dramatic new solutions to the problems of Brazilian urban life.

By 1967, ten years after construction began in earnest, Brasília had deviated significantly from the original plan. Some of these differences resulted from failure to complete parts of the city called for in that document (Costa 1957), such as an intimately scaled city center to offset the vast Monumental Axis. Others are problems of orientation, such as inconsistencies in street numbering and the social prestige of certain parts of the city, not anticipated in the plan.

The most far-reaching of the deviations, however, is that a majority of the urban population of Brasília (that is, of the Federal District) lives in areas built up in contradiction to the plan, while much of the area originally earmarked for construction remains empty. Squatter settlements, so typical of other Brasilian and Latin American cities, have sprung up in Brasília as well. They housed 10 percent of the population in 1967, but their effect on the evolution of the city's settlement pattern has been even more profound than that figure suggests.

There are four major areas of settlement in Brasília (see map 1): (1) The central planned area known as the *Pilot Plan*[1] contains the famous superblocks and some individual row houses, as well as a few individual free-standing residences like those in North American suburbs. The wealthiest and most prestigious residents of Brasília live in this part of the city. (2) The *satellite towns* (*cidades satélites*) have the largest total population. They are nuclei grouped around the central area and separated from it by expanses of open space. These settlements are recognized as permanent and legal by the government, and town plans far less ambitious than Lúcio Costa's original are being applied to them. In parts of these towns, public low-cost housing in individual units is being built. (3) Several *construction camps* operated by private companies and official agencies are licensed by government, but are considered temporary. (4) *Squatter settlements* are not legally recognized, their residents lack formal title to the land they live on, and government officials frequently proclaim their intention to "eradicate" such settlements. No term for such settlements is fully satisfactory: *Shantytown* is belied by the fact that in Rio de Janeiro and Salvador many houses in such settlements are not shanties. Even *squatter settlement* or *squatment* is not a perfect term, since the government in Brasília had a major role in localizing people who thus are only squatters in a narrow legal sense. Most important is that squatments be clearly distinguished from slums (Portuguese *cortiços, cabeças de pôrco*) where residents pay rent and the buildings are run-down townhouses or housing built for rental to poor people for profit. The largest squatment in Brasília is the Social Security Invasion.[2] On the average, its

1. This term is applied both to the proposal by Lúcio Costa (1957) and to the central area of the city built in accordance with Costa's document.
2. A translation of the Portuguese *Invasão do IAPI*. *Invasão* means "invasion" and is one term applied in Brazil to squatter settlements. The IAPI is the Industrial Workers' Retirement and Pension (i.e., Social Security) Institute, which ran the hospital behind which the invasion began. Hence the name. The IAPI has since been merged into the INPS (National Social Security Institute).

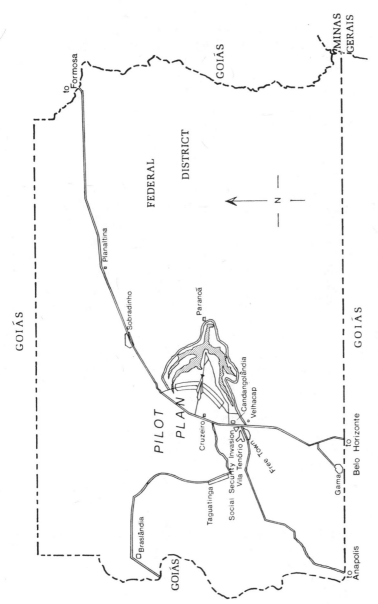

MAP 1. Major urban localities in the Federal District, 1967.

inhabitants are the poorest and least prestigious of the residents on Brasília's urban zone.

During 1966 and 1967, I observed many of these deviations in the urban settlement pattern and social life from the original plan submitted by Lúcio Costa some ten years earlier. One such type of deviation, squatting, is crucial for the understanding of some of the other deviations, such as the rise of the satellite towns. Of the squatter settlements, the one examined in greatest detail is the Social Security Invasion, the largest squatment in the Federal District, to which many squatters were transferred from other areas by the municipal government.

It is conventional for ethnographic researchers to examine social units as if they were isolated from the more complex systems of which they are a part, such as the set of neighboring societies in a region, or the more inclusive social system on higher levels of integration such as the chiefdom and the state (Steward 1955). Even the increasingly common ethnographic studies of urban areas, where the complexity and scale of the social system is an inescapable reality, often limit themselves to describing isolates in the city (neighborhoods, blocks, families, networks, associations, ethnic enclaves or "communities") with respect to their internal organization and characteristics. And generally this specification takes place from an essentially "emic" standpoint (Harris 1968: 568–604)— the effort to "get inside the head" of the informant by one means or another.

The rise of a global ecumene calls the traditional concentration on societies as isolates into question even for the most exotic and "primitive" societies. In the specific case of Brasília, this focus is certainly inadequate.

The dramatic shifts in population size and distribution in the Federal District over the last ten years indicate that the urban areas there are closely interconnected. The location, size, and nature of any given community or settlement cannot be accounted for simply, or even largely, by its internal characteristics. The daily life of most squatment residents reflects their ties to the city at large.

The founding, planning, and execution of Brasília, moreover, and the concomitant rise of segregated and socially stratified settlement patterns, can best be understood by explicit reference to the economically, politically, and ideologically dependent status of Brazil, and the direct and indirect consequences of this status for the national social and political system. In particular, the project of building the new capital itself, the monumentalist and automotive priorities reflected in Lúcio Costa's plan, and the haste with which the city was executed in the Presidency of Juscelino Kubitschek, conform to a pattern which we will call the *public works complex,* which recurs frequently in Brazilian political life. Costa's plan, indeed, was a faithful reflection of ideological biases widespread in the Brazilian upper class, differentiated and isolated as it is from the material conditions and lifeways of the vast majority of the population.

On the local level, the crucial factors in the formation of squatments were the demand for labor, the low priority given by the government to the needs of those who provide their labor (a priority reinforced by the developed underdevelopment of the regions from which the workers migrated, and the consequent low material standards and large numbers of the migrants), and the availability of resources such as land and used building materials at little marginal cost to those who controlled them. The squatter group also possessed a limited amount of bargaining power due largely to numbers and some potential for resistance under conditions of severe threat to its permanence in the squatment. A tacit bargaining process thus developed whose outcome was the toleration of squatting in certain areas of the urban space. The administration also developed certain programs—satellite towns and public housing projects—as alternatives to squatting, in spite of their deviation from the original plan.

Our view of squatting in Brasília is by no means universally held. The contrast in appearance between the middle-class apartment houses and the lower-class shacks has reinforced a number of ideas about the settlement pattern in Brasília and similar patterns in other cities. In one way or another, each of these concepts, which we will call "dualist," emphasizes the separateness or distinctiveness of the squatter settlement, its residents and their way of life, points them up as anomalous or pathological, and promotes the view that social policy should have as its goal the integration of squatters into the larger society and the transformation of their lifeways to resemble those of other urbanites.

Social workers in Brasília employ the concept of *marginality* (*marginalidade*) in talking about squatter populations. For example, a seminar organized by social workers in Brasília concluded:

The phenomenon of marginality which appears in the Latin American countries indicates the existence of a *dual urban social structure* and has in the economic factor one of the variables of its appearance. . . .

In addition to this economic variable, which assumes undeniable importance in the configuration of the situation of urban marginality, the concentration of marginalized groups in certain characteristic zones of urban space is observed (Seminário 1967: 2; emphasis supplied).

While an effort is made to give this term a technical definition, or at least usage, it should be noted that the Brazilian term *marginal* is most often used in crime reporting to refer to individuals from the lower-class criminal milieu, such as pickpockets, illegal lottery salesmen (*bicheiros*), pimps, and muggers. Use of the term, even in a professional context, must evoke in most middle-class Brazilians associations of the squatting phenomenon with crime, violence, and social pathology in general, in correspondence with their standard prejudices.

Whitten and Szwed (1968) used the concept of economic marginality in reference to intermittent or irregular income. Indeed, squatting not involving rent is adapted to marginality in this sense of the term. Use of the term *marginality* for this situation is confusing, since irregular income among sugar workers or urban squatters may be an aspect of their integration into the very heart of the functioning political economy, not of their isolation from it.

Others argue that squatter settlements are in some sense *rural,* either because of the alleged similarity of architectural forms to those in rural areas (Bonilla 1961: 2) or because of the supposed provenience and associated social and cultural characteristics of their inhabitants. Bastide, for example, suggests that the cultural assimilation of foreigners in Brazilian cities is easier than that of rural migrants: "Bearers of a folk culture, because (*a*) internal migrations are family migrations . . . [and] (*b*) the rural family in the city continues to "socialize" its children according to 1ural models" (1964: 76). Building on the concept of subculture, Bastide goes on to suggest that shantytowns are the locales of "micro-cultures" whose distinctiveness from the urban milieu as a whole he emphasizes:

Micro-cultures are translated ecologically into a distribution of the urban population into areas which are not merely ecological areas, but cultural areas in the proper sense of the term. Some of these areas, the Indian quarters of the Mexican capitals, the various types of squatter settlements [*bidonvilles*] (each country has its term) [of] the Central American and South American capitals, and more recently the *villas* or rural immigrants' quarters, have been studied . . . But it still remains to study them ethnographically as the expression of a folk culture within the capitals (1964: 76).

Other analysts are concerned with the effect on individual personality of the allegedly rapid cultural change taking place in rural-urban migration. Pye, for instance, suggests that the maladjustment and insecurity he believes associated with such migration offer a threat to the national and international status quo. This argument relies very heavily on a concept of social duality similar to the arguments of the commentators already cited. States Pye:

Urbanization is . . . a profoundly disruptive process. In nearly all transitional societies the early emergence of urban centers has produced a *fundamental cleavage* between the worlds of the more modernized cities and the more traditional and village-based people. This *bifurcation of the social structure* is usually matched in the economic realm by the development of *dual economies.* In the psychological sphere the rapid transition

from the compact and intimate world of the village to the highly impersonal and anonymous world of the city can leave people with deep personal insecurities. Thus in a multitude of ways rapid urbanization can cause
social, economic and psychological tensions which, translated into the
political realm, become sources of instability and obstacles to rapid nation
building (1963: 84; emphasis added).

Lewis's concept of the *culture of poverty* is more carefully hedged than
any of the foregoing discussions, but it also emphasizes the distinctiveness
of its bearers from the larger society, rather than the role they play in it.
While on the one hand Lewis defines the culture of poverty as a subculture
and hence presumably a product of Western capitalism, on the other hand
he states: "It is a culture in the traditional anthropological sense in that
it provides human beings with a design for living, with a ready-made set
of solutions for human problems, and so serves a significant adaptive function" (1966: 19). This emphasis on the culture of poverty as an ongoing
tradition draws attention away from those causes of social inequality which
are external to the group of culture-of-poverty bearers. Lewis is unclear
about the expected distribution of the culture of poverty. On the one hand
it is said to be a subculture found in many different geographical areas; on
the other it is not characteristic of all poor people in Western society, nor
does Lewis specify any particular subgroup of the poor to which it defi-
nitely applies.

The concept of the culture of poverty focuses attention on the relative
lack of organization and the isolation of its bearers. Yet Lewis recognizes
that many urban squatters may display a sense of community untypical
of the culture of poverty, especially when the settlements are low-rent
areas of stable residence physically and ethnically, racially or linguisti-
cally distinct from their surroundings (1966: 23).

A synthesis of the outlooks so far discussed would suggest that Brasília's
shantytowns, which contrast so starkly with the modern superblocks and
monumental architecture of the Pilot Plan, house people who, while they
may or may not be bearers of the culture of poverty, are isolated from
modern Brazilian national life, rural, marginal, and maladjusted. Fundamentally, these views would suggest, the squatters' living conditions and
their physical separation from the city derive from their failure to pass
from traditional, rural ways to modern urban society.

Such a viewpoint, however, would be largely incorrect and misleading.
Brasília's squatters are economically deprived, but, far from being marginal, they were central in the new capital's construction and development.
The squatments are not a carryover from rural Brazilian life but rather a
fundamental and by no means exclusively Brazilian or Latin American
mode of urban expansion. Such distinctiveness as shantytown dwellers
display in Brasília is due less to their failure to complete a cultural transi-

tion from rural to urban or from traditional to modern than to their inferior economic and political position relative to the urban social strata above them, a position which is advantageous to the dominant groups. The shantytown and its residents are fully integrated into Brazilian society; such settlements are natural, not pathological growths, given the economic and political system of which they are a part. As a result, attempts to "eradicate" squatter areas are not likely to succeed, and programs to promote community development or "modernization" among their residents are likely to prove unrelated to their needs and wants.

Urban squatter settlements serve as reception areas and places of residence for in-migrants and some of their descendants, and thus owe their existence to the distribution of wealth and power which underlies the migratory process. Rather than viewing such settlements, with alarm or otherwise, as the consequences of an alleged failure to diffuse urban-industrial values to the rural-oriented lower class, or as the pathological consequences of mismanagement or bad planning, we may consider the contribution they make to the supply of abundant cheap labor for the urban economy, including not only the industrial sector but the largely labor-intensive service and maintenance sector which is such an important prop to the life-style of the upper and middle classes.

In the case of Brasília we have already alluded to the role played in the building of the new capital by the social stratum from which the squatters came. These workers moved from dependent status in one part of the society to a similar status in Brasília. Their work was essential to the crash construction of the new capital, but the provisions made for their housing were minimal. As a consequence, the workers improvised their own solutions, the result being a rapid expansion of the first shantytowns. This phenomenon provoked the first governmental efforts to control such settlements and to prevent them from interfering with the city plan of Lúcio Costa. Such efforts paradoxically led to the abandonment of the more egalitarian and innovative of Costa's guidelines, giving rise to the early initiation and the rapid growth of the satellite towns.

From this point on, Brasília's settlement pattern developed in response to conflicting pressures emanating from the official "planned" construction and from the housing needs of squatters, and the type of housing provided is unattractive to many. There is scant prospect of eliminating squatting in the short or middle run.

Yet officials resist ideas such as those applied in Ciudad Guyana, Venezuela (Rodwin 1965; Peattie 1969), where planners and officials acted on the premise that the growth of squatter areas was inevitable, and set aside special zones for their installation that would permit their orderly growth and improvement without physical obstacle. Official attitudes in

Brasília may be influenced by the special ideological function of the new capital as a symbol of Brazilian nationality and socioeconomic progress, as well as by the possible loss of prestige associated with the recognition of squatment legitimacy.

Finally, squatters are not connected to the Brasília experience merely through economics, nor is their physical separateness and distinctiveness indicative of a lack of integration into the life of urban Brasília. On the contrary, the squatment is a functioning part of the life of the new capital in almost every sphere.

II. The Research

This study is based upon documentary research, interviews, and fieldwork. From September 1966 through February 1967, my wife, my infant daughter Daniela, and I lived in the Pilot Plan of Brasília in a rented row house off W-3 Avenue. During this period, I collected basic documents, interviewed government officials and others, and made many trips to the considerable number of urban settlements in the Federal District, in an effort to reconstruct the history and to verify the presnt status of the urban settlement pattern. One of he areas I repeatedly visited was the Social Security Invasion. Here I monitored the activities of the Social Service Foundation reception center for people transferred from various squatments to Social Security, made a number of friendships, and conducted many interviews.

We moved to the Social Security Invasion in early 1967 and remained there for some six months. Because we could not find a shack to rent, we were forced to buy one for some U.S.$200, from an elderly shoe peddler, who was returning to his native Pernambuco, whose capital was mainly made up from the money we paid for the house. We remained in the house, observed the passing scene, conducted formal interviews and informal ones on the many long walks we took through the settlement. At the same time, we continued to check the reports of the squatters against written evidence and the recollections of people from the Pilot Plan and governmental elite. We also made several visits to other areas of the Federal District, where we conducted interviews with the aid of Peace Corps personnel and relatives of residents in the squatter settlement.

After about six months in the Social Security Invasion, we moved to Rio de Janeiro and later to New York City and Los Angeles. I wrote this report in the latter three cities.

Any piece of research is a product of various kinds of considerations —theoretical, technical, ideological, and personal. The theoretical contribution of this research is discussed elsewhere. To some extent, these conclusions are ex post facto, as is common in ethnographic research. Rather than a test of a clearly formulated hypothesis, the research was an exploration, stimulated by the appearance of an anomaly, the unplanned and impoverished settlements surrounding an ostensibly "planned" and futuristic city, and the guess that the regional and political contexts of a Brasília would be significantly different from those of Rio de Janeiro, São Paulo, or Salvador, all regions more deeply plumbed by the social sciences than the Central Plateau.

The technical problems of urban anthropology are formidable. The present study can lay claim only to partial success in resolving them, and in fact, would not be conducted quite the same way had I the chance to carry it out again. Nevertheless it is worthwhile to discuss the reasoning behind the choice of techniques, to enable the reader to assess the basis for my assertions and to contribute to the future of anthropological studies in urban areas. In spite of fads, there are still relatively few of these, and even fewer good ones.

Traditional anthropological concerns and ethnographic techniques are quite relevant to urban research, but it is not easy to adapt these techniques to the more varied, denser, and more populous urban situation. The single anthropologist or small group of anthropologists armed with notebook and pencil, plus a few minor mechanical and statistical props (camera, tape recorder, basic survey, and census techniques), still may be capable of obtaining some kind of grasp of the culture of a small hunting and gathering band, of a horticultural or peasant settlement. The achievements of ethnography in these settings have been restricted less by technical and practical problems than by the theoretical limitations of most practicing schools of anthropology. In urban settings the sheer size and heterogeneity of the society limit the effectiveness of traditional ethnographic techniques.

Theoretical obstacles, some of which were discussed in the previous section, also restrict the achievements of the anthropology of urban society, but the limitations of traditional techniques themselves encourage errors of theory in urban settings. Urban anthropology shares with much of the rest of the field an "emic" idiographic bias (Harris 1968).

The previous chapter contained examples of urban anthropologists' propensity for ignoring the connections of the groups they study to larger sociocultural systems, a propensity they share with many contemporary cultural a: .hropologists. It is particularly inappropriate, of course, in urban society, whose heterogeneity and scale are among its most marked features. Many researchers also erroneously assume that psychological attributes, either of personality structure or belief, may be elevated to causal status without any consideration of what causes *them*.

The search for a bounded community or isolate to study is in part an effort to solve the technical problem of defining a manageable universe in which to carry out one's work on some kind of analogy with more traditional kinds of anthropological research. The traditional methods of intensive observation and interaction make necessary work with a relatively small group, since the large-scale sampling techniques of survey sociology and demography are not appropriate for obtaining the kind of global understandings ethnographers traditionally have sought. The difficulty arises when the small-scale orientation required as a matter of technique is elevated to theoretical status, when the entity studied as a matter of necessity is assumed to be more tightly bounded than is demonstrable as a matter of fact. The inevitable "naivety" (Gluckman 1964) of the urban anthropologist is unfortunately transformed, in these cases, from a necessity into a virtue.

This transformation is, however, only partly a result of technical requirements. It may also reflect a yearning on the part of members of a Western, urban, cosmopolitan intelligentsia for the stability of a bounded, cohesive community. The roots in Western thought of this search for order and stability in "native" communities may go back as far as Rousseau's "Noble Savage" and Durkheim's preoccupation with the *anomie* of industrial capitalist society. In anthropology this exotic apotheosis is clearly evident in the work of Redfield (1930, 1941, 1955) and in Turnbull's charming and utterly romantic study of the Pygmies of the Ituri Forest (1962), while Lewis Mumford's idealization of the medieval town represents a similar tradition in nonanthropological urban studies (Mumford 1961: 243–314). The contemporary usage of the term "community" in university circles in the United States (the "black community," "university community," and the undifferentiated outside "community," for example) both reflects the sincere yearning for community and disguises the hard fact of its absence or disintegration.

It was, of course, possible to study the squatters of Brasília as a "community" without romanticizing them. Such a study, however, no matter how well conducted, could not elucidate the question that I began with: why is there squatting in Brasília in the first place? That question of course involves the subsidiary question of how the squatment came into being. Nor would a relatively traditional "community study" approach speak either to the distinctively urban quality of society in Brasília, nor to the special distinctiveness of Brasília as the planned capital of Brazil. The question of the origins of squatting is historical. It also demands some kind of attention to the regional and national structure of Brazilian society. A similar difficulty would exist for many other foci of study, but the incompatibility of a bounded ethnography and my original problem was clear.

The urban ethnographer seems to be stuck with unpalatable choices.

If he gives up the strengths of traditional ethnographic work, intensive face-to-face interaction, and observation of the "natural" behavior of his informants, one alternative is to adopt some variety of survey technique, for the sake of greater statistical reliability. This was the choice of José Pastore in studying Brasília (1968, 1969), in my opinion with results which fail to justify the effort and expense of his study.

In the case of squatment studies, there are a number of obstacles to survey techniques, due both to the peculiarities of squatments, and the inherent limitations of survey methods themselves. Particularly in large metropolises such as Rio de Janeiro, where squatments are dense, comparatively old and thus architecturally and socially complex, and relatively exempt from governmental control, sampling procedures are exceedingly difficult to apply because the size of the universe is difficult even to estimate without intensive prior work. The would-be squatment survey researcher would have to map the area on foot, house by house, and conduct some kind of census in the area before drawing his sample. If the universe consists not simply in a single squatment, but in the totality of squatments within the city, the problem is multiplied. If the researcher abandons such grandiose pretensions in favor of a survey of one or a few squatments, he forswears the main advantages of survey methods, comprehensiveness and reliability, and finds himself in a bind very close to the ethnographer's.

The survey researcher, however, has still another problem in that he does not know what questions to ask, or else cannot ask the important ones. The industrialization of research techniques through computer technology which demands precoded questionnaires with stereotyped responses, allowing for no elaboration or explanation by respondents, coupled with the social and cultural isolation of the questionnaire-writer from his subjects, restricts the value of the technique. Ethnographic research has at least the potential for generating deeper insights and hypotheses.

Furthermore, in survey research the interviewer and interviewee are interacting in an artificial situation. The interviewer has no means of testing the response against behavior in the bewilderingly varied contexts of squatment life. Survey methods generate a strong bias toward verbal reports of attitudes and opinions, isolated from the context of the social and historical field in which they must become active, if they become active at all. For example, a survey on political attitudes of squatters at the time of a threat to their land tenure might be one thing; a survey at a time of apparently secure land tenure might be something else. A survey conducted in squatters' homes might give a result quite different from one conducted in bars or at religious gatherings. The emphasis on attitudes in survey research further leads to an emphasis, in analyzing data, on the relationship between one attitude and another, rather than on the social basis for the attitudes themselves. Surveys can say little about processes by which attitudes and behavior are generated.

Even survey questions about actual behavior are at best verbal reports of uncertain reliability because they are untested by any observation. And in the nature of survey research, it is impossible to return to a respondent and ask, "You said such-and-such was true; how come José and Francisco said the opposite?" Ethnographic techniques may legitimately be called into question as to the statistical reliability of the statements they generate, but they contain other kinds of internal checks. Ethnographic research makes it possible to explore a given subject in a wide variety of contexts, one-to-one, group, in different social settings and with different techniques, from formal interviewing to being a good listener. It takes long enough so that some changes over time may be noted and recorded. And, in principle, ethnographic data are as testable by other researchers, using any method they choose, as formal survey results. In other words, ethnographic research samples a variety of kinds of situation by a variety of techniques, rather than a set of carefully matched similar situations.

Another characteristic of ethnographic research that raises the hackles of positivistically oriented social scientists is the partial reliance of ethnographers on informal and intuitive kinds of knowledge. In caricature, this kind of knowledge is represented by the ethnographer's statement "I've been there, these are my people, and I know." That such statements are suspect is obvious. Every anthropologist is aware of the occasional instances of fraudulent or twisted field research, and even good faith intuitional observations can reflect biases and experience of the researcher, external to the field situation and to prior professional training.

Yet interaction between these biases and experience and the field experience also provide data. Even the most subjective reactions in a cross-cultural setting, by virtue of the common humanity of observer and observed, can provide important insights. Furthermore, much of human knowledge is not, at least at present, amenable to full formalization and testing; it is experiential. One learns a great deal through immersion in a new social setting—much that is scientifically valuable and not obtainable by other methods. Many of the instruments and methods which purport to externalize and objectify such knowledge do little more than externalize and objectify the ideological and ethnocentric biases of the researchers. The problem broached here is complex, and this is not the place to go into all its ramifications. Suffice it to say that much of the data in this study is the product of experience and intuition. Other researchers are invited to question, to challenge, and to test the statements and conclusions.

If one is convinced of the utility of ethnographic techniques, but im-

timidated by the scale and complexity of urban society, another alternative is the team approach to ethnography. Studies conducted in this manner include Redfield's four-community study in Yucatan (1941), Steward's area research study of Puerto Rico (1956), or the various studies
in Bahia coordinated by Wagley (1952). This kind of approach might
be adapted to urban research, with a group of researchers each working
in an area representative of the various settlement, class, or ethnic types.
There are problems with this method, too. The studies by Redfield, Steward, and Wagley all lacked an historical or theoretical conception of
their areas as wholes, and of the relationship of the part studied to the
whole. An urban study based on area research of this type might produce
merely a somewhat coordinated set of isolated ethnographies, and retain
the drawback of empirically unwarranted closure of the boundaries between the isolates or communities studied.

The main reason I failed to conduct such a study in Brasília, however,
was the lack of other researchers to participate in it, money to pay them,
or the time to conduct several studies myself. In principle it seemed to me
desirable, and when I first arrived in Brasília in 1966 it was with the idea
of conducting at least two intensive studies of areas within the city, with
the hope of obtaining insight into the similarities and differences in their
histories and present situations, and generating explanations for them—as
well as obtaining data for the solution of the larger problem of explaining
the deviation from the Costa Pilot Plan. Like every young researcher, I
fell into the trap of having research proposal eyes larger than my fieldwork stomach. I found it hard even to do ethnographic justice to the
Social Security Invasion.

Yet the study did not reduce itself, in the end, to simply a partial
ethnographic account of Social Security. For the problem imposed another dimension upon the research, the historical. It was the interaction
of the history of Brasília as a whole with the particular fate of Social
Security and some of the people in it that finally became the theme of my
inquiry. Each aspect of the study focused the other. Squatting was the
strategic form of settlement in generating decisions by the authorities to
deviate from the Pilot Plan; Social Security was the squatment par excellence—its fate and the fate of its residents thus providing the perspective
from which, for much of the time, I looked at, and asked about, the
evolving settlement pattern of the new capital. On the other hand, I
looked at Social Security primarily from the point of view of its place in
this evolving pattern, and in the capital's social system as a whole. A
sense of the city as a whole informed my study in Social Security; a concern with the particular fate of Social Security informed my study of the
history of Brasília as a whole. Frequent, but not intensive, visits to other

parts of the city helped me to retain a sense of Social Security's particularity as well.

To be sure, this compromise, like all compromises, was sometimes uneasy. It made both studies, historical and ethnographic, regional and local, somehow partial. Yet every ethnography has emphases and omissions. A kind of emphasis that would preserve a sense of a larger system seems a useful one, to counteract the inherent bias of intensive ethnographic methods toward emphasizing the separateness and internal cohesiveness of the group studied. It may seem that I discovered, at the end of my study, what I had set out to find—that Social Security was integrated into the urban system, rather than isolated. But in fact I was prepared, at the beginning, for it to be far more internally cohesive and distinctive from the rest of the city than it finally turned out to be, based on previous knowledge of similar communities such as the *favelas* of Rio de Janeiro and the *barriadas* of Lima. There, to be sure, the squatting phenomenon is no case of rural villages shut out from the urban system, but to all accounts squatters are more highly organized and locality-conscious than in Brasília—though it may be their urbanity, not their rurality, that accounts for it.

My study of Brasília differs from much work in anthropology in that it is urban; it is directly concerned with social stratification and the distribution of power; it is concerned with the relationship between various levels of sociocultural integration, from the international to the local; it is broadly within the "cultural materialist" research strategy; and deals with historical data and processes rather than purely synchronic material. And in eventual aim, if not in immediate content, it is comparative. The motivation for these choices is partly but not exclusively internal to academic anthropology itself.

My political views have evolved since I began the Brasília study, but then, as now, I had a strong interest in politics, and a general commitment to egalitarian, democratic, socialist, and rationalist values. That is to say, personally I am offended by many of the aspects of Brazilian culture described in this study, such as the fact that working people live in shacks, bureaucrats in comfortable apartments, and the wealthy in luxurious private homes. This phenomenon is not peculiarly Brazilian, and is as offensive (if not more so, given the greater productive potential of North American society) in New York City as in Brasília. Moreover, my objections to prevailing social conditions and public policies do not detract from my affection for Brazilians and Brazil, nor, for that matter, from my self-identification as a North American. My views do direct my efforts at scientific and human understanding toward problems which relate directly to what I see as social injustices. They may produce a certain bias in my approach to my work, perhaps even enough to counteract the biases derived from being a somewhat educated, white, male, North American intellectual in a world where all of those characteristics are associated with various kinds of privilege and status.

I have consciously tried, however, not to be partisan in my work in the sense of falsifying or omitting data. Once the problem is selected, my commitment to rationality and to scientific ethics leads me to believe in striving for sincerity and accuracy in reporting and analysis. In fact, I regard scientific accuracy as a political necessity, since only such accuracy can make it possible to find workable strategies for changing the world.

The personal motivations and experience of fieldwork are hard to discover. A few of them have some relevance to the conduct of the research.

The image of the Social Security Invasion among middle-class Brasília residents is not good. It is thought of not simply as a place where poor people live, but as a dangerous place. For example, it is sometimes hard to get a taxi driver to go to Social Security, partly because they fear damage to their vehicles on the corduroy roads there, but also because they fear robbery or worse. To me, as an American, at first the idea of living in Social Security was intimidating, and at the same time, a challenge.

It soon turned out that life there was not what I thought, and certainly not what most outsiders in Brasília think. Squatment residents are very much like other people—a varied lot of human beings, with very distinctive personalities, many problems—made worse by the prevailing poverty, in many cases. In the sense of facing danger, or hostility, living in Social Security was no challenge at all. In fact, my strongest memories are of warmth, affection, and neighborliness—sitting around in the evening and swapping stories, exchanging gifts and food, admiring children, becoming known as the American who goes around carrying a baby on his back like a Japanese.

Indeed, the ease with which I came to know and like my neighbors contributed to two of the biggest difficulties in my research. First of all, I had been in Brazil twice before. My wife and daughter were Brazilian. I was fluent in the language, and believed I had a strong intuitive "feeling" for Brazilian culture. As a result of these circumstances and my warm reception, I soon began to lose the sense of differentness and wonder that is one of the strongest assets of many ethnographers. Very little seemed unusual or worthy of note. I had begun to take life in Social Security very much for granted; certainly I lost most of my sense of the reasons why one should choose to make an academic study of such a place. Would one do a study of the corner grocery in Morningside Heights?

Second, to the extent that I retained my academic motivation, I began to feel that my research goals were an intrusion, a violation of trust. Does one take notes about one's friends? My inquiry seemed to me (if not to them) as a kind of ethnographic rape. When does friendly curiosity become espionage? In part this feeling stemmed from a measure of guilt. Guilt at coming from another, richer country, from another class, from living, even in Social Security, at a higher standard. For example, we got to know a boy of about twelve, one of eleven children. Their father earned about U.S.$50 a month in the sanitation department, and drank a lot. I hired this boy for the futile task of washing the fine red dust of the squatment off my jalopy twice a week. Occasionally I would see him and his brothers foraging in the garbage, which collected in a ravine near our house, for usable pieces of food. When we had leftovers, or a pudding didn't turn out quite right, we would send it to his family. When it came time to leave, the boy's mother thanked us for the "wonderful food" and told us she had never eaten such good things.

In a direct sense, after all, I could do nothing about Social Security. When I was mapping the area, people would come out and ask me if the mapping meant they would soon be getting houses, or be evicted. I replied that I had nothing to do with that, that I was writing a book in order to earn a promotion in my civil service—a close translation to Brazilian terms of the professional significance of the Ph.D. in the United States, at that time. I began to feel that in some obscure way I myself was exploiting, or mining, Social Security, or at least, even if I was never made to feel unwelcome, that I had no business being there.

Yet I think, if they were asked, most of the residents of Social Security would want the story told. They are proud of Brasília, proud, in fact, of their own settlement, and how they built it and by confrontation and silent resistance kept it going. They would like, I think, that there should be a book about Brasília that is about more than the architecture of the Congress or the personality of Juscelino Kubitschek. I have written this book for myself, of course; I hope in some measure I have written it also for my friends in Social Security.

Chapter II

Background to Brasília: Politics and Plans

I. The Argument for Brasília

Brasília has its defenders and detractors. To some, Brasília symbolizes Brazil's coming of age, her takeoff into mature nationhood, a break from a sleepy agrarian semicolonial past and the sweet life of the coastal centers, into a future of pioneering growth in the interior and in the realm of industrial production. The capital symbolizes the optimistic mood of developmentism and is to be at the center of a network of jungle-cutting highways such as the one between Brasília and the Amazonian port city of Belém.

To Brasília's detractors, the city is a monumental urbanistic and social disaster, a venture into conspicuous consumption on a national scale, the source of crippling inflation. It is the demagogic, megalomaniac adventure of a populist politician (Juscelino Kubitschek) bent on personal enrichment and seeking a cheap way to win a place in history. Brasília's existence by now must grudgingly be conceded, but to these critics it remains a Potemkin village in the midst of a sea of poverty, corruption, disease, and despair.

One path toward understanding why and how Brasília was constructed is to examine the public pronouncements of its promoters. While undoubtedly some of these arguments do not rise beyond propaganda of a rather trivial kind, others at least imply a more profound kind of social analysis.

The first motive was the conviction that the transfer of the capital was a means toward fulfilling Brazil's "continental destiny" (Meira Penna 1958: 304). Large in area on the map, Brazil is in fact, in terms of population, a coastal country, most of her population being concentrated within a few hundred miles of the Atlantic Coast. Some publicists for Brasília advocated a "westward march" (*marcha para oeste*), in order to

26

counter this tendency of which Brazília was to be the center (James and Faissol 1956: 306). In accord with this idea, various important highways were and are being built with Brasília–Belo Horizonte, the Brasília–Anápolis (connection with São Paulo), and, most spectacularly, the 2,276-kilometer Belém–Brasília highway, or Transbrasiliana, which for the first time provides an overland route to the vast, underpopulated Amazon Valley from the demographic and industrial heartland of Brazil to the south. In the face of the inefficiency of coastal navigation in the recent past, the opening of the Belém–Brasília highway through unsettled *cerrado* (savanna) and jungle territory vastly widens the market for São Paulo's industrial production. Other highways are in the early stages of construction or are being planned, including one reaching the far western territory of Acre and connecting with the Peruvian road system at the frontier.

MAP 2. Brazil, showing the principal places mentioned in the text.

But it was not merely the desire to populate the interior which the proponents of Brasília used to advance their proposal. There was also the idea of fleeing from the negative characteristics of the old capital, Rio de Janeiro. Rio, a port and a cosmopolitan center, was always the point of contact with foreign influences, both from the political point of view and from that of style and high culture (Pfeifer 1964: 389–390). The desire to possess a distinctively Brazilian capital, a city immune to the less constructive forms of foreign influence, was important. As Meira Penna put it:

A centrally located capital . . . might make Brazil more conscious of her role in the Americas, her terrestrial frontiers with Paraguay, Bolivia, Peru, Colombia, and Venezuela. When the attention of the elites turns from their nearly exclusive interest in Europe, the "splendid isolation" will be broken which has until now separated, in spirit and in fact, Brazil from her continental neighbors (1958: 309).

Rio de Janeiro is a city crushed by a series of urban problems, some seemingly insoluble. Locked between mountains and the sea, the city has seen its growth choked and distorted by the very geographical circumstances that give it its magnificent pictorial charm. Instead of a radial or starlike growth, typical of large cities, Rio has grown in a space shaped like a wedge of pie, increasing the distances, and especially where mountains must be crossed by roadways, the amount of money and effort spent on public works. Only in the northern suburbs has any kind of rapid transit system been put into operation, and the suburban service of the Central do Brasil and the Leopoldina is crowded, slow, and inefficient. Public utilities: gas, electricity, water, sewage, telephones, are unable to keep up with the city's growth, and combined with the jammed, undisciplined traffic make the daily life of the citizens a constant struggle. On top of this, the squatter settlements (*favelas*) proliferate all over the city, to the point where they may house as much as one-third of the population. In the face of this situation, there were many who felt that whatever the possible solutions to the problems of Rio de Janeiro, it would be best to move the national government to a made-to-order, modern, perhaps even utopian new capital.

Rio is also considered to be a center of the sweet life. The *carioca,* or denizen of the coastal capital, is thought of as an arranger and a talker, but hardly a worker; he is supposed to prefer lying on the beach, making love, and speaking ill of others and is alleged to resolve his problems on the basis of the *jeitinho,* the fix or the subterfuge. Most Cariocas would probably accept these stereotypes. Superficial observers also consider the climate of the city enervating, a conclusion vigorously protested by geographer Preston James (James and Faissol 1956: 308)—but the hot sun, a culture that accepts taking it easy if you can get away with it, and the proximity of some of the most beautiful scenery and beaches in the world hardly constitute an invitation to the strenuous life. These values probably stem from the structure of the government machinery as it functioned in Rio (Leeds 1968), but many rejected them and thought a new capital would produce a change.

Proponents of Brasília also argued that the capital's location in Rio distorted the government's view of the nation. The old capital is very different from the interior. Meira Penna (1958: 306) argued that it is Rio, seduced by a "false progress and ostentation," which "lacks real contact with the sources of national spirit and popular life," so that failure to move the capital could have led to "a dangerous break with the roots of nationality or an infantile refusal to take consciousness of present realities." The argument also noted the officially federalist regime in Brazil, suggesting that Brasília, nearly equidistant from the various regions of the country (see map 2), would be more appropriate as a capital more nearly impervious to the pull of its immediate environment.

But the desire to escape from the problems of Rio had another aspect. Rio, one of the major industrial centers and perhaps also the principal intellectual center of the country, is also one of the areas most open to the influence of radical ideas, of student and labor activity. A regime which hardly bothers to hide or to justify the extreme social inequality reigning in the country may well feel more at home in the isolated serenity of the Central Plateau than amid the agitation and demands which characterized political life in the former capital. As Israel Pinheiro, who headed the drive to complete Brasília, put it:

A city like Rio . . . obliges the Federal Government, due to the simple fact of being located there, to permanent preoccupation with matters of purely local import . . .

Asphyxiated by the wave of private interests . . . the Federal Government is forcibly divorced from those Brazilians who in the interior also build, silently, and often unsupported by any government action, the greatness of the nation.

Social agitation of a grave nature generally ferments in the great centers, stimulated by elements of indiscipline and disorder, which have there the ideal conditions for subversion . . . (quoted in Kubitschek 1962: 61–62).

Equally convincing to some was the universally shared belief in the inefficiency of the federal bureaucracy in Rio de Janeiro. The reputation of the civil servant among most Brazilians is very low, perhaps reflecting the influence of clientelism and the role of the civil service in providing a kind of middle-class dole. An armadillo in the Rio zoo, for example, was christened "Civil Servant" by the press (*Funcionário Público*) because he

spent his days sleeping. Some of this civil service inefficiency is attributed
to the vices of Rio de Janeiro. A typical denunciation of the bureaucracy
is the following by Meira Penna: ". . . this grotesquely useless, vain,
dissatisfied, cynical bureaucracy, showing all the symptoms of lack of
adaptation . . . a parasitical bureaucracy which sometimes, in its moments of lucidity, tries to govern as if we were one of the most advanced
European countries, and confronts, astonished, real conditions apppropri-
ate to Africa" (1958: 307). The problems of public administration
seemed to many to be insoluble. The civil service is protected by a phil-
osophy of "acquired rights" (*direitos adquiridos*) by which a job in the
federal or state governments is considered virtually to be a piece of private
property. A solution seriously proposed by the diplomat Meira Penna,
one of the leading apologists for the capital's transfer, was to leave the
mass of the bureaucracy to vegetate in the Rio sun and to take a few
young, technically trained civil servants to Brasília and run the country
from there:

What should be sought is not so much *more government in Goiás* [the state
from which the new Federal District was carved] but rather *less government in Rio*. Let few, very few officials move to Goiás—those few who
prefer to breathe the pure air of the plateau to living in the atmosphere
impregnated with sea air, burnt oil and cynical sensualism that weighs on
Rio! That will be enough to break, with a single symbolic act, the paralyzing
governmental paternalism, which more than any other bottleneck, impedes
national development (1958: 308).

In other words, the move in space was seen as a relatively painless means
of effecting a revolution in mentality and methods. It may be that the inefficiency of the civil service stems from political clientelism and the civil
service's function as a dole for the middle class. Many believed, however,
that the move to Brasília, by itself, could produce a change in mentality.
The egalitarian, pioneering spirit which prevailed in the first years of the
crash program to build the new capital seemed really to presage such a
transformation, as Niemeyer (1961: 61–65) implies.

It was even argued that the transfer of the capital would be a weapon
against inflation in the Brazilian economy, since it would lead to an expansion of production in the interior, and make possible the carrying out
of an anti-inflationary policy, far from the pressures of Rio: "Far from
the pressures of the great center, a more impersonal, freer, and more just
policy will be possible of restriction or selection of credit, in accordance
with the high interests of the nation" (Silveira 1957: 65–66).

Finally, there was the conviction among much of the middle class that
Brazil is a country with a magnificent future, likely to become a world
power. The need to affirm this optimism, combined with a reluctance to

combat the structural obstacles to economic development, helps to explain the symbolic significance of the construction of Brasília for large segments of the lower and middle classes. As the man who presided over Brasília's construction, Juscelino Kubitschek, put it, "The construction of Brasília was symbolic of our efforts to provide the nation with a foundation on which to build the future" (1966: 5).

These pronouncements cannot be taken simply at face value. To a degree they are the work of clients or would-be clients to patrons in high places, and thus fall into the category of public relations or apple-polishing, which the Brazilians call *picaretagem*.

More interestingly, they are a sample of a kind of pronouncement, common among journalists and in the middle class, reflecting a heady optimism about the future greatness, in economics and power politics, of Brazil. Presumably such notions help salve the frustrations provoked by the inequities and difficulties of the less-than-glorious present. Propagandists for the Kubitschek regime were particularly adept at depicting it as the agency for the transformation of Brazil from an underdeveloped into an industrial nation. The seemingly unique Brasília enterprise and the mystique created around it served as a foil to heavy doses of politics-as-usual, as will be seen in the following section; little was said about possible alternate uses of the human and material resources employed in the project.

II. The Public Works Complex

> The mayor is known by the works in the city.
> (*O prefeito se conhece pelas obras da cidade.*)
> —Saying painted on a truck bumper.

> Brasília, the city Juscelino Kubitschek built at Brazil's
> center with unlimited audacity and confidence.
> —Oscar Niemeyer (1961: 67).

I have argued for a view of Brazilian society as essentially unified, dominated throughout its breadth and depth by a network of metropolis-satellite relationships, from the clientship of the lowliest peasant in the countryside to the dependence of Brazil as a whole on the power of the United States metropolis. Similar relations of dominance and dependence are replicated on various levels of the system. One aspect of this pattern, important to the interpretation of the Brasília experience, is the *public works complex*. This phenomenon has the following features: (*a*) a relatively greater emphasis by politicians, in deeds and words, on the construction of physical public projects (*obras*), as opposed to the ongoing tasks of public administration, the institution of new programs other than public works, and changes in the pattern of social relations; (*b*) the identification of individual political personalities with the public works they sponsor, and the furtherance of their careers on this basis; and (*c*) the connection of most works only haphazardly and uncertainly with programs or plans of a longer duration and scope than a single executive term of office (*mandato*). As a result, public works that are incomplete when the politician associated with them leaves office are often abandoned. Otherwise, an effort is made to identify them with his successor. Seers (1964: 24) cites an International Bank for Reconstruction and Development report on prerevolutionary Cuba which indicates that a similar pattern, the "public works cycle," existed there.

One of the outstanding examples in Brazilian history of the public works complex is the "drought industry" (*indústria das sêcas*) in the Northeast of the country (Callado 1960; Hirschmann 1963: 70). This region's interior is frequently subject to prolonged and devastating droughts. Most instances since 1877 of these disastrous droughts led to emergency relief spending in the form of programs of public works, accompanied by the formation of a succession of agencies to deal with the water problems of the region, the first of these being the Anti-Drought Works Inspectorate (*Inspetoria de Obras Contra as Sêcas*), since 1945, the National Anti-Drought Works Department (DNOCS—*Departamento Nacional de Obras Contra as Sêcas*). Even before this agency was created, a principal program against the droughts was the construction of dams, including the notorious Quixadá Dam. According to Hirschmann (1963: 23), this dam's ". . . construction went through so many stoppages and changes in design as a result of both erratic appropriations and technical difficulties that when it was finally completed in 1906, its very name had become a byword of governmental inefficiency and waste." In addition to delays in construction, this dam fell into disrepute because inadequate drainage led to soil sterility due to excessive concentrations of salt. A large dam project of the Anti-Drought Works Inspectorate, Acarape do Meio, begun in 1910, suffered from similar delays.

Under Epitácio Pessôa, Brazil's only Northeast President until Castelo Branco (1964–1967), a vast public works program in the Northeast was undertaken in response to the drought of 1919. Pessôa rejected proposals to carry out these projects in an orderly step-by-step fashion, declaring that progress had been impeded in Brazil because "always the idea of postponement" prevailed, "in a country in which lack of continuity . . . is the characteristic note of all governments" (cited in Hirschmann 1963: 33). Pessôa's generalization was confirmed, though not in the way he had wished, for his program was paralyzed in the successor regime of

Artur Bernardes, the construction equipment being sold at a 20 percent discount from the purchase price.

A later program was the development of the valley of the São Francisco Valley Commission, modeled on the North American Tennessee Valley Authority. As Hirschmann makes clear, power over this agency from the beginning was with a federal deputy from Bahia, Manuel Novais, whose influence prevailed over appointments and projects until he got into a struggle with President Kubitschek in the 1960 political campaign (Hirschmann 1963: 52–53).

A related pattern is the continual enlargement of the legislatively defined "drought polygon" in the Northeast. This is the area in which expenditures with the announced intention of contributing to antidrought efforts must be made. As late as 1967, some deputies from northern Minas Gerais tried and failed (due to a veto by Marshal-President Costa e Silva) to get the area of action of SUDENE, the most recent Northeast development agency, extended to their areas. Both of these cases point up the connection of the public works complex to clientelism.

This pattern of emphasis on construction projects and governmental impulses is not confined to the federal level, however. In his community study of an isolated town in the interior of Bahia, Harris (1956: 181–183) reports the same emphasis on public works in the budget and the consciousness of the populace:

New buildings, roads, bridges, and paved streets are the highest expression of urban civic standards. The success of each local administration and the personal worth of the individual members of the town council are judged by the amount of construction performed under their auspices. The more new buildings, the better the record. Moreover, each councilman strives to have some particular *obra* (public work) associated with his name . . . All such construction is accepted per se as "progress." . . . Little distinction is made between basic and superficial improvements.

Harris goes on to cite the relative lack of emphasis on such matters as education and public health as opposed to the paving of streets, the construction of gardens, and the like. My own observations in Brazil suggest that Harris's community is typical in this respect.

In describing the cacao port of Ilheus, Bahia, in the boom times of the 1920s, the renowned Brazilian novelist Jorge Amado begins his paean of progress with public works: "There was an air of prosperity everywhere, a vertiginous growth. Streets were opened toward the sea and the hills, gardens and squares were born, houses, mansions and palaces went up (Amado n.d.: 32).

One of the complaints of the U.S. Peace Corps volunteers sent to one of the poorer states of Brazil was that throughout the interior, "public health centers" had been constructed some time ago, to which the volunteers were assigned. On arrival, however, they generally found them lacking in equipment and often even in staff. Many of them were reduced to following the ancient Brazilian practice of making frequent trips to the state capital, hoping to pry some assistance out of the Governor and the Secretariat of Health.

In Brazilian cities, amenities taken for granted and, indeed, vital for economic development tend to deteriorate with time, even as the politicians initiate spectacular public works projects which are often never terminated. This especially is the case when there is a change in the chief executive. The new Governor or Mayor often prefers to start new projects that will be exclusively identified with his name, than to complete those already begun and linked in the public mind with his predecessor. The result, often as not, is the presence of monumental "skeletons," the ghosts of the grandiose and unfinished projects of the past. The University City on Fundão Island in Rio de Janeiro, which includes the skeleton of what was projected to be the largest hospital in South America, has remained virtually deserted for more than a decade. For many years only the framework of the multistory headquarters of the economic information-gathering Getúlio Vargas Foundation in Rio de Janeiro testified to the pretensions of its directors, even as "for lack of funds" (falta de verbas) the project remained paralyzed.

One reason for this emphasis on public works is that they are highly profitable in the short run for the contractors and suppliers involved, who may be linked through kinship, partnership, employment, friendship, political contributions, favor-trading, or graft with those in political positions responsible for planning the projects. This characteristic of public works projects is by no means specific to Brazilian society.

The primary alternatives to public works would be efforts to improve the quality and scope of ongoing tasks of public administration, which (as will be seen below) would conflict with the career requirements of most politicians, and investment in basic economic projects—agriculture, heavy industry, education, research and development. Most forms of basic investment, however, would require the administrator to preempt the field from already established private businesses, foreign and domestic. Public works, on the other hand, permit the politician to ally himself with these same interests. The choice is obvious, and is reinforced by the hegemony of the United States, with its commitment to "free enterprise." The exceptions would seem to be in those areas deemed insufficiently profitable for private business, in the context of chronic inflation and capital scarcity. Typically, public works projects are consistent with the directions of private investment—the interurban highway network associated with Brasília, and the automotive emphasis of the city plan itself at a time that international investors were establishing an automobile manufacturing industry in São Paulo constitute no exception. These projects were also a response to the deterioration—in government hands—of coastal shipping and the railroads.

At first glance, an exception to this pattern seems to have occurred in the case of the establishment of the national petroleum monopoly, Petrobrás, over the violent opposition of the international oil companies. However, it may be observed (*a*) that the international companies continue to dominate the lucrative field of distribution; (*b*) most petroleum consumed in Brazil continues to be purchased for dollars from the international oil companies; and (*c*) the establishment of Petrobrás was a step in the gradual expansion of the military patronage subsystem, which reached its highest point so far following the 1964 coup, by which time a clear alliance between the military leadership and the private sector (and especially its international branches) had been established.

Another factor to be considered is the intense personalism of Brazilian political life—the emphasis on the person of the leader, be he a major national figure like Juscelino Kubitschek, a regional one like Pedro Ludovico (Senator and former Governor of Goiás, for many years the unchallenged political boss of the state), or merely a local one. Political program takes second place to personal leadership and image; program and ideology are tools to be manipulated in the game of personal projection, alliance, and opposition. Related to this phenomenon is an intensely personalist bias at every level of public administration, belying even the ostensibly federal structure of the nation. In any agency of government, there is a tendency to send all problems to the desk of the head man, who inevitably spends most of his time attending to matters which would be routine in a thoroughly "rationalist" bureaucracy. The President of the Republic, for instance, until recently had to sign the relevant papers every time a public employee retired or a foreign resident applied for naturalization.

This personalism implies, among other things, that a routinized career progress is not characteristic of Brazil; the young, ambitious figure cannot sit back, do his job, and hope, in the course of years, to rise to a position of responsibility. Rather he must manipulate publicity and the complex system of clienteles and informal mutual-aid groupings, keeping open a multiplicity of sources of income, power, and prestige (Leeds 1964). In such conditions, mere competence or efficiency can hardly be sufficient for advancement; hence the constant battle for publicity. He must at the same time attach himself to the figures who can afford him protection or advantages from above, and attempt to group around himself dependents from further down the ladder.

This process unfolds against a background of national penury. In any society, even the fabulously rich industrial colossus of North America, the choice of priorities implies retardation in some areas as the price of progress in others. In Brazil, beset by extreme lack of funds on all levels of government, the politician who might wish to make his mark as an administrator rather than as a builder or initiator, may find that he just doesn't have the money. At the same time the encrusted inefficiency of a civil service which serves as a sort of public dole for a middle class lacking in career opportunities, makes the task of administrative reform seem an essay in windmill-tilting. The sponsorship of a public work, as discussed above, also provides an opportunity to reward clients and allies from a wide variety of professions and other areas of interest. The multiplication of bureaucratic entities with similar or identical functions plays a similar role—and often works projects and the creation of new entities are intertwined.

Brasília is the public work to beat them all, the apotheosis of a trait of Brazilian national political culture. And the figure with whose historical reputation Brasília is linked is indubitably Juscelino Kubitschek de Oliveira. It was Juscelino, as he is known (the Brazilian custom is to firstname everybody), whose insistence and interest brought the long-dreamed-of project to fruition, Juscelino who is the father of Brasília in the public mind, Juscelino who constantly flew to the city to follow its progress, mix with the workers, and receive their adulation.

Juscelino's career began in his native state of Minas Gerais. The "Minas politician" (*político mineiro*) is famous in all Brazil for his astuteness, his propensity for supporting whatever political faction is in control of the executive branch of the government, and for his ability skillfully to manipulate ambiguous verbal formulae. This popular image is explained by the fact that the state's politics is founded upon a network of patron-client relationships that would put Tammany Hall to shame. It is perhaps to this origin that Juscelino's fame as a conciliator was due; the elements of his public personality—the famous smile, the easygoing air—contrast with the use by other famous political personalities of traits such as aggressiveness and religiosity.

The Minas branch of the now extinct Social Democratic Party (PSD) typified this patronage-oriented politics. PSD policies were unrelated to Social Democracy in the European or North American sense. Getúlio Vargas, two-time President of Brazil, fathered the PSD, which coordinated the regional oligarchies consolidated or established during Vargas's rule, and the Labor Party (PTB). The latter was the means by which Vargas and his heirs coopted the expanding urban working classes—which were relatively privileged in the context of the total Brazilian society (Soares 1968: 187–188). Each of these parties, within its own sphere, incorporated three elements of Brazilian political culture highly developed under Vargas—paternalism, clientelism, and populism.

Paternalism is the patriarchal mode of personalism—personalism as applied to relations between the classes. Political life is presented as revolving around the figure of a leader, from whom all blessings flow. The national leader is a magnified version of the local boss (*patrão, coronel*), who makes the decisions and distributes the benefits. It thus presupposes unequal control over and distribution of the benefits—a class system, and so may be seen as legitimating in an idiom of family relations the unequal distribution of wealth and power. Thus Vargas was known as the "father of the poor" (*o pai dos pobres*). The clientele is the natural complement, the machinery which distributes the benefits from on high and mobilizes support, mostly electoral, from below. It is in these circumstances that the *pelego* or dependent of the Labor Ministry (Pearse 1961: 202) and the *picaretas*—yes-men, flatterers—prevail in public life in general.

It is populism which represents the distinctively Getulian contribution to Brazilian political culture. In essence it is the appeal, demagogic if you will, of the leader, often fundamentally conservative and compromised with the interests of the dominant groups in the society, directly to the people in terms of the same paternalism we have spoken of, using emotion-laden symbols such as the rosary (used by ex-Governor Adhemar de Barros of São Paulo) or the broom, symbolizing reform and honest government (used by ex-President Jânio da Silva Quadros), appealing to deep-seated popular emotions and unexpressed demands, but arousing popular hopes far in excess of any real effort to promote social change. Populism flourished in the absence of effective ideological parties—the Communists were banned in 1947—and in the face of the tacit veto exercised through the Congress, dominated by conservative elements, and the Armed Forces, against measures which might upset the class system or Brazil's dependence on the United States. After the coup of 1964, populism itself was vetoed by the quasi-militarist government, and all of the populist figures, including Kubitschek, Jânio Quadros, and Adhemar de Barros, sooner or later lost their public offices and their political rights.

It was the politics of Minas Gerais in the Getulian era which furnished the background for Juscelino Kubitschek's career (Medaglia 1959). Trained initially as a physician, Kubitschek soon (in 1931) obtained an appointment as a medical captain in the Minas Gerais State Military Police. After serving with the pro-Vargas forces which put down the São Paulo uprising of 1932, Juscelino came under the protection of Getúlio's Interventor (federally appointed governor) in Minas Gerais, Benedito Valadares, who made him secretary to the cabinet. In 1934, Kubitschek served in the Constituent Assembly and in the Congress which succeeded it, until the coup of 1937 resulted in the dissolution of that body. By 1940, Valadares had named Kubitschek Mayor of Belo Horizonte, the capital city of Minas Gerais. One of the new Mayor's major *obras* was the development of the luxurious Pampulha section, entrusted in part to architect Oscar Niemeyer, who was later to be responsible for most of the architectural work in Brasília. In 1946, Kubitschek served in another Constituent Assembly. He remained a federal legislator until in 1950 he won election as Minas's Governor at the same time as Vargas was elected to another term as national President.

Kubitschek's campaign pledge for the 1950 gubernatorial election conformed with the public works complex. It was to provide 200,000 kilowatts of electrical capacity for the state during his term of office. Characistically, a new public agency was created for this purpose, Minas Gerais Electrical Stations (CEMIG). This agency engaged in five major dambuilding projects, while other organizations carried out a similar program of road-building.

Juscelino was the PSD-PTB candidate for President of the Republic in 1955, shortly following the coup-suicide of President Getúlio Vargas in 1954. Juscelino's candidacy represented the continuity of the Getulian system in the face of opposition from military groups and the right-wing National Democratic Union (UDN).

The line Juscelino took in these circumstances was "developmentism" (*desenvolvimentismo*). He promised fifty years of economic progress in five. Among his promises was the construction of the new capital, so long dreamed of and so often studied and postponed. Juscelino succeeded in identifying himself in the public mind with two anxieties of large sections of the Brazilian population: economic development and a stable and democratic political order. Brasília symbolized both: the former because the establishment of the new city stood for the continental scale of the nation and its optimism about a technologically advanced future, the latter because it provided a stage for demonstrations of shirt-sleeve democratic fraternization and the unfolding of the constitutional process. The spectacular, isolated Presidential Palace designed by Niemeyer marked the personalism of the political system and Juscelino's role in it and in Brasília, and its lack of fences symbolized the openness and security in power of a populist and popular President.

According to Kubitschek, in his first public appearance in his Presidential campaign,

The first question I was asked in the city of Jataí was if the candidate, should he be elected President, would build the new capital in the Goiás plateau. I want to confess that until that moment I had not considered, in all its details, the problem of transferring the capital . . . I answered that

since the transfer was determined in the 1946 Constitution . . . I would make the first steps toward the building of the new capital.
This question was repeated in every state . . . When I finished the campaign I was convinced my government would have to undertake the building of the new capital (Kubitschek 1962: 57–58).

Few, however, took this to be more than a campaign promise, to be made and soon forgotten. The promise, however, was kept.

Typical of Juscelino's style were his visits, after his election to the Presidency, to the site of the new capital, where he often stayed, beginning with his first visit on October 2, 1956, in a wooden building built in ten days and known as "Little Catete" (*Catetinho*) after the Presidential Catete Palace in Rio de Janeiro (Martins Ramos n.d.: 17). On his many visits there was a kind of fraternization symbolizing Kubitschek's role as a populist politician and builder of the new capital. Surrounded by workers, he would inspect the progress of the city. Frequently the roughly dressed men (*candangos,* Brasília's in-migrant construction workers) would press forward and hand him written requests, for such favors as free passage to visit a sick relative. Or he would lunch at a restaurant in the Free Town, unprotected by the usual heavy police detachments.

Juscelino was determined that his name should go down in history as the founder of the new capital. And to defeat the resistance that would inevitably arise, it would be necessary to make the move irreversible by the time his five-year term in office was complete. (Juscelino was the second of the two post-World War II Presidents of Brazil to complete the constitutional term, the other being Army Marshal Eurico Gaspar Dutra.)

This was a realistic judgment. As we have seen, the effects of administrative discontinuity on such projects are severe in Brazil. And in fact, in 1961, Jânio Quadros, Juscelino's successor, quickly paralyzed the construction in Brasília, which would only be taken up again in a determined, organized manner under the aegis of Marshal-President Castelo Branco, quite a different breed of politician, after the military coup of 1964.

The rather banal fact that political realism required (or condemned) Brasília to be planned and built in less than five years, is of some importance to any understanding of the development of the city and its settlement pattern. It should be remembered that the "lead time" for, say, a new airplane, is a good deal longer than five years. We know less about how cities work than we do about airplanes, which are much simpler. And Brasília is no ordinary city. So whatever one's opinion of the idea of building it in the first place, or of the result, one is forced to admit that the construction itself was a major feat. But the hasty manner in which it was performed left a considerable and perhaps indelible mark on the result.

To finance Brasília, Juscelino turned to a scheme under which the city was to pay for itself through the sale of lots in the city whose value would appreciate as a result of the very process of construction. By 1962, however, such sales had provided only 7 percent of the public expenditures for the city. Inflation soon ate away the value of the long-term payments which the purchasers were supposed to make for their lots, with the result that the construction effort was in fact financed by massive injections of government funds through various agencies, especially NOVACAP; by 1961, at that year's price levels, this expenditure totaled Cr$250–300 billion (roughly U.S.$1 billion). These funds, like those which went for big hydroelectric and road projects also carried out under Juscelino's administration, in part were provided by huge emissions of paper cruzeiros, thus contributing to Brazil's sweeping postwar inflation, and by overseas loans and credits (*Conjuntura Econômica* 1962).

The jobs associated with Brasília, even that of a recognized genius like Oscar Niemeyer, who planned almost all of the monumental buildings in the city, went to people long associated with the figure of the President. Niemeyer (1961: 28) outdoes himself in eulogy for Juscelino —with whom he was associated since 1940—who selected him for the task of architect in 1956, before the jury selected the plan for the city (1961: 12). Niemeyer in turn sat on the jury, which selected the city plan of Lúcio Costa. The task of directing the enterprise of construction fell on Israel Pinheiro, scion of an old political family in Minas and an important figure in the PSD. The examples could be continued further. The point is not to cast doubt upon the merits of the men who administered the job of building the city or on the propriety of their selection. It is merely to suggest that Brasília was a spectacular opportunity for patronage, for rewarding one's clientele, for promoting the interests of the members of one's political entourage. It was a spectacular example of the public works complex in operation.

The question of corruption in the construction of Brasília is frequently raised. I have neither sought nor found any evidence on this question though the circumstances of haste no doubt would have facilitated corruption if there were those so inclined. For all the talk of past "corruption and subversion" after the coup of 1964, the military-dominated government has—at least publicly—come up with astonishingly little hard evidence of either. The least corrupt of all governments, of course, would be one with zero program and zero budget; Adhemar de Barros's famous slogan, "He robs but he builds" (*Rouba mas faz*), makes a good deal of sense in the light of the previous analysis of the limited opportunities for government investment.

As far as Brasília is concerned, however, corruption is a side issue. What is important is the total impact of the project on the people of Brazil and upon their future.

III. From Dream to Plan

From earliest times the pattern of Brazilian society was determined in large part by Brazil's position in the global society, which was that of an exporter of agricultural products and raw materials to the European, and later North American metropolises. This position is reflected in the influence of the patriarchal slave plantations on the national character, and also in the pattern of urban settlement and growth. In direct consequence of the dependent position of the country, the large cities tended to have coastal and port locations. Late-blooming São Paulo, while not a port, was heavily dependent on coffee exportation. Belo Horizonte, the other exception to this pattern among the major cities, is a planned twentieth-century capital, in many ways a precursor of Brasília.

At the same time, central government control over the interior of the country was tenuous, much of the country's area remaining economically untouched, except for occasional forays and gathering of such forest products as Brazil nuts and natural rubber, or in the Center-West and Northeast regions, cattle-raising.

Yet an ideology of continental destiny was present from an early date. Many statesmen and thinkers regarded more effective use of the vast interior as a necessity, if only to keep other nations from taking it over. One of the constants in these discussions was the idea of bringing the capital of the country, first located in the city of Salvador, Bahia, and later in Rio de Janeiro—both Atlantic ports—into the interior of the country. While these plans were never put into practice, the idea persisted throughout Brazilian history. It represented part of the intellectual capital which President Juscelino Kubitschek de Oliveira, with whose political personality the city is identified, used to promote his project.

It is frequently stated (as by Martins Ramos n.d.: 21) that the transfer of the capital to the interior, specifically to the Minas Gerais city of São João del Rey, was one of the goals of the proindependence conspiracy of 1789, the *Inconfidência Mineira*. However, it has not been possible to document that statement.

A more reliable source reports that the idea was proposed in 1808 in the newspaper *Correio Braziliense*.[1] Accusing the members of the Imperial court of being more concerned with their own comfort than with the development of the Brazilian Empire, and citing the danger of naval

1. This was the name taken by the newspaper that in 1967 was Brasília's only daily.

attack and the difficulty of communication in the light of Rio de Janeiro's
peripheral location, Furtado de Mendonça stated: "This location, quite
central, where the capital of the Empire ought to be located, seems to us
to be indicated as the very elevated region of her territory, whence would
descend the orders [of the government], just as there descend the waters
which go to the Tocantins River to the north, the Plate to the south, and
to the São Francisco to the east" (quoted in Cruls 1957: 61). This is of
course precisely the present location of the Federal District, part of whose
area contains streams leading to each of the three great river systems.

Various other manifestations in this direction continued until in 1823
the "Patriarch" or father of his country, José Bonifácio de Andrada e
Silva, submitted to the Constituent Assembly a document proposing the
construction in the interior of a new capital with the name of Brasília or
"Petrópole," the latter in honor of the Emperor Pedro I. This idea was
supported by the historian Varnhagen (the Viscount of Pôrto Seguro) in
1834, on account of the military vulnerability of the coastal capital, Rio
de Janeiro. He too favored the site near the headwaters of the Tocantins,
Paraná-Prata (Plate), and São Francisco river systems.

While the concept of a new capital in this area remained a dream, there
were at least three other projects in the past by which the frontiers of
urban settlement were extended through the creation of brand new cities.
Each of the projects has had a modest but long-lasting success, if a continued pattern of population growth and new construction and maintenance of political status are the criteria by which the success of such projects is to be judged.

In 1851 the capital of the Northeast state of Piauí was the small city
of Oeiras, which was located on the intermittent Canindé River, a tribu-
tary of the larger Parnaíba. In that year, a new city, Teresina, was constructed on the course of the river Parnaíba, making possible the navigation which was carried out after 1858 by the Rio Parnaíba Navigation
Company, enabling the new capital to carry out a commercial as well as
a political function. Piauí, however, is the poorest of Brazil's states, and
the commercial role of the city later declined. Only now, with a new
hydroelectric project (Bôa Esperança), is there some hope for a new
departure for the region. Only Teresina's wide streets and regular plan
remind us that it is the result of an early experiment in planned urbanism
(Geiger 1963: 391).

It is in the present century that we find two important precursors of
the Brasília experience, closer to her geographically as well as in time.
These are the capitals of the two states on which Brasília borders, Goiânia,
Goiás, and Belo Horizonte, Minas Gerais.

Belo Horizonte, one of the major cities of Brazil, after the metropolises of Rio de Janeiro and São Paulo, and one of the fastest growing cities in the country as well, was built in the first years of the Republic, the works beginning in 1894 and the inauguration taking place on September 12, 1897. The new city replaced the old mining town of Ouro Prêto (formerly Vila Rica) as capital. The same features (narrow streets, mountains impeding expansion) which today make Ouro Prêto into a center of tourism and art-historical interest, were inadequate to the task of political and administrative capital of the vast state of Minas Gerais. Nevertheless, the transfer of the capital aroused ferocious resistance, so much so that the local legislature moved temporarily to the city of Barbacena to vote the law providing for the transfer within a period of four years. Opponents of the move counted on the difficulty of transport and scarcity of energy to impede the move, but nevertheless it was carried out (Geiger 1963: 226; Orico 1958: 204).

Belo Horizonte in many respects was a notable success, has succeeded in becoming an important center for banking and for industry, notably iron and steel. While much of Minas remains tied more closely to Rio de Janeiro or to São Paulo than to the state capital, from an economic viewpoint, nevertheless, Belo Horizonte's growth has been impressive.

The city is planned on a basic grid system of streets 20 meters wide, cut by diagonal avenues 35 meters wide. The city as a whole is ringed by the Peripheral Avenue (*Avenida de Contôrno*). However, her growth has gone beyond that foreseen by the planners, so that two-thirds of the urban mass lies outside this Avenue. Various urban and sururban areas have irregular grid plans disarticulated from the center. Belo Horizonte also suffers from serious problems of public services, notably water; less than half the city has access to purified piped water.

Another aspect of the Belo Horizonte experience is that the implantation of the city, successful from the point of view of urban growth, contributed little or nothing to the settlement of the rural northern region of the state. This area, with a landscape similar to that around Brasília, still does not enjoy the kind of dense population typical of the southern region of Minas, nor even the pioneering growth typified by the Triangle region, radiating from São Paulo. It remains to be seen whether Brasília, located in advance of the front of dense settlement, will have a more positive effect in this regard than Belo Horizonte, located on the front's outer margin.

More recent than Belo Horizonte and still closer to Brasília is the city of Goiânia, planned capital of the interior state of Goiás. Begun in 1933, and inaugurated on March 23, 1937, Goiânia was in part a product of the 1930 "revolution" that installed Getúlio Vargas as Brazil's President. Its local manifestation was a shift in the Goiás political situation, dominated by a local oligarchy. Pedro Ludovico, federal interventor in the state and to this day chief of one of its two political factions, was the major instigator of the transfer. The former capital, Goiás (now Goiás Velho, or Old Goiás), is, like Ouro Prêto, an old mining town, and something of an historical site, but equally unsuited as a capital from the Brazilian point of view. It was condemned as early as the last century by Couto de Magalhães, provincial governor under the Empire and explorer, who suggested moving the capital to the banks of the Araguáia River, which he saw as a future inland waterway of great importance.

Goiânia, a pleasant if somewhat provincial place, is built on a classical concentric pattern: a central square from which streets go out like spokes on a wheel, intersected by other streets on a concentric fashion. The variant is that there are two such central squares, and in the north an area of straight line streets. North, center, and south contain respectively the commerce, industry, and railway station; the government buildings; and the residential zone. Attached to the city is the preexisting locality of Campinas. Though it has enjoyed a modest prosperity, Goiânia has been rivaled by Anápolis, a nearby city, also served by a spur of the Center-West Railway.

Although the idea of a new national capital remained present during the nineteenth century, it ran up against the technoenvironmental obstacles of the lack of easy communications from the coast, over the mountains and into the interior, and the reality of the limited resources of a technologically backward, stagnant, and dependent political economy. It was not the fact that the proposals of men of vision were willfully neglected, such as that of Couto de Magalhães who explored the Araguáia River and proposed a great system of canals and internal navigation between the Amazon and the Paraná-Prata basins; it was rather that the social conditions in a country that remained a dependent outpost in the international economic system made such talk completely impractical.

With the coup d'etat that established the Republic in 1889, the idea of a new site for the capital gained greater impetus. The Provisional Constitution of 1890 provided for the transfer of the capital and for the granting of statehood to Rio de Janeiro, formerly the "Neutral Municipality" (*Município Neutro*). This proposal was repeated in Title I, Article 3 of the Republican Constitution of February 24, 1891: "Once the transfer of the capital has taken place, the present Federal District [Rio de Janeiro], will come to constitute a State" (*Imprensa Nacional* 1948: 87). The document also provided for the demarcation of an area of 14,000 square kilometers in the central plateau for the eventual construction of the new capital.

In accordance with this provision, President Floriano Peixoto appointed a Commission to Explore the Central Plateau. The Cruls Commission (known for its leader, Luís Cruls) left Rio de Janeiro on July 9, 1892. It included astronomers, doctors, military engineers, a geologist, and a botanist and constituted an authentic scientific expedition. The Commission demarcated a vast quadrilateral within which, at some future date, the new city was to be built (Cruls 1947; Geiger 1963: 427). Little, however, came of this immediately.

It was only in 1922 that the first abortive attempt was made to give life to the legal provision for the transfer of the capital. The Congress provided in Decree 4494 of that year that the foundation stone of the new capital should be laid within the Cruls Quadrilateral on September 7, 1922, the one-hundredth anniversary of Brazilian independence. This was done in the small town of Planatina, Goiás, which has become part of the Federal District since the construction of Brasília. Nothing more than the foundation stone was ever built, however (Martins Ramos n.d.: 22).

The 1934 Constitution, enacted in the wake of the "revolution" of 1930 and the abortive São Paulo revolt of 1932, included, again, provisions for moving the capital (*Imprensa Nacional* 1948: 204), but these were years of tumult in Brazil's political life. In 1937 the Constitution was replaced by Getúlio Vargas's "New State" (*Estado Nôvo*) decree, which contained no provision for the transfer of the capital. The provision was restored, however, in the 1946 Constitution, and promulgated when Vargas's overthrow led to the return of liberal-democratic forms in the wake of the Allied victory over the Axis in 1945. Article 4 of the "Transitory Dispositions" of the 1946 Constitution stated:

(1) The President of the Republic, within sixty days of the proclamation of this act, will name a commission of technicians of recognized merit to study the location of the new Capital.

(2) The study provided for in the foregoing paragraph will be directed to the National Congress, which will deliberate in regard to it in a special law and will establish the time for the beginning of the delimitation of the area to be incorporated into the Domain of the Union.

(2) After the demarcation is complete, the Congress will set the date for the transfer of the Capital (*Imprensa Nacional* 1948: 356).

The result of these provisions was the creation of the Commission for the Studies of the Location of the New Capital of Brazil, headed by General Poli Coelho.

This body acted with a despatch far from typical in the history of past efforts toward the creation of a new capital. An expedition was organized under the leadership of the French geographer François Ruellan. This expedition covered 1,750 kilometers in sixty-five days, gathering detailed information about possible sites for the new capital (Ruellan 1948).

Seven sites were selected, four in Minas Gerais, and three in Goiás—
including the present Federal District. Among the criteria for site selection were an altitude sufficient to provide an amenable climate and to
reduce the incidence of malaria; a moderately sloping terrain, with a sufficient gradient to allow for an efficient drainage system; nearby water and
hydroelectric potential (110,000 to 120,000 kilowatts within 100 kilometers); a modest distance to a supply center; and available construction
materials.

Ruellan reasoned that the location of the new capital would depend on
what was expected of it. If it was to be a purely political and administrative center, it should be located in an already populated area in the southern part of the Central Plateau. If, on the other hand, it was to be a pole
of expansion of the frontier and a base for future settlement, it should be
located on the edge of the vast unsettled region, further to the north and
west (Ruellan 1947: 41). In this case, Ruellan emphasized the importance of ". . . the site selected . . . permitting the easy construction
of a star of roads and railways" (Ruellan 1947: 43).

According to James and Faissol (1956: 311), a majority of the professional geographers employed on the expedition preferred the former alternative. They proposed a site near Tupaciguara in the Minas Triangle,
the western projection of that state between São Paulo and Goiás. A
majority of the members of the Coelho Commission itself, however, were
swayed by the desire to have a capital nearer the geographical center of
Brazil, and called for a site within the old Cruls Quadrilateral in Goiás.
This impasse was resolved by a commission of the Chamber of Deputies,
on which each state had one vote. The fact that the Northeast is divided
into more states than any other region of the country led to a preference
for a site nearer that region, since it was recognized that the Minas Triangle is within the economic sphere of São Paulo (James and Faissol
1956: 313). This Congressional decision took the form of Law No.
1803 of 1953, and specified a location lying within the state of Goiás,
between Latitudes 15°30' and 17°South and Longitudes 46°30' and
49°30' West.

The United States firm of Donald J. Belcher and Associates, Inc. was
contracted on February 25, 1954 to do photoanalysis and interpretation
on the broad area chosen the previous year, in order to choose the best
site within it for the actual construction. Later in 1954 Marshall José
Pessôa Cavalcânti de Albuquerque was named (in Decree 36,598) by
President Café Filho to head the Commission for the Localization of the
New Capital.

On April 30, 1955 this Commission selected the present site, which
was declared of "public utility" (*utilidade pública*) by the state governor

of Goiás. This was the first step toward expropriation. Table I shows the criteria, each given a percentage weight, on the basis of which the choice among the five possible sites indicated by Belcher and Associates was made.

For each of the criteria, each of the five sites, denominated by a color, was graded on a scale. The Brown (*castanho*) site was finally chosen, located in an area outside the centers of settlement in southern Goiás. This area was low in population density and presumably easier to expropriate (Ludwig 1966: 191). The emptiness of the region would also

TABLE I
Criteria for the Final Selection of a Site for the New Capital

Criteria	Percentage weight
(1) A favorable climate with no extremes of temperature or rainfall and no violent winds, and at an elevation high enough to offer freedom from malaria.	20
(2) A water supply adequate for a city of half a million people, preferably available by gravity flow.	15
(3) Gently sloping terrain—not too steep, not too flat.	15
(4) Access to ground and air transport.	10
(5) A source of low-cost electric power located within 100 kilometers.	10
(6) Locally available building materials, including lime for cement.	10
(7) A subsoil suitable for building foundations and for the excavation of sewers and subways.	5
(8) Nearby forested areas where agriculture can become established for the supply of vegetables and milk, and where wood can be procured for fuel.	5
(9) An attractive landscape and nearby recreation areas.	5
(10) Ease of disappropriation.	5
TOTAL	100

Sources: Orico 1958: 54; Ludwig 1966: 182–191; James and Faissol 1956: 313.

Note: The point values are taken from Orico, and diverge slightly from those given in James and Faissol; the latter also fails to include items (4) and (10), though Ludwig mentions both in his more extensive treatment. Since Orico's treatment is summary, we have in other respects followed James and Faissol.

make it easier for the planners to mold a specialized political-administrative center according to their taste.

It was still necessary to delimit exactly the area to be incorporated into the future Federal District. According to the law, the District was to have an area of 5,000 square kilometers. The approved final borders, however, included 5,850 kilometers, and the Green as well as the Brown site. It was established that a dam would be constructed in order to provide both a source for at least some of the needed electricity and an artificial lake 48 kilometers long and up to 4 kilometers wide (Orico 1958: 61). The site, just as had long been advocated by proponents of the new capital, included portions of the watersheds of the Tocantins, Paraná-Prata, and São Francisco rivers.

Early in his administration, President Kubitschek had decided to press the construction of the new capital with special vigor. On April 18, 1956 Juscelino went to the city of Anápolis in Goiás, and signed a message which was the first step in the creation of NOVACAP, the Company to Urbanize the New Capital of Brazil (*Companhia Urbanizadora da Nova Capital do Brasil*). On October 24th of the same year, Dr. Israel Pinheiro was named as president of this body.

Since the city had virtually to be completed, at least to a degree sufficient to make the transfer of the capital irreversible, in the five years of Juscelino Kubitschek's Presidential mandate, many aspects of the city's future development were not considered in detail by any agency. The relation of Brasília to th Center-West geographical region, for instance, was studied only in terms of highway and rail connections; in spite of the *marcha para oeste* as a justifying slogan for the city's construction, no overall program of colonization or regional development was made with Brasília as its center.

The first tasks of NOVACAP were those which did not depend on the details of the Pilot Plan of Brasília, which was only to be selected on March 12, 1957. This early work included the soundings for the Paranoá Dam, which would create the artificial lake and provide electrical energy; the water and sewage system, the former of which was initiated; and the transportation network which was to link the new capital with the rest of the nation and especially with the industrial heartland, Greater São Paulo. The most important part of this network was the road between the city of Anápolis, railhead of the Estrada de Ferro Goiás (now Viação Férrea Centro-Oeste), and the future Federal District. Of the monumental works, the Presidential Palace was to have a lakeside location independent of the Pilot Plan, the airport site had already been selected, and work was begun on a luxury hotel near the Presidential Palace (Orico 1958: 61–62). In view of the later consequences of the failure to provide adequate housing for the construction workers in this period, the decision to build a luxury hotel at this early stage is perhaps a significant example of the priorities which reigned from the beginning of the Brasília project.

IV. Lúcio Costa's Pilot Plan

The overall plan which would guide the construction of the new capital was to be selected by an international jury among competing plans by Brazilian architects and city planners. Those participating in the contest were given a great deal of information, including maps, charts, and aerial mosaics, and had an opportunity to visit the prospective site. They were expected, however, to submit only two basic documents:

(a) A basic layout of the city, indicating the position of the main items of the urban structure, the location and interconnexion of the various sectors, centres, installations and services, the distribution of the open spaces and lines of communication, to the scale of 1:25,000.

(b) A supporting report (Holford 1957: 397).

This left a great deal to the discretion of the contestants, and as a result the proposals ranged from the detailed one of the firm M. M. M. Roberto, of which William Holford, a British town planner and member of the jury, recalls, "I have never seen anywhere in the world a more comprehensive and thoroughgoing master-plan for the new capital city on a cleared site" (1957: 397), to the submission by Lúcio Costa, presented on five medium-sized cards including not a single mechanical drawing, model, land-use schedule, or population chart.

It was nevertheless the Costa proposal that was chosen by five of the six jurors—Holford, Oscar Niemeyer, the architect already chosen to design major government buildings, Horta Barbosa of the Society of Engineers, André Sive of the French Ministry of Reconstruction and Housing, and Stamo Papadaki. These jurors chose Costa's plan because in spite of its extreme economy, it seemed to have the thrust and unity required to orient the growth of a capital city. Paulo Antunes Ribeiro, the juror who represented the Brazilian Institute of Architects, dissented, calling Costa's proposal far too slight even to merit consideration. Ribeiro proposed as an alternative that the ten leading competitors share the total prize money of Cr$2,400,000 (a bit less than U.S.$17,000). His protest was disallowed, however, and it was the Costa plan that oriented much of the construction of the new capital (Holford 1957; Orico 1958: 111–112).

Costa, one of the pioneers of modern architecture in Brazil and a defender and student of the Brazilian architectural heritage, presented a plan calling for a city in the form of a cross, variously described by commentators as an airplane, a bird, or a dragonfly. One axis, the Monumental (see illus. 2), constituting the fuselage or body of the city, would concentrate the official political-administrative functions, while the other was to contain the residential and associated sectors in its two wings (see fig. 3). At the juncture of the two axes was a great multilevel highway interchange, including the bus station (illus. 5). The railway station (unbuilt as of 1967) eventually would be located at one end of the Monumental Axis (see map 3).

Evidently, one of the characteristics of the plan was the monumental emphasis on the government buildings, an effect heightened by broad

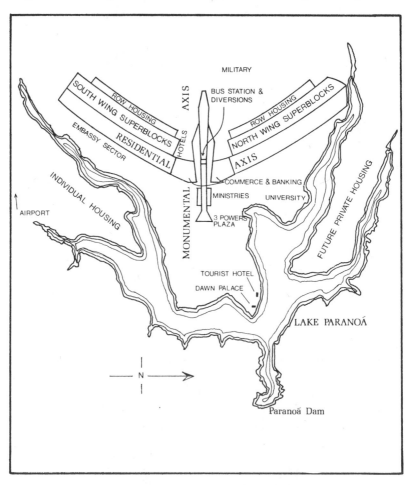

MAP 3. Main features of Costa's Pilot Plan.

vistas, formal in a bare way, and by the constant impression of great distance. The style of the buildings, uncluttered, glass-surfaced, and high, today contributes to this effect.

This monumentality was much criticized in the name of humanitarian values—Brasília was seen as a throwback to nineteenth-century conceptions of grandeur, the exhibition of civil and military power. Costa responded by denying that Brasília is monumental in any pejorative sense, and defended its right to grandeur:

As for the concept of monumentality, I don't see why in Democracy the *city* must necessarily be lacking in grandeur. In ostentatious and emphatic grandeur, yes; but not in that which naturally results from a simple and functional layout, conceived with high intentions. The more so when dealing, as in this case, with a capital, a singular city no matter how socialized the country. It isn't breaking [the city] down into units of a provincial rut that one will symbolize this singular role urbanistically.

One ought not to forget that besides this business of "welfare" the human condition has, in spite of everything, *grandeur,* and it is awareness of this that gives us strength to carry life on to the end . . . (Costa 1962).

And again, in response to Antonio Callado, a noted journalist who compared (unfavorably) the priorities of the Brasília plan with those of the more social-welfare-oriented British New Towns, Costa affirmed: "The *monument,* in the case of a capital, is not an afterthought, that can be left for later, as in the modern little English cities,[2] the *monument* here is intrinsic to the thing itself, and as opposed to the . . . city which one wishes discreetly inscribed into the landscape, the capital city must be imposed, and command [the landscape]" (Costa 1962).

This very desire, to command, to "take possession" as Costa puts it, inspired the plan's symbolism: "[The solution] was born of the primary gesture of one who indicates a place and takes possession of it: two axes crossing at a right angle, or the very sign of the cross" (Costa 1957: 41).

Everywhere in his writings Costa seemed concerned with the special functions of Brasília as capital and symbol. Brasília can be analyzed in terms of these assumptions and of the political and cultural imperatives behind its construction. In doing so we choose the first of the alternatives pointed out by Paul and Percival Goodman (1947: 20–21) for the discussion of a city plan: (1) analyzing the *ends* of the plan from a philosophical or humanistic perspective, or (2) looking at it technically, in terms of the elegance and economy of the means chosen to carry out a given purpose.

The capital, said Costa, must be not only *urbs,* "capable of fulfilling satisfactorily and without effort the vital functions proper to any modern

2. The diminutive, *cidadezinhas,* is employed here in quite a pejorative sense.

city," but *civitas,* with the special virtues, the "dignity and nobility of *intent*" of a great capital. Residents of Rio de Janeiro suffering from lack of water, rationed electricity, and floods; or Londoners whose lives are shortened by smog; or New Yorkers crushed in the subways like sardines, living in constant fear of sudden violence or social explosion may all wonder at this seeming dismissal of the problem of planning a city in which the vital functions of daily life can be performed "satisfactorily and without effort." Even in Brasília it has proven far easier to build some of the world's loveliest monuments than to solve practical problems of this kind.

The second feature of Costa's plan, and according to Ludwig that which distinguished it from other proposals actively studied by the jury (1966: 191), was that it called not for a pattern of growth and expansion, but presented a city whose shape, pattern, and future extent would be evident from the earliest possible moment. The city would be born with an adult skeleton. The openness and even desolation that impresses some visitors to the new capital are partly attributable to this characteristic. Of course this feature fits perfectly with the desire to complete enough of the city in President Kubitschek's term to make the transfer of the capital irreversible.

The full-blownness of the city plan was a partial antidote to the danger that future administrators, even if they were to prove unable to prevent the transfer of the capital, would succeed in undoing the lucidity and authority of the plan. Thus in Brasília one comes frequently upon asphalted streets in the midst of virgin *campo cerrado*; elsewhere one block of apartments may be separated from the next by a kilometer or two of unbulldozed lots, empty of all signs of urban life. The effect was to inoculate the city against future efforts by pressure groups, vested interests, politically well connected speculators, and vain administrators, aimed at undermining the integrity of the plan. Rather than merely providing in the plan for the nucleus of a future metropolis, outside of which such forces would have free play, Costa's plan provided for an entire street network, laid out and paved in accordance with his design. A situation much harder to undo.

Costa himself recognized this necessity, and in a reply to the criticisms of General Menezes Côrtes, former head of Rio de Janeiro's traffic department, he defends the extensive paving of large numbers of streets not immediately put to use for buildings:

I do not agree that there was any waste of paving material. I believe that the criterion adopted by the President of attacking at once, in articulate and organized form, the whole structure of the city in the appropriate scale, was essential, not only so that, barely born, she would inspire all

Brazilians—even those from the old metropolises Rio and Sao Paulo—
with a sense of really being in the Capital, but also because *neglecting to
do it now* because it might seem superfluous, *he would have run the risk of
never having it done,* reducing forever the integrity of the original conception [last two emphases added] (Costa 1962).

The other side of the coin of course is that the plan is also that much
harder to adapt and mold to circumstance, in the light of the finality of
the skeletal form. And in fact, when the pressures became unbearable the
solution chosen was simply to leave the planned area to one side and
attempt the solution elsewhere, in the satellite towns and squatter settlements.

Many details of the plan derived from a basic preoccupation with the
passenger automobile and the problems of its circulation. A principal aim
of the plan was to permit the free flow of auto traffic. It was the same
Juscelino Kubitschek whose administration marked the installation of a
national automotive industry in Brazil that led the installation of the automotive city par excellence as Brazil's capital.

This automotive emphasis had certain implications. Protestations to the
contrary, it suggested that the city would for a long time attend, in the
very practical matter of getting around, much more to the interests of
that relatively small segment of the population able to acquire cars, than
to the less well-to-do majority condemned to foot, bus, and bicycle travel
(see table XI). Even in 1967, ten years after the national auto industry
was installed, the family car is a dream for most, and those who have access to one are still in the first flush of excitement and fascination. The
planning emphasis given to auto traffic led to the lengthening of distances,
the dispersion of sectors (also the consequence of the decision not to build
the city out from a nucleus), and the placement of the retail stores on
W-3 Avenue (see illus. 10), which has turned out to be the main commercial street, on only one side of it, increasing the distance between
stores from what it would be under a more centralized arrangement.

Brasília is no exception, either, to the rule that planned or "artificial"
cities are organized hierarchically into sectors, subsectors, and so forth. In
fact this sort of planning sometimes amounts to nothing more than a kind
of bookkeeping, a neat compartmentalization of supposedly separate categories of activity carried out by people in cities. Perhaps it could not be
otherwise; we have not progressed analytically or practically to a point
where another conception could be translated into "planning" in the conventional sense, whose tools are after all drastically limited.

Yet there is considerable doubt that cities can work effectively when
organized hierarchically into sectors—what Christopher Alexander
(1966) calls *tree* organization. Jane Jacobs, in her iconoclastic book

(1961), argues that the most vital and psychologically healthy neighborhoods of American cities are those which diverge the most from the conventional planning wisdom. Far from being delineated into sectors, or orthodoxly zoned (zoning is an attempt, ex post facto, to divide a city into sectors), such neighborhoods are typically areas of mixed uses, industrial, commercial, and residential; of different types of traffic in a somewhat frenetic juxtaposition; more crowded than is supposed to be healthy; stylistically eclectic and made up of buildings of varying ages; and lacking in a geometric street plan, being cut up instead into short, irregularly disposed blocks.

A healthy modern city, says Christopher Alexander, is not, in mathematical jargon, a hierarchically organized "tree," but a "semi-lattice," composed of a complex series of connections, not merely between part and whole, or subpart and part, but also between the various parts and subparts, a veritable spider's web of connections. Asserts Alexander:

For the human mind, the tree is the easiest vehicle for complex thoughts. But the city is not, cannot, and must not be a tree. The city is a receptacle for life. If the receptacle severs the overlap of the strands of life within it, because it is a tree, it will be like a bowl of razor blades on edge, ready to cut up whatever is entrusted to it. In such a receptacle life will be cut to pieces. If we make cities which are trees, they will cut our life to pieces (1966: 55).

Lúcio Costa's plan divided Brasília into two principal parts, the Monumental Axis and the Residential Axis, the latter in turn being divided into what have come to be called the South and North Wings (*Asa Sul, Asa Norte*). Conceptually, the plan has four parts: (1) the government buildings, (2) the residential zones of superblocks, (3) the vehicular circulatory system, and (4) the city center. The government buildings largely correspond to the Monumental Axis, the superblocks to the Residential Axis, the city center to their intersection. Axes, intersection, and the local feeder roads constitute the vehicular circulatory system.

The Monumental Axis of 1967 follows Costa's plan with great fidelity. At one extremity are the official centers of the three branches of government, executive, legislative, and judiciary. These are grouped around Three Powers Plaza (*Praça dos Três Poderes*), which from the intersection of the Monumental and Residential Axes is hidden from view by the Congressional complex (see illus. 1). To one side of the Plaza, the Presidential Office Building, the Plateau Palace (*Palácio do Planalto*); to the other, the Supreme Court, fronted by a stone sculpture of Justice. Also in the square is a windowless building whose flat facade is broken by an enormous head of Juscelino Kubitschek. This building is a museum commemorating the construction of the new capital. Inside, carved in the walls in enormous letters, are the texts of speeches, some by the precursors of the Brasília idea discussed in section III of this chapter, but most by President Kubitschek himself. President Quadros's wife had a tall wooden dovecote installed in the square.

Hiding the Plaza from the mall above it is the group of buildings housing the legislative power, the Congress. This group of buildings is dominated by the twin twenty-eight-story towers of the Congressional office buildings, known to Brasília pioneers simply as "the twenty-eight" (*o vinte-oito*); a reflecting pool links the towers to the paved part of the Plaza. Geese, brought in as a tribute to the geese which once saved the Roman Senate, live in the pool. Plenary sessions of the Senate and the Chamber of Deputies are held in the two wings of the lower section of the Congressional complex, surmounted by a dome and a contrasting bowl shape respectively. Access to these buildings is by a series of ramps.

The Mall (*Esplanada*) dominated by the Congress is flanked on either side by the identical green-glass-and-concrete matchboxes of the Ministries buildings. By 1967 the number of ministries in the government has grown beyond the number in Juscelino's day, and the correspondence is not so neat as in the original plan between the number of buildings and the agencies in them. Two ministries, Justice and Foreign Relations, have buildings nearer the Congress and of different form and location from the others. The Palace of Arches (*Palácio dos Arcos*), seat of the Foreign Relations Ministry, completed in 1967, is perhaps the finest and most classical of Niemeyer's buildings.

Further up the Monumental Axis is the junction with the Residential Axis, followed by a fairly steep rise surmounted by a tall television tower whose base was designed by Costa himself. Beyond the tower the plan called for a series of facilities, including the organs of local government, the army barracks, and finally the railroad station. But in 1967 the asphalt here narrowed and the area remained largely deserted; this part of the plan has not so far been executed. The Prefecture of Brasília is located in offices ceded by the federal social security authorities in an out-of-the-way location. For all practical purposes, the Monumental Axis remains truncated.

The monumentality implied by the name is achieved in a number of ways. The first of these is the dramatic skill of Niemeyer as an architect. The second contribution to this effect is the careful and expensive manipulation of the angles of view, effected by massive earth-moving, well enough done so that the casual visitor to Brasília may never realize just how much was involved. The flatness of the Mall between the rows of the Ministries, the abrupt drop behind the Congress were both carefully manipulated with this end in view (Niemeyer 1961: 51). A third factor is the simple

use of open space in the most generous sense, augmenting the impression
of height and breadth in the buildings; this use of space does, however,
contribute to the difficulty of walking around the government area, particularly in midday or in the rainy months. Finally, the cruciform plan of
the city and the restriction on high building in the residential zones make
the government buildings, especially the Congressional and television towers (and to a lesser degree the Ministries) highly visible and impressive
from fairly great distances. Clear air and strong light contribute to this
visibility.

Costa (1962) insisted that the Residential Axis's two wings, unlike
the Monumental Axis, were to contain areas of a "retiring and intimate"
character. He adopted as his principal solution for housing and related
functions—schooling, local commerce, some kinds of recreation, church-
going—the superblocks (*superquadras*), "so called not so much because
they pretend to be superior as because they are large" (see illus. 6 and 9).
The plan called for ninety-six such superblocks, plus fourteen superblocks
of doubled area whose elevatorless buildings were to be limited to three
stories as opposed to six in the single blocks. The blocks were to be laid
out in double rows on either side of the highway access, with its fourteen
lanes of traffic, paralleling the Residential Axis, and dividing it into upper
and lower segments.

The cul-de-sac roads in these superblocks were to be isolated from
through traffic. The blocks were to be equally isolated from direct view
from outside by a wide belt of tall trees and a supplementary curtain of
lower vegetation; from any external viewpoint the buildings were to appear absorbed in the landscape. The plantings were to serve the function,
also, of providing shaded areas for walking and leisure.

Each superblock was to be made up of a series of residential apartment
buildings (*blocos*), in a single style for each superblock, and a uniform
planting distinguishing it from its neighbors. This latter provision was never
carried out. For some purposes, the single superblock was to serve as a
single neighborhood unit; for others, each group of four superblocks was
to form a unit. Between the superblocks would be the low buildings devoted to local commerce, opening onto the blocks, with a rear access road
for deliveries and parking. Each group of four blocks, at the point of
juncture, was to have a church, and behind the church there would be
located a secondary school, and near the main highway axis a movie house.
This location would facilitate access for those coming from other neighborhoods. An area was set aside for a youth club, with appropriate playing fields. Thus within the neighborhood area, the intention was to facilitate the creation of a neighborhood unit (*unidade de vizinhança*). A series
of activities centering on domesticity and education were to take place on

a local scale, obviating any need for automotive or mass transportation for their execution.

Costa did not ignore the social "gradations proper to the current regime" and attempted to provide for them in his plan, though he specifically asserted that so far as he is concerned, the authories must "provide within the scheme proposed decent and economical accommodations for the *whole* population" [Costa's emphasis]. He insisted that "the encystment of squatments [*favelas*] must be prevented, both within the urban periphery and the rural." The planner, then, at least in his declaration of intentions, wanted to reconcile the social inequality of the present system with measures that would alleviate some of the extreme manifestations of it found in other Brazilian cities.

Costa suggested that one of the means of "dosing out" inequality, as he put it, was to attribute greater value to certain superblocks, those nearer to the embassy section located below the Residential Axis toward the lake, and also those closer to the main highway axis. Yet grouping the blocks four-by-four in neighborhood units would "propitiate social coexistence to some degree, thus avoiding excessive and undesirable stratification." Another source of differentiation would be differences in density and in the living space per person or per family. Finally, Costa would employ more or less expensive materials and use various types of finishing, according to the social level of the residents. At the same time, he seemed to hope that the stratification he considered himself impelled to provide for would be neutralized by the layout of the city, and certainly not "affect the social comfort to which all are entitled."

The implied assumption behind this solution is that differences in class—at least among the vast majority, who were to be apartment dwellers—were, or at least ought to be, essentially economic within fairly narrow limits. Different life-styles and different types of functions fulfilled by the residence for the different social strata were not provided for or even considered. Costa, in line with the tendency of his plan to provide for the form of the completed city, but not for its growth, concerned himself but little with who was to pay for the "social comfort" to which he said all have a right, but which only a small minority of Brazilians possess in the degree he suggested is desirable. If the residents of the apartments were to pay for them, very little was said about the nature of the architectural economies required to make them available to the members of the lowest social strata. If the government was to pay for them, in spite of its limited financial capabilities, Costa did not consider either the criteria for selecting the beneficiaries of such largesse, or the need for control of the influx of benefit-seeking lower-income migrants which was almost sure to result in view of the lack of similar programs in the many areas of widespread poverty in the country. Costa's preventive measures against the growth of squatting, such as they were, were all in the realm of physical planning prescriptions about the types of buildings and their locations. The social and cultural causes of the growth of squatting in other Brazilian cities were not examined, and the life-styles and needs of the various strata likely to compose the population of the new capital were not considered. As it turned out, this emphasis meant not merely that the city was to turn out to be inconvenient or less than perfect for many of its residents: it made Costa's plan impossible to carry out in full in the light of prevailing demographic and economic conditions.

It should be noted here that the conception of the contest for the plan of Brasília and the composition of the jury made the neglect of social considerations almost inevitable. Underlying both was a conception of city planning (*urbanismo*) as an offshoot of architecture, supported by engineering in regard to such matters as water supply and electricity. It would be silly to deny the importance of both architectural and engineering considerations in the planning and building of cities. The task of these professions, however, tends to be defined as the drawing of maps and the placement of lines on paper. Often the main concern is with esthetics— form, lines of sight, the visual flow and articulation of the sectors of the city.

Yet we must remember that the city dweller generally experiences his (man-made) urban environment as natural or given (Goodman and Goodman 1947: 3), and of all the physical apparatus surrounding him, finds that the brick-and-mortar world of the city is the slowest changing (Doxiadis 1963: 25). Thus the power and responsibility of the city planner in a case such as Brasília extends beyond mere esthetics to the totality of the human experience. If the planner intends to solve the social problems of the city's residents, he should be prepared to consider such matters as the culturally and socially determined needs of the city's first residents and the probable mix of social strata in the future. The lines on the map can have social as well as esthetic consequences.

The problem of urban squatting, for instance, is one of extraordinary gravity all over the world, and may in fact prove insoluble. The planner of Brasília dismissed it—or perhaps imagined that he had dealt with it effectively—in a sentence. The result has been, as we shall see, more squatter settlements.

For the well-to-do, however, the plan made explicit provision, providing an alternative to the apartment houses of the superblocks, both in the form of closely regulated row housing of several types (see illus. 8) and in the more distant areas, private houses, sufficiently separated so that their owners could give vent to personal caprice and build houses free from the detailed restrictions on the superblocks and nearby areas.

The cul-de-sac access roads of the superblocks were to be eddies in the main flow of traffic. In a north-south direction, parallel to the Residential Axis, through traffic was to be funneled through a six-lane South Highway Axis, intermediate traffic being routed through two four-lane highways parallel to and immediately alongside the Axis, access to the superblock roads being by means of incomplete cloverleafs, so that nowhere in the city would four directions of traffic intersect. The Monumental Axis was to have two six-lane highways, each one-way, in contrary directions on either side of the Mall. Beyond the Three Powers Plaza on one end and the television tower on the other, these highways were to be reduced to undivided two-way roads. In the original plan, trucks were to be routed along special service roads to the back of the double rows of superblocks, along which were to be grouped garages, repair shops, and warehouses on one side and a greenbelt beyond. The superblock access roads were to feed alternately from this service road and from the Highway Axis cloverleafs.

It was at the juncture of the Monumental and the Residential Axes' circulatory systems that Costa proposed to locate the nongovernmental city center. Here would be the bus station, at the center of a vast system of cloverleafs and viaducts, linking the north-south and east-west traffic trunks. On the upper level, as Costa (1957) put it:

The crossing of this Monumental Axis, of a lower elevation, with the Residential-Highway Axis, imposed the creation of a great platform free of traffic except that headed for parking there, a calm area where logically were concentrated the amusement center of the city, with movies, theatres, restaurants, etc. . . .

On this platform, where . . . the traffic is only local, was situated the amusement center of the city . . . on the front side were concentrated the movies and the theatres, whose height was made low and uniform, the group thus constituting a continuous architectonic body, with a gallery, broad sidewalks, terraces and coffee houses . . . The various theatres will be linked together by lanes of the traditional genre of the Rua do Ouvidor,[3] of the Venetian streets or covered galleries (arcades), and articulated to small patios with bars and cafes.

The obvious intention here was to modify, as in the superblocks, the monumental tone of the city, to provide a different scale and rhythm by means of a different disposition of space. Near this amusement center, in the four quadrants formed by the two axes at their crossing, were to be located two banking centers, to the southeast and northeast, and two hotel centers, to the southwest and northwest. North and south of the hotel

3. A narrow shopping street in Rio de Janeiro, reserved to pedestrians.

sectors were to be placed two commercial centers composed of office buildings of some considerable height.

Again we see the sectoral tendency of the plan, segregating all the banks, the office buildings, the amusement center. To a certain extent, such concentration was practical; banks do do business with other banks. People do go to a part of town noted for night life without a specific destination, and so forth. But it is also true that someone on the way to the bank drops off for an hour's work at the dentist; women go window shopping en route to a matinee. In short, there are reasons one might wish to concentrate certain urban functions, but there is also a good case for what Jane Jacobs (1961: 152–177) calls "mixed primary uses," which can attract people with different purposes and different schedules who will use certain facilities in common, and sustain an area economically. In Brasília's plan, the central sectors, each fulfilling a different function (government, banking, hotels), were to be contiguous, but as observation in 1967 demonstrates, far enough apart and separated by enough empty space—superhighways, grass, and vacant lots—to make walking between them a chore. Brasília is very large compared with some other well-known cities, in spite of its much smaller population. There is parking space set aside for the car-owning minority to drive from place to place, but the city in 1967 was unfinished, and when it fills up even the privileged may have trouble getting around. It remains to be seen if Brasília's plan is as successful on the human scale as it is on the monumental.

CHAPTER III

The Pilot Plan and the Rise of the Satellite Towns: 1957-1967

I. The Rhythm of Brasília

> Juscelino's called me,
> Juscelino's calling;
> Israel is paying.
> I'll walk, I'll take a plane—
> But somehow or other, I'll go.[1]
> —Popular song (Orico 1958: 178).

Brasília was built in an extraordinarily short time. The approval of Lúcio Costa's city plan in early 1957 left Juscelino only the four remaining years of his Presidential term to complete Brasília, since the constitution forbade him to succeed himself. If he was to inaugurate Brasília by the date set (by Law 3273 of 1957) for that ceremony, April 21, 1960, he had an even shorter time.

In that period, vast sums had to be appropriated and disbursed, labor had to be found and transported to Brasília, and equipment and materials had to be provided expeditiously and in a continuing stream. This was the consequence of the decision, fully congruent with established custom and political realities, to make the transfer of the capital a fait accompli within the limits of the five-year Presidential term.

The haste imposed by that decision underlay the gold-rush atmosphere of the new capital in those early days. Instead of a reward in precious metal, there was the fiat money which flowed off the presses of the American Bank Note Company and Thomas de la Rue and Company at the orders of the Brazilian government.

In these first years, many elements contributed to the general atmos-

---

1. Juscelino me chamou/Juscelino está chamando/Israel [Pinheiro, NOVA-CAP'S President] está pagando/Eu vou a pé, vou voando/Mas de quarqué [*sic*] modo, eu vou.

phere—feverish haste, the desire to get rich quick, the provisional flavor of almost everything, excitement, hope, and violence. Great machines cut into the red earth, leaving seas of mud and clouds of dust in their wake. New arrivals driven by poverty and drawn by hope and ambition slept almost anywhere and were soon set to work on a dozen fronts, or began to seek an easier road to wealth in the thriving and often profiteering commerce, which ranged from the sale of hot coffee on a construction site to shady dealing in the scarce raw materials of the building trades. Some fortunes were made.

At the same time there was a kind of frontier democracy. Architects, administrators, and simple construction workers rubbed elbows, lived under similar conditions, and wore the same kind of informal clothes. As Oscar Niemeyer describes this period:

That human solidarity . . . gave us the impression of living in a different world, in the new and just world we had always wished for. At that time we lived as if in a great family, without prejudice and inequality. We lived in the same houses, ate in the same restaurants, frequented the same places of amusement. Even our clothes were similar. We were united by a climate of fraternization resulting from identical discomforts (Niemeyer 1961: 64).

Niemeyer goes on to lament the diminishing of this spirit in more recent times. For instance, he himself was recently barred from showing some visitors the Plateau Palace because he was not wearing a tie and jacket. There was a much more egalitarian, fraternal atmosphere in the chaotic environment of the early days of the city than after the plan had been partly translated into bricks and mortar.

Brasília in the period of its construction was the object of tremendous publicity. Some of that, promoted by the political opposition, was adverse, but as the Brazilian geographer Milton Santos tells us, whatever the technical reservations raised in the fields of economics, city planning, and geography, and, we may add, whatever the hostile rumors that may have been spread about the new capital, "The psychological balance was favorable: perhaps the Brazilians paid dearly [for her], but they are happy to have Brasília" (Santos 1964: 398). And particularly outside of Rio de Janeiro, Brasília exercised a tremendous fascination on the man in the street. One result, actively sought after, was the accrual of considerable prestige to President Kubitschek. Another result, attributable in part to the publicity, was the attraction of many internal migrants to the site, as the result of radio, magazine, and word-of-mouth publicity.

As the arrivals of migrants snowballed and work became more and more intense, legends grew up around the haste, confusion, and opportunism of the times. One, told me by a young small businessman very proud of being a "pioneer," or old-timer in the city, is of small truckers who would arrive at a construction site to deliver sand, brought in from some distance away. After receiving a receipt from the checker, they would drive off without unloading the sand, and through the negligence or conivance of the checker, return an hour later with the same sand, check it off again, selling the same sand several times in a day.

Other stories deal with the personnel policies of NOVACAP, the official construction company. A typographer (*tipógrafo*) applied for a job, was hired, and before he knew it was assigned to do surveying: he had been confused with a topographer (*topógrafo*). Another version of the same story deals with a common laborer who was assigned to count bricks. Classified as a *contador* (which means both "counter" and "accountant"), he received several times his own correct salary for months, even though his job was to count bricks and not money.

The bulk of the migrants, of course, had no such luck. They provided the hands for the job of building the government buildings and superblocks of the Pilot Plan. In 1959, 54.5 percent of the labor force was employed in construction—and this figure does not include the many employees of NOVACAP, also partly involved in construction. Only 5.2 percent were engaged in commerce involving merchandise.

These workers were attracted to Brasília, among other things, by the relatively high wages. The legal monthly minimum wage is an important yardstick of prevailing wage rates in Brazil, because it and its multiples actually fix the wages of many workers who are on jobs registered with the Ministry of Labor in the labor passport (*Caderno de Trabalho*) each worker must carry in order to be eligible for official health and retirement benefits. While unregistered employment is common even in urban areas, the minimum wage, which varies from region to region and is periodically readjusted to reflect inflationary changes, does furnish a rough indication of prevailing rates for unskilled and low-status jobs. In Brasília, the minimum wage was close to the nation's highest, and nearly twice that prevailing in the northeastern state of Piauí. The frenetic "rhythm of Brasília" also provided opportunities for overtime work. Recalls newspaper editor Ari Cunha: "Nobody wanted to work on a job that didn't go for eighteen hours. ((To work on the Congress, I'll only go for a double shift." "Are they hiring people as unskilled laborers? No. They're putting them down as carpenters [a higher-paid category]." The *candango* [slang for a worker of Brasília] went to the Free Town, bought a hammer and a sack of nails, and was hired" (CB December 18, 1966).

Although many of the migrants were uneducated, they were, like most who choose to make a major move, better educated and more ambitious than their fellows who stayed behind. Brasília had 55.6 percent literacy in 1959; 58.4 percent among men and 49.7 percent among women. Though low, this was much more than the percentage of literacy in any of the regions which provided large groups of migrants, and greater than the national average of 1950. It was also greater than that recorded in 1950, before construction was initiated, in the municipios of the area of the new capital (Luziânia, Planaltina, and Formosa) (IBGE 1959: 27–29).

While the pay was good, social conditions were atrocious. Prostitution flourished, since in this early period there was a great preponderance of men in the population, in 1959 two men for every women and three men for every woman in the age group 20–29 years. In some construction camps, there were more than five men for every woman, and more than ten for every woman in the 20–29 year age group (IBGE 1959: 7–8). This disparity, combined with the relatively full pockets of the workers, produced a vigorous market for members of the oldest profession. As one *candango* describes it, "They lined up in front of the whorehouses like dogs." Others recount—perhaps with a touch of embroidery—that any woman who appeared in public attracted groups of men seeking her favors, and that even accompanied females were approached, giving rise to fights.

Sexual needs were not the only ones difficult to fulfill. Since the plan made no provision for temporary housing, improvised solutions were repeatedly called into being. The Free Town (see section IV of this chapter) was the tolerated area of shacks where Brasília's commercial center was located. Eventually it was to become established as one of the capital's satellite towns.

Construction Camps

Besides the Free Town, from the earliest days construction camps appeared in Brasília with the permission of the authorities. Located near the construction sites, these camps were built and administered by the various private firms engaged in work on the new capital. In addition, one large camp about two kilometers from the Free Town was the original headquarters of NOVACAP. It soon became known as Velhacap, or "old capital," as opposed to Novacap, "new capital." An extension was christened Candangolândia (*Candango*-land).[2] While there were some separate private residences—in wood—for the professional employees the typical building in the encampments was a long barrackslike bachelor quarters, or, less frequently, a similar building divided into family residences. Many

2. The suffix *-lândia* (-land) is common in Goiás and Western Minas Gerais (the Triangle) place-names: Uberlândia, Radiolândia, Cristalândia, etc.

encampments, including Candangolândia and Velhacap, still exist.

Many workers in the camps ate the mess provided by the construction firms; others purchased food from women who supported themselves filling lunchboxes.

One *candango,* a squatment resident from Piauí, recounts a fatal incident arising from these conditions, Some workers in the encampment near the Dawn Palace complained about the food they were getting in the mess, and as tensions rose the police were called, and reacted violently. Shots were fired, including machine guns, according to this worker, and several of his coworkers were killed, including some who were in another building writing letters or resting; this informant saw two killed by his side. Later, he recounts, an inquiry was held, and he was called before a major, who asked him whether he stuck by his story that machine guns were used. Didn't he know that the police didn't have machine guns? He asked permission to leave, and went and gathered some shells, returned, and asked the major what revolver used those shells; he had served in the army for many years and never saw a revolver that used shells of that type. With that, they called him aside and offered him free passage to Rio or São Paulo, and a job with the same company. He refused: he had come to build Brasília and in Brasília he would stay. So he was fired.

Vila Amaurí (Bananal)

As the crowding of the Free Town became more intense, a second Free Town was created, known formally as the Bananal Nucleus (after the watercourse Ribeirão Bananal) and familiarly as Vila Amaurí. Located to the north of the Monumental Axis, in the opposite direction from the Free Town, on low ground that was to be flooded by the rising waters of artificial Lake Paranoá, Vila Amaurí never had the opportunity to fight for permanence. Yet by 1959, Vila Amaurí contained over 6,000 souls, more than half the total population of the Free Town at the same juncture (IBGE 1959: 4, 79). It was never, owing to its impermanence (guaranteed by its location), an area for any kind of investment. In 1959 it had the highest proportion (67 percent) of houses lacking sanitary installations of any of the areas in the future Federal District, the second highest proportion (95 percent) lacking in electrical installations (after the miniscule rural nucleus of Braslândia), and the highest proportions lacking water supply (71 percent), radio (95 percent), or sewing machines (81 percent) (IBGE 1959: 73). With the rising of the waters, this community disappeared from the map, leaving a sizable remnant on high ground, known as Vila Planalto, which as late as 1964 had 6,500 people (FSS 1964: 3).

Squatments

Even the proliferation of construction camps, the Free Town, and Vila Amaurí failed to provide for all those who came to Brasília in search of work. In the area of the Free Town, near construction camps, and in the many "holes" in the Pilot Plan where the cerrado vegetation had not yet been replaced by the skeletons of superblocks, migrants took advantage of the vast open space and the complaisance of the government, and put up their shacks and sometimes tents improvised from truck canvases. Later, when some companies ceased supervision of their camps, and in 1961 when President Quadros called a halt to all construction work in Brasília, these areas continued to be host to a de facto community.

As in Salvador (Pendrell 1968), these settlements came to be known as "invasions" (*invasões*), in spite of considerable question as to whether they manifested the degree of illegality and unilateral occupancy that this term implies.

It was the growth of these squatments, more than any other factor, which (with the reaction to them of the authorities) led to the disfigurement of the Pilot Plan and the creation of a different Brasília of row houses, satellite towns, and seemingly eternal squatments.

II. The Establishment of Taguatinga

In the gold rush atmosphere of Brasília in the late fifties, with the government preoccupied above all with the rapid completion of the main government buildings of the capital and masses of migrant workers and get-rich-quick operators flocking to the region, the orderly growth of housing and amenities for the lower classes was impossible. The solution these people adopted for their pressing need for shelter was an expedient familiar from other Brazilian cities and, indeed, one of the standard forms of urban expansion in all the underdeveloped countries: squatting. While a Free Town had been established with commercial interests especially in mind, this zone and other encampments soon proved inadequate, and squatments began to appear in various regions of the future Federal District. Such squatments were largely tolerated by the authorities since the workers housed in them were required for the achievement of the goal of completing the new capital on time, so long as they did not seem to pose a massive threat to the public order or to the eventual execution of Costa's plan.

However, eventually they did begin to pose such a threat, and the emergency expedient adopted to deal with them proved as fateful for the future of urban Brasília as the outcome of the original contest for the city-plan itself. The largest area of squatting was across the Brasília–Anápolis highway, the main route from São Paulo, whence came most of the supplies for the construction effort. Ernesto Silva, one of NOVACAP's directors and a participant in the events, recounts: "Nearly four thousand people installed themselves in less than a week. They lived in the most precarious manner: *barracos* [shacks] of old wood, cans, zinc sheets, cement sacks. There were no sewage pits. Nor water. Promiscuity and lack of hygiene. Everything built in a few days, especially at night, to get around the vigilance of the inspectors" (Ernesto Silva, CB June 4, 1967). That Saturday, the President was visiting Brasília and had been invited to dine in the JK Restaurant[3] in the Free Town. A mass of people, perhaps as many as four thousand, were gathered around the restaurant, waiting for the President and bearing signs saying, "We want to stay where we are!" "Viva President Juscelino!" and "We have founded Sara Kubitschek Town!" Dona Sara was the President's wife, and the choice of the name was obviously a maneuver to gain the sympathy of the authorities and even a subtle form of blackmail, to prevent any move against the invasion.

It was necessary to do something rapidly, to avoid an incident that would not look good at all in the newspapers, and could even threaten the construction timetable if things got serious enough. Israel Pinheiro, President of NOVACAP, asked director Ernesto Silva to go and try to calm the situation. Recounts Silva:

I climbed onto a wooden box and addressed the demonstrators. I told them that Novacap had already arranged for the creation of a satellite town, 25 km from the Pilot Plan, and in this place each worker would have his own lot and could acquire it for a reasonable price over a long term. I arranged, with the committee or representatives of Sara Kubitschek Town, a meeting for the next day—Sunday, at 7 AM—when we would show them the plan of the new planned city and examine the means by which the transfer would be made.

The President's dinner was nevertheless canceled, and the next day the meeting did not go too well. Silva promised that NOVACAP would "move everybody, put up the shacks," and take steps to provide medical care and schools.

Silva puts part of the blame for the resistance on some businessmen in the Free Town who stimulated invasions because their residents were customers for building materials and later for food. He charges that they were among those who incited "indiscipline and resistance." Another reason for the resistance was the fact that the Free Town was one of the principal points for odd jobs and petty commerce; living near it represented a form of security for recent migrants. To be moved summarily to a distant, empty location, dependent upon the whims of the authorities—

3. JK—Juscelino Kubitschek, as in FDR, JFK, LBJ, etc.

preoccupied with the timetable for Brasília, more than workers' welfare
—would be at best a leap in the dark.

So the following Monday when the attempt to persuade the invaders
to move was begun with the aid of two nuns trained as social workers, only
one family accepted the idea. That night a hundred people marched to the
provisional headquarters of NOVACAP, still demanding the right to stay
where they were, while some, allegedly, proposed setting fire to the offices.

A series of additional attractions were offered to those willing to move.
A mobile hospital was sent to the new city, Taguatinga. NOVACAP
bought wood, nails, zinc, and provided them to the workers to improve
their shanties. The shacks were located in the back of each lot, as a symbol
of the hope of future stucco construction in the front. Writes Silva:

> We dismounted the shacks, transported them, rebuilt them, transported
> furniture, utensils, men, women, and children. We built nearly a thousand
> sewage pits, one for every lot. We demarcated every lot so that each person
> already occupied his own lot. We put in a provisional water network, God
> knows how (He will forgive us!). We instituted daily transportation for
> the workers in NOVACAP and construction company trucks. We assured
> a minimum of medical assistance (CB June 4, 1967).

In effect, then, the move was finally carried out (in ten days) because a
series of advantages were offered, as well as because the dialog between
the government officials and the workers was essentially unequal, since
the former were invested with legitimacy and potential police backing.

Perhaps because the difficulties of the transfer had put the fear of God
(or of social tumult), into it, the administration moved, in the next six
months, to consolidate the new, hastily installed satellite town. A school,
a hospital, and houses for the schoolteachers were put in. A few months
later an Industrial School was built. One should note the difference in tone
and orientation between the original Pilot Plan of Brasília and the immediate, improvised, down-to-earth process ("plan" would be saying too
much) by which Taguatinga was instituted. On the one hand, an esthetic
ideal, the lofty sweep of monumental design and its rhetoric; on the other,
harried administrators, workers seeking a chance so far denied them, in an
often grinding interaction, produced a solution that pleased nobody, but
met pressing and immediate needs.

The improvised creation of Taguatinga set the precedent for the creation of satellite cities outside of the watershed of the artificial Lake
Paranoá. Taguatinga itself became the fastest growing segment of the Federal District, with the exception of the Social Security Invasion to be discussed later. As shown in table II, from a modest 6 percent of the total
population of some 64,000 in 1959, the town grew to include 26 percent
of a total of some 270,000 in 1964, second only to the Pilot Plan, and

TABLE II

Population of the Federal District by Locality: 1959, 1960, and 1964

Locality	1959		1960		1964	
	Population	Percent	Population	Percent	Population	Percent
Pilot Plan	18,071[1]	28.10	68,665[2]	48.45	89,231	33.26
Free Town (pioneer nucleus)[3]	11,565	17.98	21,033	14.84	22,772	8.49
Taguatinga	3,677	5.72	26,111	18.42	68,947	25.70
Planaltina	2,245	3.49	2,917	2.06	4,223	1.57
Braslândia	355	.55			616	.23
Sobradinho			8,478	5.98	19,205	7.16
Gama			—[4]		27,524	10.26
(Subtotal: satellite towns)	(17,842)	(27.74)	(58,539)	(41.30)	(143,287)	(53.41)
Velhacap[3]	1,318	2.05			4,572	1.70
Candangolândia[3]	2,868	4.46			4,807	1.79
Bananal (Vila Amaurí)	6,196	9.63				
Other encampments	5,763	8.96				
Social Security Invasion[3]					8,084	3.01
Paranoá					1,351	.50
Rural	12,256	19.06	14,538	10.25	16,983	6.33
TOTAL	64,314	100.00	141,742	100.00	268,315	100.00

Sources: IBGE 1959: 79; IBGE 1961: 2; PDP-SEC 1965: 4.

1. Includes "Three Powers Encampment" (population 7,064, 10.98 percent).
2. Includes "Brasília: Suburban" (population 15,334, 10.81 percent).
3. Totals for the greater Free Town agglomeration at the intersection of the Brasília–Belo Horizonte and Brasília–Anápolis–São Paulo highways, made up of the Free Town proper, Velhacap, Candangolândia, Social Security Invasion, and (subsequent to the collection of the 1964 figures) Vila Tenório: 1959: 15,751, 24.49 percent; 1964: 41,235, 14.99 percent.
4. Estimated population in September 1961: 16,472.

threatening to overtake it in the near future. When Taguatinga was founded, the only communities recognized as permanent by the authorities were the Pilot Plan, not yet completed, and the preexisting communities of Planaltina and Brasília. Even in 1959, these latter towns accounted for only 5 percent of the total population. With Taguatinga, and the Free Town, which only in 1961 was to be recognized as permanent, the future satellite towns accounted for less than a third of the total population. A year later, with population growth and the addition of the town of Sobradinho, they accounted for 41 percent of the population, and by 1964, with Gama added, they made up more than half (54 percent) of the population total.

The growth of these towns and their sponsorship by the governmental authorities reflects the continuing pressure of population increase, mostly through in-migration, and the consequent growth of squatter settlements. Faced with the prospect of seeing the monumental capital surrounded by a ring of proletarian hovels, the planners opted for removing what they could not eliminate. In interviews, officials frequently assert that the locations of the satellite towns outside the lakeshed reflect a desire to prevent th accumulation of pestilential sewage in the lake. In fact, however, sewage facilities for the accepted urban concentrations within the lakeshed have not been completed as of 1967. Suburban-style homes dot the lakeshore.

The de facto segregation of the lower strata of the society on the urban periphery in fact mirrors the settlement pattern of most of Brazil's major cities, including Rio de Janeiro, São Paulo, and Salvador. The onus of commuting in Brazil falls upon the less affluent, while the well-to-do maintain apartments and private residences nearer to the central business district.

The development of Taguatinga's layout was marked by frequent outbreaks of squatting, which took two forms: *defensive squatting,* the seizure of land by those who had no other recourse, and *speculative squatting,* the occupation of land by the economically secure in the hope that in the course of events the seizure would become legalized and the land appreciate in value. The defensive variety predominated in the cases of Vila Dimas (FSS n.d.) and Vila Matias (FSS 1965). These areas were eventually incorporated into the officially recognized plan for Taguatinga, though some of the inhabitants were removed. Speculative squatting was common, and was aimed at the acquisition of lots in the direction of the town's growth. During the Presidency of João Goulart (1961–1964), many of these lots were given to the squatters in return for modest monthly payments which soon became trivial in the face of constant inflation.

The full complement of lots in Taguatinga as of 1967 was 15,314, of which 13,947 were residential. Of the buildings in the town, over 60 percent were wooden shacks (*barracos*), while the owners of only 2 percent of the buildings had obtained occupancy permits (*habite-se*) signifying that they met full legal standards. Since there were 14,885 buildings on the 15,314 lots in Taguatinga, there was little room for the expansion of the town on recognized lots. If growth was to take place, the alternatives were (*a*) construction of multiple dwellings, (*b*) opening up of additional areas to subdivision (*loteamento*), or (*c*) renewed squatting.

Taguatinga developed as a kind of imitation Pilot Plan. Like the Pilot Plan it has the form of a cross, the main street, divided by a mall, separating two long residential axes. A single Commercial Avenue lies near the outer edge of one of the two wings. Unlike the Pilot Plan, however, there is little monumentality in Taguatinga. Low stucco buildings, largely commercial; some few stucco houses; and a vast array of wooden shacks, increasing in frequency toward the outer ends of the residential axes, set the tone. Many secondary streets are unpaved, muddy in the rainy season, and dusty in the dry.

III. The Pilot Plan

The "rhythm of Brasília" continued. Heavy materials arrived by airplane; work went on under the lights. By inauguration time, April 21, 1960 (anniversary of Brazil's discovery), enough of the city was ready to make the dream appear to have come true. The main buildings on the Monumental Axis—the Congress and the Ministries—the bus station, the bulk of the highway system, several superblocks put up by various federal agencies (especially the pension and retirement funds, the so-called IAP's —Institutos de Aposentadoria e Previdência), were built. Red mud and dust were everywhere; euphoric confusion reigned. The promotion of the new capital's symbolic value was at its height. Proclaimed President Kubitschek: "With the New Capital there will come, God willing, an era of abundance and genuine brotherhood which will permit to all Brazilians, without distinction, the enjoyment of the advantages of culture and of progress" (quoted in Martins Ramos n.d.: 12).

Already, however, the realities of urban life in Brasília had begun to give the lie to these heady and optimistic words. For the distribution of the people in the urban space clearly reflected social class distinctions, in spite of Lúcio Costa's proclaimed intention to limit this kind of segregation.

As we have seen, the workers lived in construction camps, in the Free Town and Vila Amaurí. Some were living in the satellite town of Taguatinga, founded to reduce the pressures of continued squatting. Both Taguatinga and the Free Town also housed commercial people and some lower-level civil servants.

Thus the satellites began to fulfill some of the functions of the dormi-

tory suburbs of Rio de Janeiro, providing cheaper and less desirable housing for the lower strata of the population. As in Rio, these were less convenient areas to live in. Distant from the place of work, they subjected
the commuter to a long trip in overcrowded, rickety buses to the center
of the city, at considerable expense given the low incomes which prevailed. Public utilities were fewer: there was virtually no telephone service, water was often nonexistent or only available in improvised public
taps, and electricity was only available in some districts and subject to
frequent blackouts.

The satellite towns were planned largely for individual habitation. Most
of the houses were mere shacks, and lacked official occupancy permits.
The Pilot Plan, on the other hand, depended on governmental initiative or
on the incorporation of condomina on a large and expensive scale. The
gvernment, in the face of the reigning political instability, was in no position to plan and finance a systematic transfer of the various ministries and
their employees to the new capital. Brazilian private construction initiatives all over the country were restricted by inflationary expectations, rent
controls, and scarce long-term credit. In the case of Brasília, few could
acquire first-class housing except by governmental favor (even professionals often work at least part-time for the government, or have wives who
work for the government). Of this small number, many preferred individual houses.

The highest stratum of the population was housed in individual houses
on large lots along the lake, an arrangement reminiscent of some North
American suburbs. Here people such as ministers, supreme court judges,
and businessmen could indulge their individual tastes and their desires for
conspicuous display, unhindered by restrictive codes such as prevailed for
the row houses along W-3 Avenue in the Pilot Plan.

In the Pilot Plan itself, the Monumental Axis was largely complete
from the bus station east, including the Three Powers Square and the
Ministries. Several superblocks had been built, and the little Church of
Our Lady of Fátima designed by Niemeyer had been completed, although
on a scale much smaller than the architect had envisaged. Most of the
residential construction was concentrated in the South Wing (South Residential Axis), so that the city, instead of an airplane shape, had the form
of an ⌊. A considerable number of row houses had been built along the
W-3 Avenue by the so-called Popular Housing Foundation (*Fundação
da Casa Popular*), although the name of the agency was belied by the fact
that in the area it was active: "The resident family groups were constituted
nearly exclusively by families of technical personnel and administrative
functionaries of the construction organization" (IBGE 1959: 72). Superblocks had been constructed in the South Wing by the various social se-

curity institutes (IAP's), including those for the civil service, industrial workers, banking employees and transport workers (Rodrigues 1967: 166).[4]

Brasília was able, however, to grow without the intense crowding at the center and the uninterrupted sprawl at the outskirts which typifies other Brazilian cities with similar class segragation. Open spaces covered with the indigenous *campo cerrado* vegetation were preserved, for the time being at least. The underpopulation of the region and the governmental control of the land and the construction process made this possible.

The proposed central commercial area and recreation zones, unlike the Monumental Axis and some residential areas, were not even represnted by building foundations. As late as 1965 Brasília's Pilot Plan boasted two movie houses. As a result of the neglect of this aspect of the plan, W-3 Avenue soon became the de facto downtown for the Pilot Plan area.

Rapid population growth between the 1959 and 1960 censuses (see table II) reflects a second migratory stream to the new capital composed of civil servants transferred from Rio de Janeiro, the former capital. In view of the acute housing shortage, Pilot Plan superblock apartments, like the row houses, went almost exclusively to civil servants and professionals. Had they not been offered good housing, these people would have remained in Rio, and an ideal excuse provided for the enemies of the new capital to retard or even reverse the move.

Even for this relatively prosperous and influential group there was a pressing housing shortage, so that the assignment of apartments, the responsibility of the Brasília Working Group (GTB—*Grupo de Trabalho de Brasília*), depended largely on political influence or connections. The GTB was composed of the President of NOVACAP and representatives of the Armed Forces General staff and each of the civilian ministries.

So great, in fact, was the pressure for housing that in the North Residential Wing, after the original occupants had been asked to leave some buildings considered unsafe, some civil servants "invaded" and occupied the apartments until the government legalized their presence. The former occupants at the same time were housed in the luxurious Brasília Palace Hotel at government expense. Some allege that the former occupants and the "invaders" had acted in collusion.

Aside from these housing problems, there were other sources of the resistance on the part of many civil servants to make the move from Rio

4. The acronyms for the participating agencies are IPASE, IAPI, IAPC, IAPEFESP, IAPB, IAPETC, and IAPM. The Bank of Brazil (*Banco do Brasil*) also carried out some construction. The IAP's were the equivalent of the U.S. Social Security Agency, though until they were combined into a single National Social Security Institute (INPS) under Marshal-President Castelo Branco, each institute dealt only with a particular category of worker.

de Janeiro to the new capital, a resistance not always overcome by the lure of the *dobradinha* or bonus for those who made the move. Many, especially women, felt that Brasília was a huge construction camp, which seemed all the more desolate once Jânio Quadros halted all construction work in 1961. Even the completed parts of the city were full of "holes" or open spaces where the plan had not yet been implemented; these holes included most of the cultural and commercial areas that might have made the city seem more inviting, more human. Many middle-class people report that the city looked like a city on the moon, a mausoleum, lacking the hustle-and-bustle (*movimento*) of a real capital. In this kind of competition, Brasília, small, lacking in street corners, beaches, and sidewalk cafes, distant from the worlds of fashion, theater, and art, could not hope to compete with Rio's fashionable Copacabana or its downtown. As one famous samba put it,

> I'm not an Indian or anything,
> Don't pierce my ears,
> Or wear a ring in my nose.
> I didn't use a feather loincloth.
> And if my skin is brown
> It's from the sun of the beach where I
>   was born and happily raised.
> I won't, I won't go to Brasília,
> Not me, or my family either,
> Even if it's to make a pile.
> There's no comparing the life,
> Even hard, expensive—
> I want to be poor without leaving
>   Copacabana.
> (Billy Blanco, from Orico 1958: 174).[5]

Another reason many preferred to remain in Rio is that multiple job-holding is common, both as a source of extra income, influence, and personal promotion (Leeds 1964). Many civil servants would not or could not give up their jobs in private companies or second government jobs in Rio in order to remain with a single job in Brasília. The private sector was insufficiently present, and the public sector too new, for multiple job-holding to be widespread in Brasília in this period.

5. Eu não sou índio nem nada,/Não tenho orelha furada/Nem uso argola pendurada no nariz./Não uso tanga de pena./E a minha pele é morena/Do sol da práia onde nasci e me criei feliz./Não vou, não vou para Brasília,/Nem eu, nem minha família,/Mesmo que seja para ficar cheio da grana./A vida nao se compara,/Mesmo difícil, tão cara,/Quero ser pobre sem deixar Copacabana.

These sources of passive resistance to the transfer were more effective in the case of the massive Executive branch bureaucracies. The Congress and the Supreme Court were able to move rapidly. The institution of two-hour shuttle flights to Rio, the "air bridge" (*ponte aérea*) on which legislators could travel free, did much to ease the transition for the doughty solons.

IV. The Free Town Becomes Permanent

One of the first tasks NOVACAP had faced after its foundation in late 1956[6] was the preparation of a base area for the drive to build Brasília. Lúcio Costa's plan provided only for the form of the full-grown city, not for the process by which it would grow. Planning this process was the job of NOVACAP, and in its course the shape of the new capital was to be radically altered.

It fell to the engineer Jofre Mozart Parada to select a site for the base camp. This he did on December 17, 1956, when he arrived at a point near the confluence of the two watercourses Riacho Fundo (Deep Creek) and the Córrego Vicente Pires. A short way beyond, the Riacho Fundo reached the level of the future Lake Paranoá while through the area ran the old unpaved road from Luziânia, a nearby county seat in Goiás, to Planaltina (CB December 18, 1966).

The choice was confirmed on December 26th, when Bernardo Sayão, a member of the NOVACAP directorate, ordered the concession of lots, for a four-year period, for all commercial establishments which would sustain and supply the construction camps. This was the beginning of the Free Town (*Cidade Livre*), the principal center of Brasília during construction. Sometimes the Free Town was given the more formal title "Pioneer Nucleus" (*Núcleo Bandeirante*). Table III shows how fast the Free Town grew and how important it was in the early months. If we consider that perhaps only half of the 12,200 population of the Federal District in 1957 was made up of people attracted by the construction effort, the Free Town's centrality is further emphasized. Most of the other people in this category were living in construction camps.

So rapid, in fact, was the Free Town's growth that NOVACAP issued orders to prohibit new construction in the area. It was also about the same time (1957) that the spillover from the Free Town, in the form of invasions across the Brasília–Anápolis highway, led to the creation of Taguatinga.

6. In a ceremony officially founding Brasília, held there on October 4th, Juscelino Kubitschek presiding. The decree creating NOVACAP was no. 40,117 of 1956.

This rapid growth, the frenetic atmosphere, and the official preoccupation with the completion on time of the Pilot Plan led to the neglect of the Free Town's own planning problems. After all, the contracts (a type known as *comodato*) provided for the immediate vacation of the site when its functions were no longer essential; the bulldozers would eliminate it and all of its defects. The result of these circumstances was a very informal system of distributing lots: "The cession of lots obeyed the decision of the mayor [an appointed official] or a note from Dr. Israel [Pinheiro, NOVACAP's President], [Bernardo] Sayão or Ernesto Silva. Dr. Iris [Meinberg, another NOVACAP director] rarely got involved with this, since he represented the opposition, was financial director, and didn't want to get involved [*não queria muita conversa*]" (Ari Cunha, CB December 18, 1966).

The special characteristic of the Free Town was the heavy representation of major retail and wholesale commercial interests (see fig. 11). Its location at the convergence of the two main auto routes into the Federal District made it a natural site for such activity.

The presence of these commercial interests, some of which belonged to important figures in the Chamber of Deputies, became an obstacle to the Mayor (*Prefeito*) of the Federal District, Paulo de Tarso Santos, appointed by President Jânio da Silva Quadros, Juscelino's successor. Paulo attempted to carry out the removal of the Free Town in accordance with the original plan. Initially, he forced commercial establishments to move to the largely empty North Wing of the Pilot Plan and to Taguatinga. Some residents also moved. Police presence insured that the Mayor's orders were carried out. A few larger establishments moved to the commercial areas of the South Wing or to Taguatinga at their own expense, convinced that the extinction of the Free Town was only a matter of time.

TABLE III

Population of the Free Town Compared with the Federal District
(Census Data 1959, 1960, 1964 and Estimates 1957, 1958, 1961)

Date	Free Town population	Federal District population	Free Town as percent of Federal District
June 1957	2,200	12,200	18.03
April 1958	7,000	28,800	24.30
May 1959	11,600	64,314	18.03
Sept. 1960	21,033	141,742	14.82
Sept. 1961	15,000	199,188	7.53
Nov. 1964	22,772	268,315	8.49

Sources: IBGE 1959: 4, 79; IBGE 1961: 2; PDF-SEC 1965: 4.

The move was disastrous for many, however, The North Wing, lacking in residents and the Free Town's reputation as a commercial center, far from the main traffic routes, proved to be a graveyard for commerce. The departure of many firms also reduced the attractiveness of the Free Town to residents of other areas in the Federal District. They began to make purchases nearer home or on the W-3 Avenue in the Pilot Plan.

Some indication of the degree of success of the campaign to remove the Free Town can be had from table III, which shows a decline in this period of some 6,000 souls in the Free Town, in the face of a steeply rising population for the Federal District as a whole.

Many firms, especially wholesale firms and warehouses, were not to be dislodged so easily from the Free Town. These business interests—some with important political connections—launched a campaign against the removal of the Free Town: The Movement for the Fixation and Urbanization of the Pioneer Nucleus.[7] This conflict provoked a running debate in the Chamber of Deputies. The leading advocate of the cause of the Free Town was Breno da Silveira, a deputy from Rio de Janeiro (State of Guanabara), who had introduced a bill in favor of the permanent fixation of the Free Town as early as October 1960, when Kubitschek was still President (DCN May 31, 1967: 3627).

Breno accused President Quadros and his Mayor, Paulo de Tarso, of violating previous pledges in favor of the Free Town. Several rallies were held in the Free Town, and support was mobilized from student groups, the Civil Construction Union (large in Brasília because of the large size of its sector), various impromptu residents' associations from various areas of the Free Town, and, significantly, the Brasília Commercial Association.

Paulo de Tarso and the Prefecture relied on legal tactics, police action, and harassment to remove the Free Town. On June 8, 1961, for example, the bus line serving the area was withdrawn. Lawsuits to regain possession (*mandatos de reintegração de posse*) were pursued, for example, against the politically well-connected firm of Paranoá Agricultural Implements. A Baptist church and several houses were demolished in July. In August, the police threatened an area known as Mercedes Signs (*Placas de Mercedes*—the name derived from a nearby billboard advertising a line of trucks), as rumors spread of the demolition of the market, the bus station, and the movie theaters (DCN May 31, 1961: 3627; June 8, 1961—

---

7. *O Movimento pro-Fixação e Urbanização do Núcleo Bandeirante.* "Urbanization" (*urbanização*) refers to the provision of public works and services, and legal recognition of an area, not to the technical sense of the word in English-language literature on demography.

supp.: 5; July 5, 1961: 4578; July 29, 1961: 5203; August 10, 1961: 5661; August 24, 1961: 6101–6102).

As this local agitation reached its height, President Quadros unexpectedly resigned, and after an attempted military coup and a confrontation, Vice-President João (Jango) Goulart assumed the Presidency under a modified form of parliamentarism.

This shift in power had local repercussions. Breno was now able to press his case effectively, given Jango's populism and his precarious political position and need for parliamentary support. Argued Breno:

The Free Town, in the conception of the architects and planners of the present Federal District, should have disappeared with the installation of the Capital, so much so that only wood buildings were permitted . . . Nevertheless the town continued to grow, becoming economically powerful, a true satellite of the new Capital, helping supply her, a veritable commercial emporium, offering the most varied articles to the consumer. As a consequence, there arose the dispute as to whether it should be destroyed, eliminated, or remain, provided with a better and more urban appearance. In this still recent struggle, the President of the Republic himself participated, determining finally that it should remain there.
A historical landmark in the construction of Brasília . . . it will be, with an improved appearance, the visiting card of Brasília, an example of how such a grandiose capital can rise from such a small center . . . (DCN September 5, 1961).

This statement makes evident the role of both the commercial interests and the new President in the conflict. Breno himself was accused of harboring ambitions—which he vigorously denied (DCN September 13, 1961: 6571)—of becoming Mayor of the District.

It was not until December 20, 1961 that the law embodying the decision to allow the Free Town to remain was finally passed. This law, no. 4,020 of 1961, reads as follows:

Article One. The so-called Pioneer Nucleus in the present Federal District is considered a satellite city of Brasília.
Paragraph. The locality treated in the present article may not be moved to any other area; the construction or reconstruction of wooden real property is not permitted there . . . (Imprensa Nacional 1962).

The law also allocated funds for the permanent installation of the Free Town, though in fact this work was not begun for some five years.

The reference to wooden property also has considerable bearing on the social significance of the law. Wooden construction in Northern and Central Brazil is looked on with disfavor, though it has significant advantages, discussed below, for those whose life-style is lower class. Only wood construction was permitted in the Free Town before the passage of Law 4,020, on the theory that it would be easier to demolish. Thus, the ele-

vation of the Free Town to permanent status was accompanied by a prohibition of the building material that had symbolized its provisional status.
Later, when this prohibition began to be enforced, the victory of fore-
stalling the demolition of the town proved to be, for the poor, a Pyrrhic
one indeed.

The decision to retain the Free Town was received with bad grace in
the circles involved with architecture and planning in Brasília, in part
because the Free Town's frontier look was hardly in keeping with the
monumental tone of the Pilot Plan. Whatever the adjustments eventually
made in its layout and appearance, the confirmation of the Free Town's
permanence was another come-down from the logical purity and monumentality of the original plan.

The face-lifting called for in the 1961 law was slow in coming, due in
part to the passive resistance of the planners and architects, as well as to
the administrative discontinuity that characterized the Goulart government. The Free Town continued to be a settlement composed almost entirely of rough wood shacks (*barracos*), the exceptions being a few of
the commercial establishments along Central Avenue. It was only after
the military coup of 1964, which led to the appointment of Plínio Catanhede as Mayor of Brasília, that a plan was approved for the urbanization
of the Free Town.

This plan, however, provided a number of residential lots wholly inadequate to provide for the permanence of the then-resident population.
On official estimated to me that of 22,000 Free Town residents as of
1966, only 12,000 would be able to remain after the plan was put into
practice; another source maintained that as few as 37 percent of the residents are provided for in the urbanization plan, leaving 63 percent to
make their homes elsewhere. In addition, the new plan called for major
changes in the town's layout, including a large civic square whose construction would require the removal of dozens of houses. Once again, the
result was the creation of a de facto settlement without legal status, though
with evident official sanction. The site was the same one whose residents
had previously been moved to found Taguatinga, across the Brasília–
Anápolis highway from the Free Town.

This settlement reportedly was founded by the chauffeur of Federal
Deputy Tenório Cavalcânti, an operatic figure from the state of Rio de
Janeiro who sported a black cape and reputation for violence and illegal
gambling connections—a reputation which cost him his seat and his political rights in the wake of the 1964 coup d'etat. To this day many refer
to the area as Vila Tenório.

In theory, who was to stay and who was to go was to be determined
by a complex system of selection. Preference was to be given to those
candidates who (*a*) had lived the longest in the Free Town prior to pas-

sage of Law 4,020, (b) were married people, widows, or widowers, with
the largest number of dependents, and (c) held ownership of a given
shack (with the proviso that if the shack was rented the preference went
to the tenants). From a legal point of view, the residents were either
squatters or had signed contracts pledging them to return their lots to
NOVACAP following the inauguration of the new capital. Law 4,020
referred only to the fixation of the Free Town as a whole, leaving the details to executive discretion.

This discretion was often exercised to the detriment of the poorest residents. For example, in the Brazilian lower class, rural and urban, it is
common—and socially respectable—for couples to live together without
benefit of civil or church sanction. Such couples are said to be *amasiados*;
their unions suffer only from a slightly lower status among their fellows
than those sanctioned by state and church. Yet the allocation of lots in
the Free Town excluded from the "married" category couples who lacked
such sanction for their unions. This measure redounded against the lowest stratum of residents, among whom the institution of legal marriage is
rarest, often for lack of appropriate documents and money, often as an
adaptive response to economic insecurity and the lack of property.

Many residents claim that political favoritism was also involved in the
administration of this program. One informant complained bitterly that
a prostitute friend of a NOVACAP agent was favored with a lot in spite
of her failure to meet the official criteria.

Still another obstacle to those wishing to acquire lots was the requirement that the beginning of permanent construction take place within
ninety days, and that the construction be completed in six months. Financing for this construction was virtually nonexistent, the time short,
and the legal standards to be met exceedingly high. For instance, houses
with an area over sixty square meters must have a registered professional
engineer or architect legally responsible for the job. Since regulations prohibit any such professional from taking on more than ten such jobs at any
one time, be they private residences or skyscrapers, rigid adherence to
this criterion would make it impossible for construction to continue at
more than a snail's pace, given the lack of professionals. The few houses
that we were able to observe actually under construction belonged to
moderately wealthy members of the local commercial bourgeoisie.

Vila Tenório

Those who were unable to meet the criteria and whose residences happened to be in the way of the bulldozers were summarily informed that
they had to move to Vila Tenório, where a representative of the Free
Town Subprefecture allocated them a lot, again, to be sure, on a legally
temporary basis. One man, the owner of a "hotel"—a ramshackle wooden

rooming house—camped miserably in the rain in the remains of his establishment, which was demolished by the Subprefecture's carpenters, attempting to protect the roofing material and lumber from the elements and from thieves. He waited several days and complained repeatedly to the Subprefecture, which finally provided a truck to dump the materials in the Social Security Invasion, where he had chosen to move instead of the Vila Tenório. No help was provided for the reconstruction of this building, or any other. In Vila Tenório, the only service provided was piped water at public taps, although in parts of the Free Town electricity was available as well.

Mercedes Signs, referred to earlier, had been removed even before the more central areas discussed above, to a part of Vila Tenório known as Hope Town (*Vila Esperança*), much of which was flooded throughout the rainy season. The name Hope Town, for perhaps obvious reasons, did not stick.

By early 1967, Vila Tenório had grown to contain about 2,000 shacks, including some substantial commercial establishments, an attribute it did not share with the Social Security Invasion, where virtually all the commerce was petty. Vila Tenório's growth from this base of some 9,000 people is likely to be stimulated by another factor, in addition to the continuation of the forced exodus from the Free Town: the construction of the railroad line linking Brasília to the national rail network through the town of Pires do Rio. The official ceremony inaugurating the line was held in March 1967, in the last days of the Castelo Branco administration, in Vila Tenório, where the temporary station—which is likely to be the only one for many years—will be located. Only later was the line to reach the stations designed by Oscar Niemeyer, at the extreme west end of the Monumental Axis in the Pilot Plan.

The crowds which patiently waited in the mud for the ceremonial first train, whose "Smoky Mary" (*Maria Fumaça*) locomotive pulled it into the town several hours late, seemed to understand the likelihood of long delays in initiating service. In fact, by early 1968 rail service had still not begun. When it does, however, Vila Tenório and the Free Town's position as transportation and distribution centers should be further enhanced (CB March 11, 15, and 19, 1967).

V. Other Legal Peripheral Settlements

Planaltina and Braslândia

The Federal District, prior to its acquisition of that august status, included only two small settlements: Planaltina, a county seat (*sede de município*), and Braslândia, a small rural nucleus which in 1959 housed only 350 people (IBGE 1959: 79). Planaltina was the home of some 2,000 souls.

Probably originating with the *bandeiras* (exploratory expeditions setting out from São Paulo) in the latter half of the eighteenth century, Planaltina received official status only in 1859, when it was organized as a district (*distrito*) of the nearby city of Formosa. Transferred to Santa Luzia (today's Luziânia) in 1863, the town later returned to the orbit of Formosa, winning a position as a separate municipality in 1891. The original name was Mestre D'Armas (Master Armorer), probably derived from the profession of one of the local residents. In 1910 the name was changed to Altamir, and in 1917 to Planaltina (IBGE 1958). In 1922, centenary year of Brazil's independence, the fundamental stone of the new capital of Brazil was laid, symbolically as it turned out, in Planaltina.

A cattle town, Planaltina remained undeveloped due to the poor communications and transportation which prevailed until the creation of Brasília. As Furtado points out, the cattle civilization of various Brazilian regions stagnated as far as exports were concerned without losing population, since meat and leather are among the few staple products which can be consumed locally if not exported (1959: 70–76). The cattle culture referred to here was a local manifestation of a regional pattern typical of much of the Center-West.

In essence, Planaltina retained the character of an eighteenth-century town, lacking in water, sewage, paved streets, and electric power. Socially it was dominated by cattle latifundists and a small middle class, the majority of the population belonging to the lower class. The typical ranch was self-sufficient, there being, besides cattle-raising of the extensive variety on unimproved pasture, a subsistence agriculture based on slash-and-burn cultivation (*roça*) of such crops as manioc, rice, beans, and squash, and small-scale tree culture. The community was afflicted by various endemic diseases, especially Chagas's disease (whose propagation was favored by the predominant adobe construction), "wild fire" (*fogo selvagem*), a skin disease; and endemic goiter, due to iodine deficiency, in some victims so severe as to produce a characteristic type of retardate (*bôbo*) of the Brazilian Central Plateau.

In spite of this situation of generalized underdevelopment, within the limits imposed by the environment and the cultural level, there was an effort to keep up with the times, to maintain a certain minimum of cultivation and learning. This concern was frequent in isolated Goiás communities.

With the creation of the new national capital, Planaltina suffered a considerable cultural impact, "a culture shock as if there were a new colonization," as the regional administrator put it to me. In the first years of the aroused the concern of the administrators. These, however, felt that the

Brasília project, Planaltina's population showed only a modest increase —from 1,900 in March 1958 to 2,900 in September 1960. Nevertheless there arose a clear cultural separation between the older residents and the new arrivals, many of them from the Northeast, a separation reflected in the distribution of the residents in space. Most of the migrants live in a newer area of the town known as Vila Vicentina, and fifty-five families in a property known as Fazenda Sucupira, subdivided irregularly by a local official for speculative purposes. Official plans call for the elimination of the latter settlement and the transfer of the families to the town proper.

Politically, the construction of Brasília led to the loss of Planaltina's local autonomy and her incorporation into the Federal District as an Administrative Region or Subprefecture. The town has benefited from the new asphalt highways and the heavy subsidies received by the Federal District government, which trickle down to Planaltina in the form of improved public services and educational opportunities. With the lack of a regional plan for the area of Brasília, at least as of early 1968, Planaltina remains a town turned half toward the cattle culture of her past and half toward the special relationship with Brasília, which will undoubtedly bulk larger and larger in her future.

Cruzeiro

The problem posed by the scarcity of housing in the Pilot Plan also aroused the concern of the administrators. These, however, felt that the construction of new superblocks, as called for by the Pilot Plan, was not an adequate solution, and began, under the auspices of the Brasília Working Group (GTB), the construction of a new neighborhood close to the future railroad stations and the Industrial and Supply Sector (*Setor de Indústria e Abastecimento*). This neighborhood, composed of row houses similar to those along the W-3 Avenue, was known as Cruzeiro or Gavião (Hawk). The proposal to build Cruzeiro at a time when relatively few superblocks had been completed or even begun aroused vigorous protest from Lúcio Costa, in a letter he sent to the President of NOVACAP on July 19, 1961:

Allow me to clarify the following in regard to the housing problem in Brasília.

What characterizes the city plan approved in the contest and executed in reality, is *residential concentration* in apartments in the so-called super-blocks, each four of them constituting a *neighborhood unit* . . .

The plan foresaw in these neighborhood units housing of different economic standards so as to make possible to the population of civil servants *in general* the use of the city as planned, thus avoiding the division of the urban area as such into "rich neighborhoods" and "poor neighborhoods," thus occasioning the normal convivium of the population in the schools and the public streets . . .

[Due to the indiscriminate sale of the superblock areas arose] the general mistake of considering the superblocks areas destined *only* to a certain category of tenants, in consequence creating the present problem, artificially, and the resulting proposal for "economic" solutions that are really an aberration, like this one of spreading in the urban areas available thousands of little houses, without taking into account how expensive this is . . . and not only expensive, but serious . . . for such dispersive solutions counter the original scheme of the plan, conceived exactly with the intention of avoiding the usual problems of rarefied urban reticules . . . *No* civil servant ought to live outside the residential area concentrated along the residential axis; if he does, let it be caprice and personal initiative, not compelled by the circumstances (Costa 1962).

Costa goes on to urge the abandonment of the proposed neighborhood of Gavião, and the elaboration of new solutions in the superblock areas; the transfer of projects from the South Wing of the Pilot Plan to the North Wing, in order to free the internal superblocks for low-cost housing in both wings; the cession of these internal superblocks to those disposed to construct such low-cost housing; and the elaboration by the Department of Urbanism and Architecture of the appropriate proposals for economical apartments.

Costa's appeal was to no avail, however, and the Low-Cost Housing Sector (*Setor de Habitações Económicas*) was eventually built in Gavião. Largely inhabited by middle-level civil servants, it suffers all the difficulties foreseen by Costa, especially lack of public transportation, because the low density of population does not permit frequent bus service.

The internal superblocks built earlier, the so-called "JK" neighborhood (*Bairro JK*), composed of three-story walk-up buildings, do not have much of an advantage over Gavião. Also difficult of access, they remain dirty, jerry-built, and gardenless.

Sobradinho

The same pressures which led to the rapid growth of Taguatinga, the passage of Law 4,020 fixing the Free Town as permanent, and the Cruzeiro project, also motivated the elaboration of additional projects for satellite towns. The most orderly growth of any urban segment of Brasília was enjoyed by the satellite town of Sobradinho.

This town, located on the site of a ranch on a height to the northeast of the new capital, along what will evenutally be the Brasília–Fortaleza highway, is distant enough from the center of Brasília to discourage squatting, yet not so far as to make vain any inducement which the government may offer to people to settle there. Much of the housing in

Sobradinho is that which was put up by NOVACAP for its employees, for instance. A few industries, such as a factory which produces modern furniture, have also been established.

According to the Regional Administrator, Sobradinho will be permitted to expand to the point where there will be 7,432 buildings of various types, 6,099 of these being residential. In late 1966, only 1,897 of these residential lots were built up according to official standards or had construction going on on them, amounting to only 35.6 percent of the total lots, although all but 200 of the residential lots had been sold or otherwise distributed. The 4,000 lots not provided for in this account were in many cases occupied by "temporary" buildings of one kind or another, most of them wooden shacks. One-quarter of the streets were paved; electricity, water, and sewage systems were largely installed, and a teaching hospital to be operated in conjunction with the University of Brasília was largely complete. On the other hand, telephones were lacking except in the Subprefecture office, and the transportation service provided by the municipal bus line was quite unreliable.

Gama

Gama is the victim of its own location and its distance from the Pilot Plan. Located some 45 kilometers from the Pilot Plan, off the Belo Horizonte–Brasília highway, Gama is so inaccessible that on several occasions people moved there by the government have found it necessary to leave. Squatters from Vila Planalto, a Pilot Plan site which remained on dry ground after the flooding of the Bananal Encampment (Vila Amaurí), were moved to Gama at government expense; soon their shacks in Gama were found to be locked and empty. The people had left for the Social Security Invasion and other squatter settlements in the Pilot Plan. One area of Gama, inhabited largely by ex-squatters, came to be known popularly as Vampire Town (Vila Vampiro) because of the desperate living conditions and unemployment.

The lack of efficient public transportation is undoubtedly the main reason for this state of affairs. The 45-kilometer distance is nearly twice that from Taguatinga—25 kilometers—and half again as large as that from Sobradinho—30 kilometers. In addition, Gama itself is a dispersed locality composed of three main nuclei with intervening open space. This fact makes it still harder to provide decent bus service. On the road one can often see extremely overcrowded buses breaking down or crawling precariously along the road from Gama to the Pilot Plan. Workers must rise at 5 or 6 in the morning—or even earlier—to be sure of arriving at work on time. Often they must transfer at the bus station, paying an additional fare, to reach their final destinations. In the early days, people report, they were "starving" (*morrendo de fome*) in Gama. Brasília's main source of employment—construction—is characterized by rapid labor turnover, partly a result of many companies' policy of firing people frequently so they fail to qualify for the legally mandatory indemnities when the job is over. Many other workers rely on petty commerce, odd jobs, day labor, or on the domestic employment of female dependents to eke out their wages. To live in Gama is to cut oneself off from most of these opportunities; so for many, having to move to Gama was the unhappiest destiny of all within the Federal District.

The dispersed character of the town further resulted in a very sluggish commercial sector and a virtually nonexistent street life, decreasing still further the attractiveness of the settlement.

The three main nuclei of which Gama is composed are Vila São João (the remains of the largely unsuccessful attempt to remove Vila Planalto); Itamaracá, which is an area abandoned by a construction company which had been induced to set up facilities there on what proved to be the misleading promise that a major development would arise there; and Little Gama (Gaminha). Of the three, the latter has the most active street life and commercial sector.

Gama's plan provides for 13,175 lots, of which 3,398 are vacant, 1,290 are stucco houses (*alvenaria*), and 6,620 wooden shacks. There are 760 dwellings, wood and stucco, that are closed and unoccupied. Additional lots are allocated to commerce. Buildings are distributed approximately in equal numbers in the East (Itamaracá), South (Vila São João), and West (Gaminha) sectors.

Rural Settlements

Table I shows that the rural population expanded at a very slow rate compared to many of the urban settlements. This reflected the continued lack of a regional plan or any large-scale effort to develop the rural sector in the area during the early years (for details see Mandell, in press). Though agrarian reform was the subject of impassioned debate on the national political scene, it remained largely in the talking stage. In the Federal District there was some migration of Japanese truck gardeners. There were also at least two small attempts at rural squatting, in Alexandre de Gusmão (near Braslândia) and Taquara (near Planaltina). The eventual legalization of both squatments and the assistance offered to their residents by various governmental agencies and the U.S. Peace Corps (one of whose members helped construct a small hydroelectric plant near Taquara) hardly amount to a serious agricultural development program.

The small scale of the agricultural sector in Brasília can be underlined by the presence of miniscule plantings of sugar cane and vegetables in the gallery forests along the courses of the Côrrego Vicente Pires and the Riacho Fundo in the vicinity of the Free Town, Vila Tenório, and the Social Security Invasion, all clandestinely cleared.

The bulk of the food supply continues to come from São Paulo and Anápolis, much of it under the auspices of the Cotia Agricultural Cooperative, a Nippo-Brazilian enterprise which packs considerable commercial wallop.

VI. Housing Plans After the Coup

The period immediately following the military coup of April 1, 1964 was occupied by a purge of the nation's political life and public administration. Brasília was no exception; there, power was handed over to Lt. Col. Ivan de Souza Mendes (Rodrigues 1967: 34). The Mayor's office intervened in a series of officially controlled but nominally autonomous organs: NOVACAP, the official food distribution company, and the Hospital Foundation.[8]

Several major political figures were arrested, including Federal Deputy Francisco Julião, an agrarian reform advocate. The reformed University of Brasília was surrounded by military contingents and searched for arms and subversive literature. This institution was a special target because of ex-Rector Darcy Ribeiro's position as head of deposed President João Goulart's civilian staff.

Once the mechanics of a forceful political transition were out of the way, the regime was faced with the problem of what to do about Brasília. The city was still only partly the capital of the country in the practical sense, since the majority of the ministries had only token representation there. Brasília was also the subject of much hostility on the part of important groups in the new administration, dominated as it was by the National Democratic Union Party (UDN—*União Democrática Nacional*), a conservative group; orthodox economists around Planning Minister Roberto Campos; and the "Sorbonne" group of military men.[9]

These groups were hostile to Brasília not only because of its association with Kubitschek, with whom they had old scores to settle, but because they regarded the construction of the city as having been the occasion for the initiation of the inflationary spiral they contended was the root cause of the nation's economic difficulties. Yet by the time these groups reached

8. The food company is SAB—*Sociedade de Abastecimento de Brasília* (Brasília Supply Company). The relevant decrees are 289 and 290 (1964), DOU April 14, 1964 and 295 (1964), DOU April 20, 1964.
9. "Sorbonne" is the nickname of the National War College (*Escola Superior de Guerra*) in Rio de Janeiro where the group is supposed to have been formed.

power, Brasília had also become a reality in spite of its incompleteness as a city. A return to Rio de Janeiro would have been disastrous, both as a symbolic retreat from what had become an incarnation of national progress and aspirations, and as an economic loss of the considerable sums invested in the enterprise. The government was, an Marshal-President Castelo Branco is apocryphally alleged to have said, torn between the "folly of finishing Brasília and the crime of abandoning her."

The though of abandoning the city soon was given up, and the question became how much money would be invested in her completion, and how rapidly the task was to be accomplished. The problem was handed to a new Mayor of the Federal District, a civilian technician, Dr. Plínio Reis de Catanhede Almeida (Rodrigues 1967: 34). It soon became apparent that nothing approaching the original "rhythm of Brasília would be reestablished, but through administrative reforms and a continuing program of activity, the city was able to move a considerable distance forward. Not much, however, was to be accomplished in the way of transfer of new federal organs from Rio de Janeiro, until Castelo Branco was succeeded in 1967 by his former War Minister, Marshal Artur da Costa e Silva.

Dr. Plínio's program dwelt initially on the completion of what had been left half finished by the previous governments. He became known as the "gardener-mayor" in the press, because one of his principal programs was the planting of grass and gardens in the city, previously marked by mud and dust coming from the bare red earth left by the bulldozers. This activity was concentrated in the Pilot Plan, and had the psychological effect of diminishing the construction-camp appearance of much of the city. The television tower, called for by the plan of Lúcio Costa, was completed according to the planner's design, along with the vast garden of the Monumental Axis, which includes an illuminated fountain that plays instrumental music at night while colored spotlights illuminate the play of the water. This particular program obviously did not reflect any reversal of the monumentalist priorities of the prior administrations.

It is true, of course, that an attack upon the housing shortage would depend upon financial resources of quite another order, and on political decisions in the national sphere. Some action was taken, however, in the area of providing the satellite towns with water, electric power, and sewage; plans were announced for telephone service expansion, but as of early 1968 not much had been achieved in that field.

The National Housing Plan (*Plano Nacional de Habitação*) was enacted as Law 4,380 of 1964, on August 1st of that year. It was partly by technical and partly by political considerations. The government had adopted an "anti-inflationary" policy which hit hardest at the lowest social strata. Eliminating subsidies and price controls for such items as petroleum derivatives, basic foodstuffs, and suburban railroad commutation (largely a recourse of the poorer segments of the urban population in Brazil), while maintaining a relatively strict limitation on wage increases, throttling the labor movement, the Castelo Branco group had made itself exceedingly unpopular with the less well-to-do sections of Brazil's urban population. While at times government spokesmen boasted of its unpopularity as a sign that it was not "demagogic," it was nevertheless the conviction of the coup leaders that some tangible sign of social concern was necessary until the hoped-for success of the anti-inflationary policy would make the country realize the wisdom of Castelo's economic policies. Another aspect of the economic orthodoxy of the Castelo-Campos group was the policy of gradual decontrol of rents. Rates had in many cases become nominal due to the rapid inflation without corresponding increases in rentals; the planners of the Campos school argued that this pattern had resulted in the paralysis of residential construction for rental purposes. Since the decontrol was a gradual one, investor pessimism about housing as an investment was bound to decline gradually also. As a result, the average tenant simply noted an increase in rents without any corresponding increase in the supply of housing. Again, the government had to supply some kind of compensation to those who suffered from the immediate consequences of its economic policies.

There was also a more strictly economic motivation for the enactment of the National Housing Plan. The restriction on credit that was a part of the anti-inflationary policy and the decline in demand due to the reduction in real wages consequent upon the incomes policy of the government, combined to produce recession conditions and unemployment in the industrial sector. Residential construction, an industry which with current methods uses a relatively large labor supply, was a hoped-for source of jobs for the unemployed and a stimulus for the lagging economy. The principal agency assigned to execute the new plan was the National Housing Bank (*Banco Nacional de Habitação*), which was to operate indirectly with the cooperation of other agencies in the different regions of the country. At the same time, as part of another reform, the Social Security Institutes, unified as part of the National Social Security Institute (INPS—*Instituto Nacional de Previdência Social*), were to remove themselves altogether from the housing field, selling their existing units to the lawful occupants on a long-term payment basis. The hope was to eliminate favoritism and political influence in the distribution of the up-to-then scarce public housing which had been built under the auspices of the Institutes. The legal system of security of employment (*estabilidade*), which obliged employers to pay indemnities (*indenização*) to most workers discharged without cause, according to the length of service, was to be substituted on an optional basis by the Seniority Guarantee Fund (*Fundo de Garantia de Tempo de Serviço*), to which a contribution was made each month, and was deposited with the National Housing Bank, to be withdrawn by the worker only in case of emergency or for the financing of housing.

A Federal Housing and City Planning Service (SERFHAU—*Serviço Federal de Habitação e Urbanismo*) was created to be the research and planning arm of the National Housing Plan. Later the Constitution of 1967 would provide for the establishment of metropolitan area unit authorities to help deal with the problems of areas such as Greater São Paulo, Greater Rio de Janeiro, and Greater Recife.

In the beginning, one inspiration for the policies of the government in the housing field was the precoup squatment eradication program of Guanabara (city of Rio de Janeiro) Governor Carlos Lacerda, who mobilized U.S. aid funds to create distant neighborhoods composed of tiny individual houses for the former residents of several *favelas* (squatter settlements), notably some situated in conspicuous locations (USAID 1966: 139). One of Lacerda's associates, Sandra Cavalcânti, was chosen to head the National Housing Bank. Each state, under the plan, was to create a special company modeled after Guanabara's COHAB, which Srta. Cavalcânti had headed, to deal with the housing needs of the lower social strata.

The Rio program, however, turned out to be a success only in the sense of having eliminated the target *favelas* by heavy pressure from the government. Distant from the labor market, served only by very expensive and time-consuming public transportation, lacking in many public services, the new developments such as Vila Kennedy neither satisfied their residents nor resolved their most pressing problems. The political dividends which the United States authorities had hoped for from the projects, moreover, were not forthcoming; Lacerda's hand-picked successor, Flexa Ribeiro, was trounced in the gubernatorial elections of 1965, with the opposition candidate, Negrão de Lima, carrying the new projects such as Vila Kennedy. United States officials indicated that they would be most hesitant to support future projects of this type (Salmen 1966).

As a public work, however, and a highly touted model for solving one of Brazil's most serious urban problems, the project did provide short-run political prestige to Lacerda and Srta. Cavalcânti. Nevertheless, Lacerda soon found himself in opposition to the military-dominated regime, and Srta. Cavalcânti was soon removed from the National Housing Bank, for reasons which remain unclear. Nevertheless, the Rio solution had gained considerable momentum and would be tried in Brasília.

There was another element to the National Housing Plan, however, which affected Brasília with great force: the compulsory sale of the real estate belonging to the Institutes to their lawful occupants. In the case of Brasília, a special Rotating Housing Fund (*Fundo Rotativo Habitacional de Brasília*) was created from the funds derived from the tenants' monthly payments toward purchase of their apartments on a condominium basis. They would have thirty years to pay the full price of the apartments, at prices periodically increased to allow for the effects of inflation (*correção monetária*). The first area this money would be invested in was the 2,316 housing units whose construction was paralyzed in various stages of incompletion from the time Jânio Quadros ordered work in Brasília halted in 1961 (Rodrigues 1967: 166–167). Later, additional funds from this source would be invested in new housing. As each unit was completed, payments by its occupants would be invested in more new housing. The fund would be administered by the Brasília Working Group (GTB), later renamed the Brasília Development Corporation (CODEBRAS—*Coordenação de Desenvolvimento de Brasília*). The principal beneficiaries of this program would be civil servants.

The opening of the apartments to purchase, subject to certain conditions, led to a considerable volume of transactions in which apartments were traded or the rights to them sold. Since the financing was very generous by Brazilian standards, the mere cession of rights to an apartment was worth as much as Cr$10,000,000 (a bit less than U.S.$5,000), even though the new resident would have to buy it over a fifteen instead of a thirty-year period.

In part this activity was due to the fact that under the inspiration of the egalitarian ideas of the Costa plan, in exceptional but not infrequent cases, people of radically different incomes were neighbors in apartment buildings in which all paid only nominal rents. The low-income residents were mostly civil servants (chauffeurs, etc., rather than workers). With the compulsion to buy, those who did not have sufficient resources to meet the monthly payments chose the considerable cash they could obtain by selling or trading their rights.

One difficulty with this policy of sale of apartments at very favorable prices is the fact that large numbers of people in high positions live in Brasília only temporarily. Deputies, subject to electoral defeat, had the right to acquire their apartments very inexpensively. As a result, in 1967 when a new Congress took office, there were not enough apartments in the city available for allocation to the new deputies, a lack which is being remedied by the construction of additional apartments. Meanwhile, the Brazilian taxpayer is shouldering the bills of many deputies at the luxurious National Hotel.

A third aspect of this housing program in Brasília was the financing activity of the Federal Savings Bank of Brasília (*Caixa Económica Federal de Brasília*), which would finance houses worth up to four hundred times the monthly minimum wage (Cr$33,000,000 in late 1966, or about U.S.$15,000), though at least 40 percent of the funds must go for houses worth up to 100 times the monthly minimum wage, which are financed for 90 percent of cost, while those worth from 300 to 400 times minimum wages receive only 70 percent financing. Since the buyers are eligible only for houses for which they can contribute up to 30 percent of their income over a thirty-year period, with periodic correction for inflation (*correção monetária*), it is clear that this program was designed primarily for the middle class, or such of it as were not civil servants waiting for government apartments.

There had already existed in Brasília an agency called the Brasília Low-Cost Housing Company (SHEB—*Sociedade de Habitações Económicas de Brasília*), designed to deal with the housing shortage at the lowest social level. This agency was incorporated into the plan as the local version of Guanabara's COHAB, its name being changed to the Company for Housing of Social Interest (SHIS—*Sociedade de Habitações de Interêsse Social*). It would deal with the housing problems of those whose incomes were below 2.5 times the minimum wage, which in 1967 was about NCr$100, or U.S.$37, so that 2.5 times it would be a little under U.S.$100.

One of the points on which the planners of the new housing program insisted, however, was that the program would have to pay for itself, not depending on governmental paternalism. Hence the correction for inflation in the payments for the house, and a series of requirements designed to insure that the recipients would be willing and able to keep up with them. These requirements would soon eliminate, in practice, those either earning less than the amount necessary to participate in any program, unable to prove their ability to participate, or unwilling to do so.

By early 1967, SHIS had completed 666 popular houses in Gama, 622 in the southern sector of Taguatinga, and 1,008 in the north sector of the same town. This was the first stage of a projected 10,000 units; some units were already under construction in Sobradinho, along with additional ones in Gama (Rodrigues 1967: 158–159).

These houses are "core houses" (*casas embrião*). That is to say, they comprise only a very small area (27 square meters), including a kitchen and bathroom. The house is conceived to be a minimal unit providing for hygienic necessities. It is designed to be expanded in accordance with the needs of the occupants as time goes on. The difficulty is that the carrying charges already tax the incomes of many of the occupants to the breaking point. Many of them are neither willing nor able to construct the additions themselves. Those most able financially to pay for materials for the additions are least able to contribute their own labor, for they have work obligations. Many people prefer the free and clear "ownership" of a shack in the squatment, which is also capable of being expanded if need be, and at less expense, to the long-term obligation of paying 15 or 20 percent of their wages, with the constant threat of eviction and loss of their home.

Another objection frequently voiced to the SHIS developments is that the rules, which seem to be fairly strictly enforced, prohibit commercial activity in the dwelling units. Since many urban lower-class Brazilians supplement their incomes with small commercial craft and maintenance enterprises run from their homes, this prohibition is a considerable disability.

In spite of these limitations, the SHIS program has meant political success for its executors. The Mayor appointed in 1967 by President Costa e Silva, Wadjô Gomide, and his Secretary of Social Services, Domingos Malheiros, are both ex-executives of the SHIS program. The problem of squatting, as we shall see, remains.

VII. Class and Space in Brasília, 1967

Ten years after the jury selected Lúcio Costa's Pilot Plan, the realities of the city's development presented a picture distinctly different from that foreseen by the planner. It has not in reality been possible to prevent the "encystment of squatments" or to provide for the coexistence of various social classes in neighborhood units. Inspired by European ideas and standards, obeying the dictates of esthetics and symbolism rather than being grounded in empirical social and regional reality, the Brasília plan in practice soon betrayed the gap between the plan's pretensions and the social and geographical reality to which it would be applied.

The rigid precepts of the Pilot Plan had to be filtered through the hard reality of Brazilian society, whose nature and needs even as directly affecting the new city hardly are mentioned in the plan's text. Thus, for instance, the prospect that massive migrations of unskilled laborers from the poorer regions of the country might direct themselves toward Brasília must have been imagined, and the differences between construction camps at a damsite, for instance, and in a new city that tends to create a life of its own, as in the case of the Free Town, cannot have been as subtle as to escape notice. A planner who like Lúcio Costa had for years lived in Rio de Janeiro cannot have ignored the tenacity with which *favelas*—the Rio term for shantytowns—cling to the hillsides and other sites in resis-

tance to gravity, erosion, and official hostility (or at least inconsistency).
The most we can say with assurance, on reading the document that
guided the construction of the new capital, is that the author did not deal
with the life of the lower class, either during the construction process or
after it, with the realism and depth that would have been necessary for
a major improvement in the urban existence of this class. As a result,
the lower class was virtually eliminated from many aspects of the life of
the planned center of Brasília; it is segregated less formally but just about
as completely as black North Americans or the African population of
Durban, South Africa (Kuper and others 1958). The people who built
Brasília are permitted to look at the city and to serve there in menial
tasks, but rarely do they live there or participate in the social, political,
or—except in a restricted way—economic life of what was grandly proclaimed as the future *civitas* of Brazil. While calling for an equality not
existing elsewhere in Brazilian society, the planner produced, it turns out,
a blueprint for a city of inequality and class separation.

Symbolic of this inequality and separation is the Bus Station at the
center of the Pilot Plan. The result of a massive earth-moving and construction effort, the station is located at the confluence of the two highway
axes that form the skeleton of the Pilot Plan. The station is surrounded
by a vast traffic circle, shadowed by two viaducts, and undercut by still
another superhighway. On a rise above it is the television tower; below
it are a vast expanse of lawn and Oscar Niemeyer's monumental government buildings. Even as this modernistic, monumental environment strikes
the observer, he cannot fail to notice the long lines of impoverished workers and their families awaiting public transportation to their homes miles
away. At the rush hours, the lines of people awaiting the creaky buses
assume proportions as monumental in their own way as the architecture
surrounding them. At times one observes newly arrived migrants, their
belongings in sacks, still dazed by their new surroundings, in the midst
of the confusion. Innumerable barefoot boys hawk newspapers, from
Brasília and Rio de Janeiro, with only occasional success in making a
sale. A few ragged beggars, most of them steady fixtures of the station,
make the rounds.

Brasília's social structure mirrors the contrast described here. Those in
cars speeding over, under, and around the Bus Station belong to one
group; those who must wait on line, in general, belong to the other.

The Pilot Plan of the city, originally intended to house the whole population, is dominated by the middle class. A large number of domestic
servants sleep in the maid's rooms with which most apartments and houses
come equipped. There are also some day workers, mostly laundresses. A
large number of these live in the Social Security Invasion, and some in

Taguatinga; many of the domestic servants are young unmarried girls whose families live in squatments and to a lesser extent in satellite towns.

Table IV shows the different sectors, corresponding to housing types, in which the housing units of the Pilot Plan are located. It does not include all the housing types which may be found in the Pilot Plan; it omits the airport-lake neighborhood, the many rented rooms in the SHIGS houses, and the many apartments installed in what are technically commercial establishments. It is, however, accurate with respect to the great bulk of the housing units which exist. Most importantly, it does indicate the relatively large numbers of the apartments, all of which are grouped into superblocks according to the Lúcio Costa plan.

During the period we lived in the Pilot Plan, we rented a SHIGS house off W-3 Avenue. These houses themselves come in two major types, and ours was an example of the simplest variety, originally constructed by the misnamed Popular Housing Foundation (*Fundação da Casa Popular*) (see illus. 8). Most of these houses are owner-occupied, but a few are held by small investors as income property or as a reserve asset in case they should have to return or bring relatives to the capital. Our house, for example, was the property of a retired Army officer from Northeast

TABLE IV
Housing Units in the Pilot Plan by Type and Location, 1966

Type and location	*Number of units*
Apartments	(10,259)
Elevator	(5,579)
SQS[1] 100–300	4,047
SQS[1] 200	860
SQN[2] 300	672
Walk-up	(4,680)
SQS[1] 400	3,144
SQN[2] 400	1,536
Row houses	(3,747)
Cruzeiro	1,406
SHIGS[3] (W-3)	2,343
Commercial north wing	840
TOTAL[4]	14,846

Source: Mr. José Pastore (see Pastore 1968)

1. South Wing superblocks (*Super Quadras Sul*).
2. North Wing superblocks (*Super Quadras Norte*).
3. Individual Row House Sector, South (*Setor de Habitações Individuais Geminadas, Sul*).
4. Omits airport zone, some invasions within Pilot Plan area, rented rooms in SHIGS, and commercial buildings.

Brazil, who had been active in the establishment of Brasília's telephone network, but with the change of administrations had returned to his native state to work in the same field. This man owned four houses in the vicinity. His agent, also an ex-officer, with family connections of some importance in one of the Northeast states, had become established, and then failed, in coffee planting enterprises in the frontier area of Paraná. He himself lived in a stucco house, which he owned, in one of the better areas of Taguatinga, but traveled to the Pilot Plan on business, which provided income to supplement his pension.

The block we lived on was fairly typical in appearance. Like most of the SHIGS blocks in which a majority of the lots were built up, there were two rows of houses fronting on a common garden, planted with grass and shade trees by the city government. At the W-3 end of the block was a brick and concrete bus-stop shelter; to the other end was a church belonging to a North American missionary group. To the rear of each house there was a backyard, which in every case was walled, and in many cases had been built up either with rooms for rental, additional rooms for the family, or covered garages. A cul-de-sac alley to the back of the houses provided automotive access. Each house had a small plot in front of it, and in many cases fairly elaborate gardens were planted with roses, dahlias, *ficus* trees ("rubber" trees), and other plants. Usually the work on these gardens was done by men who daily passed from door to door soliciting work; in some cases, a regular arrangement was made for the gardener to return weekly or on some other schedule.

These itinerant gardeners were not the only members of the lower class to make their appearance in the SHIGS area. The residents of the row houses were constantly called to their doors by beggars, peddlers, and seekers of work of various kinds. Most of the beggars were either women, usually accompanied by one or more small, ragged children, or groups of children in twos, threes, and fours, who would come to the door asking for *auxílio* ("aid," as opposed to *esmola*, "alms," the standard Portuguese word). Often the youngest child of a group would be sent to the door, to clap hands rather than to knock, for the former is the polite way to approach a house in Northeast Brazil, and ask, "for the love of God" (*pelo amor de Deus*), for leftover food, for clothes, or for money. This begging is as much a pattern of the rural interior as of the cities.

Others, usually men, came to sell, some on regular routes. A few of the more prosperous peddlers came by bicycle selling fresh vegetables they had bought wholesale in the Free Town. Others carried sacks of oranges, caramel (*doce de leite*), cheese, or bottled honey. A popcorn cart and hand-drawn ice cream wagons made the rounds regularly. Small boys would make the rounds selling homemade candy or lollipops, which they would usually carry on trays suspended by a string from their necks. Periodically the Minors' Judge (*Juíz de Menores*) would begin a campaign to prohibit minors from traveling by bus except in school uniform or accompanied by an adult, but in this event the young peddlers would hitch rides on private cars and trucks.

The range of itinerants is by no means exhausted by the foregoing, however. Purveyors of services also made their appearance with some frequency; among the tasks they would undertake to perform were knife-sharpening, repairs of gas stoves and electrical equiment, light carpentry, and construction work. Women would appear, often with children, seeking employment as domestics, either by the day or on a more permanent basis: frequently this served as a transparent cover for begging, but often it was sincere.

This ambulant commerce and odd-job seeking provide an important part of the income of squatters and other members of the lower class. Some of those who engage in these activities are full-time specialists; others are only occasional participants, weekly or when they are out of work. In both cases, however, their activity and their relations with the middle-class residents of the Pilot Plan suggest that they are integrated, albeit on terms of inequality, into Brasília's urban economy and society. This integration is particularly crucial to the maintenance function in the economy. The assymetry in wealth, power, and status between the lower class and the more prosperous members of the society is the result not of a *failure* of integration, but of the *terms* of integration and the polarized structure of the society as a whole.

The residents of the SHIGS blocks, the potential customers for the goods and services offered by the ambulants, included, in addition to a foreign anthropologist, his wife and child, several modestly well off members of Brasília's urban middle class. Not all of them, however, lacked connections with the rural sector. Thus one neighbor, of Syrian ancestry, had considerable holdings in ranch property in Goiás. Although urban residence on the part of landowners is a secular tradition in Brazil, he claimed to be a man of the soil, and blamed his wife and daughter for the need to live in the capital. His wife preferred the comfort, and his daughter could acquire a secondary education, for a teaching certificate.

Other residents were more strictly urban in their orientations. Thus there was a woman, whose husband was a retired civil servant, whose spinster daughter taught science at the University; across the way, the manager of a store that catered to tourists visiting the posh National Hotel; a Hungarian refugee, who with several relatives had left São Paulo to start a small construction company specialized in planning and building schools; and an officer of the Federal Police. In other blocks, many of the residents were doctors and dentists, some of whom maintained their professional offices in their houses. Even at the social level represented here, the residence often becomes a place of business, whether for liberal professionals, for housewives doubling in brass as seamstresses, as an occasional restaurant or boardinghouse (*pensão*), or as a source of rental income. This is another example of the widespread occupational multiplicity characteristic of Brazil at all social levels.

A less frequent type of residence is the flat above a store; however, in the smaller businesses along W-3 Avenue and in the local commercial areas, it is not uncommon. One man we came to know had a small business in construction and maintenance supplies, sustained mainly through an occasional successful bid for a government contract. Originally from eastern Minas Gerais, this man, a devout Protestant, had come to Anápolis, a nearby city in Goiás, some years before Brasília's construction began. When Juscelino initiated the drive to build Brasília, he had moved to Taguatinga, and later, after his business had become established in the Pilot Plan, to W-3 Avenue above his store, in a rented two-story building, in order, he said, to be near the business. His youngest daughter also studied in the Pilot Plan, and his oldest worked as a teller in a bank there, though she had originally worked in Taguatinga and had arranged a transfer when her family moved. A young girl, a cousin, from Eastern Minas, had come to live with the family in order to benefit from the relatively abundant secondary education in the capital; in return, she served virtually as an unpaid domestic servant. In addition to its commercial interests, this family also held a plot in Taguatinga, acquired through political protection from the government, and a small, though not miniscule, rural property in Goiás near Anápolis, which was farmed on shares by a family which lived on the site. Frequently, when we visited them, this family would be slaughtering a pig from the farm or making a cauldron of dessert from fruit, such as guava, that was in season there.

By far the most common sort of residence in the Pilot Plan, however, is the apartment house. A few of these are privately owned; one very elegant superblock caters to the few embassy personnel living in the new capital (the Foreign Office—*Itamaratí*—not having moved from Rio while we were in Brasília); another has been mostly rented by the University for its junior faculty and instructors (graduate students on fellowships). More common, however, are the superblocks associated with government agencies; as a result of this affiliation, the social composition of the apartment house superblocks is somewhat different from the SHIGS row houses, notably in the even greater preponderance of civil servants.

The distinction between elevator apartments (six stories) and walk-ups (three stories, with and without *pilotis*—open air, collonaded entryways) is important both architecturally and socially. The latter category include the "JK" (Kubitschek again) apartments in the South Wing of the Pilot Plan (see fig. 9) and the "Residential North Wing" apartments. These are inferior in terms of architecture, construction, maintenance, landscaping, and public services, and in practice are the domain of a lesser category of the middle class, and are viewed as such by both their inhabitants and other residents of the Pilot Plan. The North Wing, *Asa Norte* in Portuguese, for instance, is sometimes called the *Asa da Morte,* or "Death Wing." The commercial blocks in the walk-up areas are almost entirely composed of empty lots, in contrast to the humming commerce of the 100 and 300 superblocks (elevator apartments). In the Residential North Wing, the only commerce is the official SAB supermarket and a few wooden establishments more or less irregularly installed in the nearby cerrados. The Commercial North Wing (W-3 North) is largely the product of an abortive attempt to transfer some Free Town residents and businesses to that sector, and is an area of mud, shacks, auto repair shops, and warehouses, with only a few concrete and other permanent buildings. In 1967 the Mines and Energy Ministry was building some row houses in the Wing, and there was talk of financing some permanent buildings for merchants in the area which had not come to fruition.

The distinction between the elevator and walk-up buildings is part of one of the most direct contradictions between the plan of Brasília and the 1967 reality. In fact, the 100 and 300 superblocks, on the opposite side of the Highway Axis from the lake, are much more "alive" and much more valued than those on the lakeside. This is due, we suspect, to the contrast between the marginal avenues L-2 (east, that is to say, toward the lake) and W-3. The former is a busy thoroughfare, but on the east side of it there are nothing but secondary schools. W-3, on the other hand, has a solid bank of storefronts on its east side, and behind them superblocks, and across the street the row houses of SHIGS. W-3 is the center of the city's street life, to Brazilians an important attraction. Transportation, in turn, is easier, because the bus routes were of necessity shifted to where so many of the passengers are found. Thus Brasília, planned to be symmetrical, in fact is centered on its South Wing in general, and particularly the southwestern quadrant.

We have already seen that socioeconomically the southeastern quadrant's "JK" walk-ups are inferior to the elevator apartments more common to the west; this distinction further accentuates the imbalance between southwest and southeast. Lúcio Costa's prediction that the major social distinction would be between "internal" and "external" superblocks is thus disconfirmed; it is the "upper" and "lower" ones that are so distinguished—the upper ones to the west of and above the lower ones taking visual advantage of the gradual slope of the city toward the lake.

The plan has also not been followed by the local commercial zones between the superblocks. These shops were to have fronted away from the access roads, along which parking and deliveries were to take place. Access to the stores would be from the grassy superblock side, following the general principle of the separation of pedestrian and automotive traffic. In practice, however, perhaps because of the delay in planting grass and construction of the necessary walkways in many of the super- blocks, the pedestrians walk on the sidewalk on what was to have been the back entrance, violating the principle of separation of the two kinds of traffic. In consequence, the display windows and public entrances are on this side, and the superblock side is usually partly or totally closed off.

It has not been practical to make each superblock or group of super- blocks largely autonomous in terms of commerce; many of the super- blocks, especially those to the east of the Highway Axis, as we have seen, lack nearly all the stores of their planned commercial streets. A few streets to the west of the Highway Axis, on the other hand, lead all the rest, and their stores (along with those on W-3) attract buyers from all over the Pilot Plan and the satellite cities. On the most important of these, known as "Little Church Street" (*Rua da Igrejinha*) after the Niemeyer chapel of Our Lady of Fátima which is at its head, it is often impossible to find a parking space. The sector of private office buildings and stores, South Commercial Sector (SCS—*Setor Commercial Sul*), is only be- ginning to become important, and not principally for its retail commerce, which is limited.

It turns out, indeed, that the projected orderly compartmentalization of many aspects of urban life has to a large extent not taken place. The elementary schools, located in the superblocks, are one exception, though even in this sphere the large number of private schools drawing students from the whole Pilot Plan make the compartmentalization incomplete. In no sense does the compartmentalization extend to secondary education. And only two of the neighborhood clubs really function, the weekend at country places and at various lakeside clubs having assumed greater im- portance.

One reason for this pattern, in addition to the simple noncompletion of the neighborhood clubs, is that since many apartments are assigned by virtue of employment in a single agency, many people are neighbors of their work associates, and do not find it congenial to mix work and leisure associations. This is a subtle problem; the typically urban dissociation of roles implies freedom of association, privacy, a certain liberty in choice of life-style, the stimulation of diverse contacts, but also loneliness, insecurity, and a predominance of affectively neutral interpersonal relations. One suspects, however, that any version of the company town, like some ministry superblocks in Brasília, removes more advantages of the "urban" configuration than it succeeds in eliminating disadvantages—perhaps because it extends the social relations typical of the work-place into the neighborhood. Since work-place relations tend to be stratified and formal, tense, and generally disagreeable, the proximity of the same people in another context is not very attractive to the majority. This differentiation of participants in different forms of interaction is one of the characteristics of urban life in most cities, and is reflected in Alexander's distinction (1966), discussed earlier (pp. 53–54), between "tree" and "semi-lattice" urban plans.

Another example of this simplifying or rationalizing tendency was the numbering system of Brasília. Numbers were chosen, among other reasons, to get away from the usual Brazilian habit of naming streets, buildings, and almost anything else after public figures of greater or (frequently) lesser importance, President so-and-so, Major this, or Doctor that. Presumably the *rationality* of the numbering system would serve as a brake to the temptation to honor the dead or the living with a street name or a superblock. The fundamental element in the Brasília numbering system is a three-figure number, preceded by an acronym, in the case of superblocks either SQS (*Super-Quadra Sul*—South Superblock) or SQN (*Super-Quadra Norte*—North Superblock). Then the first figure of the number refers to the location of the block in the east-west direction, odd numbers to the west of the Highway Axis, even numbers to the east, the lowest number to the blocks closest to the Axis, the highest to those farthest away. The second and third figures of the number refer to the location in a north-south direction, the lowest numbers to the blocks closer to the Monumental Axis, the highest to those farther away. Thus, for instance, SQS 308:

> SQS—south wing
>> 3—(odd number) west of the Highway Axis;
>> (second in the odd series)—in the second
>> row of superblocks west of the Axis
>> 08—the eighth superblock in the north-south
>> row, out (south) from the Monumental Axis.

The north-south avenues are similarly numbered, with reference to the compass direction; thus W-3, the third west avenue[10] and L-2, the second east avenue. In addition, special sector acronyms were established in cer-

10. The English W was chosen because the "O" of Portuguese *oeste* would be confused with zero.

tain cases and combined with building names, as in Edifício Maristela, SCS, named for ex-President Kubitschek's daughter, an indication of the persistence of "personalist" naming habits.

The pattern has been broken, however, along W-3 Avenue. The stores along the east side of the street are included in blocks which follow the superblock numbers' last two figures, but the initial "5" has been dropped for the expression "commercial W-3," to contrast with the "residential W-3" row houses on the west side. These, originally "714," "706," and so on, now have a numbering system completely distinct from the superblocks'. Sometimes they are referred to as "W-3, Quadra (Block) 17," sometimes as SHIGS (from *"Setor de Habitações Individuais Geminadas Sul"*—roughly South Sector of Individual Housing in Rows), Block 17.

The official numbering system, however, has not been consecrated in popular usage. In general, the residents of Brasília orient themselves and give directions to others by means of named landmarks, usually buildings or commercial establishments. Thus one frequently hears such expressions as "the street of Supermarket number one," "opposite Dom Bosco Chapel," "near Ponto Frio" (an appliance store). Most of these points of reference are on W-3 Avenue, reflecting the role of that street as a "downtown" and also as a thoroughfare for public buses and private cars. Even when people give numbers, as in the case of the superblocks, they will usually specify "it's the bus stop opposite the swimming pool," or "one stop before the hospital."

This emphasis on landmarks parallels the reaction of many visitors to Brasília and recently arrived residents that the buildings are "all alike." People complain of never knowing where they are. This of course is an impression, and a first impression at that. Brasília is generally characterized by excellent visibility, due to the climatic conditions and to the regular, slightly eastward-sloping lay of the land. The different sectors of the city—Three Powers Plaza, the Ministries, W-3, the superblocks, the row houses, the University, the TV Tower—are spatially distinct, highly visible, usually at a distance, and set off from one another by all the resources at an architect's command, some so well known that they are recognized by people who have never seen them, as are Notre Dame, the Capitol in Washington, St. Peter's, or the Kremlin. Some of the buildings, then, are highly individual, and "imageable" as Lynch (1960) puts it. Within certain sectors, however, it is very difficult to orient oneself. The Ministries, for instance, are identical externally, and can only be distinguished by their position or by tiny signs. The commercial streets between the superblocks follow a single mold; within each subarea, the row houses must follow a single profile. One man told me Brasília was "communist" because he was forbidden to put up a second story.

The superblocks, each composed of ten similar apartment buildings, are not as differentiated from one another as the original plan specified, with different layouts and landscaping; it is here that the impression of sameness seems to be formed, and is most justified. The architectural sameness is accentuated by a rectangular and repetitive street plan (the slight arching of the north-south axis is not easily perceptible at ground level), so that the angles of streets, special squares, or intersections do not usually help one to recognize a place one has been to before. So smaller clues are seized upon; a particular store, an unusual church, a gas station. We should add here that the largest Brazilian cities are the opposite of Brasília in respect to orientation: within a neighborhood, like Rio's Copacabana, multiple clues (tunnels, squares, forks in the avenues, curved streets, a particular hotel of distinctive design) orient one, and the succession of neighborhoods along certain routes is easy to remember, but conversely few can map the actual shape of the city or the compass orientation of the neighborhoods. Brasília, as we have seen, has easy-to-distinguish sectors, but within certain of them orientation is very difficult.

Another factor contributing to the seeming sameness of the residential buildings in Brasília is the uniformity of style of these buildings, invariably done in a boxy "contemporary" style harking back to the Bauhaus, with the addition of pilotis out of Le Corbusier. Plane surfaces, right angles, and an absence of adornment typify these buildings. The commercial buildings are also similar to one another, typically two-story whitewashed boxes, arranged in rows.

Brasília's retail stores reflect the underlying provincialism of the city. In terms of ideas, communications, fads, the center of Brazil is the Rio–São Paulo axis, from whence magazines, television soap operas, intellectual innovation, and industrial products emanate. Small, distant, almost entirely administrative but not yet containing even the whole upper echelon of the government, Brasília has the feel if not the appearance of an interior city, a receiver rather than a transmitter of novelty. Lacking a real upper class, populated, at least at the lower levels of society, by people from the country's poorest regions, Brasília wears its international, modern appearance unconvincingly, as one discovers if one tries, for instance, to buy white, undecorated cups and saucers. Popular tastes run to plastic flowers, formica furniture, and last year's fashions; and all of these are available at prices much above those in Rio or São Paulo.

This is not to say, however, that Brasília is isolated from the consumer economy which has grown up with Brazil's industrialization, at least for the national upper and middle classes. The basis of the game is the installment plan, which relies, in Brasília, heavily on the secure, if limited, incomes of the bureaucratic employees. The novelty of the products and the difficulty of acquiring them, plus the saturating effects of advertising, especially on television and radio, give rise to an appetite and an admiration for material goods—notably automobiles and electrodomestic equipment. It is common, for instance, to find people putting a refrigerator in the living room.

In Brasília, the middle class is primarily composed of middle and upper-echelon civil servants, liberal professionals (such as lawyers, doctors, and architects)—many of these employed part-time or full-time by government, and the owners of commercial enterprises. There is no doubt that in Brasília the largest of these groups is the civil servants, whose presence in a sense justifies the existence and growth of the city, and whose mentality and values dominate it. This phenomenon is probably typical of all cities whose function is mainly administrative, like Washington, D.C. or Canberra, Australia. The Brazilian civil service, whose study would be a good subject for another volume, should be understood in reference at least to the following:

(a) Functioning in terms not only of economic or technical rationality, but socially as a sort of middle-class dole in a country whose labor market is relatively restricted, and politically as one object in a complex system of patronage (*empreguismo*), clienteles, and favoritism.

(b) The accentuated importance of bureaucracy in view of a socio-economic system which some students have gone so far as to call *patrimonalism* (Faoro 1958, who took the term from Max Weber) and bureaucratic capitalism (Caio Prado, Jr. 1966). Whatever the name, historically and at present the system is accentuatedly interventionist and more recently there has grown up an important sector of state-owned enterprises within the overall capitalist framework (Ianni 1965). Bell (1966) furnishes an introduction to the study of Brazilian public administration.

The lower class, on the other hand, depends mostly upon construction employment. To a lesser degree, other sources of employment, including commerce, menial civil service jobs, and domestic work (especially for women), are also important.

Correlated with this differentiation is a wide disparity in formal education, which is also a clue to the distribution of the classes in the urban space.

Table V provides an indication of the illiteracy rates in the various areas of the Federal District in 1964. This table confirms a number of generalizations about stratificational differences in the Federal District. Most notable is the relatively low illiteracy in the Pilot Plan, which houses the middle-class population. The rural areas show a rate higher than even the poorest urban area. Among the other urban localities, Candangolândia and Velhacap, where NOVACAP employees predominate, show relatively low rates, followed by Taguatinga, the most prosperous of the satellite towns. The lowest rate of all the urban areas is displayed by the Social Security Invasion, identified with an almost exclusively lower-class population, earning low incomes.

It is the middle class that makes its home in the Pilot Plan proper—in the superblocks, in the row houses along W-3 Avenue, and in the individual houses between the airport and the lake. This group is also present in small numbers elsewhere, in the satellite cities, especially Taguatinga, but as a minority. The lower class, with the exception of domestic servants, makes its home in the satellite towns, especially their less central areas, and to the virtual exclusion of the middle class, in the invasions, notably Social Security and Vila Tenório. Even much retail commerce of these areas is in the hands of people originating from, and in most respects similar to, the lower rather than the middle class. The owners of the larger businesses in the satellite cities show a corresponding overall similarity to the middle class. In other words, with minor exception, the Pilot Plan is middle class, the rest of the Federal District is lower class. It is to the lower class, as represented in Brasília's largest squatter settlement, that we now turn.

TABLE V
Illiteracy in the Federal District
Expressed in Percent, by Locality, for People over Seven Years

Locality	Illiteracy rate (percent)
Pilot Plan	12.3
Candangolândia	19.3
Velhacap	21.9
Taguatinga	23.0
Free Town	29.0
Sobradinho	34.2
Planaltina	36.1
Gama	40.4
Braslândia	40.7
Social Security Invasion	41.4
Rural Zone	46.7
Federal District (average)	24.4

Source: PDF-SEC 1965: 4.

CHAPTER IV

The Spontaneous Settlements

I. The Lower Class Social Security Invasion

The hill hasn't got a chance
And what it's done already
Is already too much.

(O morro não tem vez,/E o que êle fez/Ja foi demais.)
—Popular song.

The Social Security Invasion is the polar opposite to the Pilot Plan. The gross differences between the Pilot Plan and the Social Security Invasion appear almost by inspection. The streets of the Pilot Plan are paved in asphalt; the streets of Social Security are unpaved, and as a result are muddy in the rainy season and dusty in the dry. Houses in the Pilot Plan are of glass and cement; in the Social Security Invasion they are wooden shacks (*barracos*). In the Pilot Plan automatic sprinklers daily water the lawns of the superblocks and row houses; in the Social Security Invasion women carry drinking water on their heads from public taps, or else collect it from barrels to which it is delivered by tank-truck. The parking lots of the Pilot Plan are filled with Volkswagens and other private cars; the residents of the Social Security Invasion, rain or shine, trudge fifteen minutes on a footpath and cross a busy highway to sweat out a line in order to gain access to crowded public buses. In the Pilot Plan, women shop in brightly lit, hygienic supermarkets; in the Social Security Invasion, they must be content with tiny rat-infested shops or scabrous open-air markets. To do their laundry, women in the Pilot Plan have running water, and sometimes washing machines and maids. In the Social Security Invasion, they must do their laundry in a stream, or carry the water on their heads in order to do their washing in the yards of their shanties. In the Pilot Plan, there is street-lighting and electricity in every home; in the Social Security Invasion the moon and stars provide what street light there is, while kerosene and candles light the shacks.

The Social Security Invasion is a bounded settlement, everywhere surrounded by physical barriers and open space, and largely hidden from the view of the casual passerby on the two main highways that frame it (see illus. 12). It can be reached by automobile from the Brasília–Anápolis highway via a steep, rutted road, unpaved, with no sign indicating the existence of the settlement. Here the wood buildings and cyclone fence of the Juscelino Kubitschek de Oliveira Hospital and the ri:e in the terrain hide the settlement.

The hospital is now run by the National Social Security Institute (INPS). Formerly it was run by the Industrial Workers Retirement and Pension Institute (IAPI), whence the name Social Security Invasion (*Invasão do IAPI*).

To enter the automobile access road to the settlement one risks overturning into the drainage gully which parallels the main highway. In the rainy season, flowing water adds to the hazard here, and small boys play at filling it in whenever a car appears, hoping for tips from the drivers.

The other road leading to the Social Security Invasion is also unpaved, and runs into the Brasília–Belo Horizonte highway at a considerably higher altitude than the route near the hospital. Here too, the existence of the settlement is hidden from the casual observer, in this case by the terrain of an inactive athletic club on one side, and by a Catholic convent and day school on the other. Though level, this access road is even more deeply rutted than the other and exacts a heavy toll on springs and kidneys. Where the access road and the highway meet, there is a flourishing petty commerce, for it is here that the buses heading to and from the Pilot Plan, the Free Town, Gama, and Taguatinga make their stops. Stands abound whose owners sell coffee and snacks to the passersby on their way to wait for the bus. Some of these establishments are rough wooden edifices of some permanence; others are smaller and equipped with wheels so that they can be moved if the police, as they occasionally do, insist on clearing the area of its petty commerce.

For the pedestrian, there are still other access routes. The two most traveled of these lead to the Free Town and Vila Tenório over log bridges which cross Vicente Pires creek. The pedestrian makes his way through the narrow back streets of the Invasion, down the hill through the pastures and gardens which line the creek on either side, over the bridge, where he can see the washerwomen in one place and the young boys swimming in another, among the tall trees lining the stream bank, until he arrives on the highway at the lower edge of Vila Tenório and across the road from the Free Town. This route is a favorite of women who go to shop in the markets of the Free Town, and of the young men who go there to pick up the wagons of ice pops they hawk in the streets of the Social Security Invasion.

The main street of the Social Security Invasion is generally known as

just that, *Avenida Principal* (see illus. 13). An effort is occasionally made
to curry favor with the powerful of the moment by changing the name to
that of some politician, such as former Prefect Ivo de Magalhães or
Marshall-President Humberto Castelo Branco, but these efforts seem to
be of largely ephemeral effect. This wide street is the continuation of the
access road which passes by the hospital, and for most of its length can
accommodate a lane of traffic in both directions without crowding the
pedestrians. About two hundred meters from the beginning of the settlement, however, there is a deeply eroding gully a good twenty meters deep,
where most of the drainage from the invasion, when it rains, comes surg-
ing across the road. This cliff intrudes on the road and adds to the haz-
ards of driving in dark nights. At least one woman is bedridden because
of paralysis resulting from a fall into this canyon, but the fill the authorities provided after the incident soon washed away. Besides its use as a
landmark, the gully provides many residents with a place to throw garbage of all kinds, and an occasional playground for small boys, some of
whom once in a while scavenge among the debris.

For its whole length, the Main Street rises, at times steeply and elsewhere less so, though nowhere is it so spectacularly steep as the squatments located on the hills of Rio de Janeiro or the dunes and hills of
Salvador.

The landmarks along the length of the Main Street are mostly the
larger buildings used for some public purpose. There are three schools,
one near the gully known as the Interplanetary School in impartial tribute
to the sputniks and satellites, the two others—located in the middle of
the street, which widens to accommodate them—provided by the Education Secretariat. All are of wood. Further above them a church of the
Pentecostal Assemblies of God, with a Potemkin-village or movie-set
facade facing down the hill, proving to be false only when one passes
alongside the church to see that the building itself is not much higher
than any other. Behind the church are the small post maintained by the
Social Service Foundation, which was staffed during the early part of our
stay, and a police post which was usually empty or provided a place for
NOVACAP work crews charged with reassembling shacks moved to the
invasion to carry on conversations when (as frequently happened) they
were not working.

On Sundays, a small but animated market (*feira*) is held just above
this post, housing some fifty stands dealing in meat, vegetables, rice and
beans, cheap plastic goods, and staples such as cooking oil, salt, and
sugar. During the week the only stand operating is a small one which
deals in sugarcane juice which is ground on the spot, by hand, on a
wrought-iron mill built for this purpose.

Aside from these landmarks, the overwhelming presence in the Invasion, on the Main Street as everywhere, are the shack dwellings of the inhabitants. Some of these, in higher proportion on the Main Street than elsewhere, have stores at the front, with the multiple doors characteristic of small stores throughout the Northeast and in other parts of the country as well. (Often the importance of a businessman is established by the number of doors in his establishment.)

The architect Constantinos Doxiadis points out that basing the estimate on very liberal assumptions, ". . . existing architects do not design more than 5 per cent of all buildings created all over the world. It is much more probable that they really control much less, perhaps no more than 2 per cent . . . Even this assumption of 2 per cent is misleading if we think of real architectural creation . . ." (1963: 73). Even in Brasília, where the creation of a new city would seem an architect's gilded paradise, so far it would seem that as great an influence on construction was had by the anonymous creators of the Free Town's buildings as by Niemeyer and the other professionals who designed the city's monuments. The *barraco* or shack (see illus. 15, 16, and 17) is at least as typical of Brasília as the collonades of the Dawn Palace, the towers of the Congress, or the rectangular apartment buildings of the superblocks.

Although wood construction enjoys very low prestige in Brazil, with the exception of certain areas of recent European immigration in the South, it is widespread in many areas, especially in the squatter settlements—the *favelas* of Rio and São Paulo, *alagados* and *invasões* of Salvador, *mocambos* of Recife, etc. The *barraco,* however, is far from universal in the squatments of Rio and Salvador, which is the main reason the term "shantytown" has not been used in this study.

The basic characteristics of the type are everywhere similiar, though minor variations abound. A framework of beams (the North American "two-by-four" would do fine), buried a few inches into the ground, supports a roof of any one of a number of standard varieties of corrugated roofing material, sloping down from facade to the back. The house is then faced, usually with boards attached vertically to the frame's outside, the spaces between the boards often being closed in with stripping. A wooden shutter may be cut into the wall here and there and hung on hinges. The building can then be subdivided, usually by standard panels up to about seven feet in height. Ceilings are rare; the principal refinements in the more prosperous houses are in the choice of roofing materials and the use of concrete floors.

Its association with poverty and obvious distance from international and official Brazilian architectural standards, plus the use of wood, which in Brazil is an untraditional and low-prestige building material, have made the *barraco* an object of opprobrium in Brazil, and even more so in Brasília, where it is a negative reflection upon the modernity, which, along with the position of national capital, is the city's principal claim to importance. Yet it would be well to consider the *barraco* not so much as a problem, but as an adaptive solution—even an architectural solution—to certain problems. The cultural ideal, stuccoed brick construction (*casa de alvenaria*), can hardly compete. In comparison with the latter, the *barraco* has the following characteristics:

(1) *Rapidity of construction.* A fairly large one-family *barraco* that can be built in two working days by two men, sufficiently complete to be inhabited in relative comfort.

(2) *Inexpensive materials.* While new, first-class materials are not by any means bargains, considerable economies are possible with a *barraco* as opposed to a stucco house. New material for a one-family shack could be bought in 1967 for NCr$600.00, six months' wages at the local minimum. It is also possible to use secondhand material, or castoffs from construction jobs.

(3) *Flexibility.* Large or small alterations are easy to make in the *barraco*. One can change the internal divisions, enlarge the house in various directions, cut space for windows or doors directly out of the walls and nail them up. A three-door commercial establishment, for instance, can become a private residence just by nailing up two of the doors; a private residence can be made into a store by doing the reverse. The *barraco* has a surprising resemblance to Doxiadis's proposal for a growing or expandable house:

> In rural areas or neighborhoods of single houses and relatively low density, it is possible to provide each family with a plot which will suffice even if that family reaches maximum size. In such cases we can follow the policy of making our houses grow and expand . . . This kind of idea will lead to a radically different design of house, one allowing for natural and gradual growth, to be followed perhaps by its redivision and re-allocation among more families, yet still providing for its final reunification into a single house if and when that proves necessary (1963: 115).

In many cases the builders of *barracos* also follow the "core" or "embryo" house policy now in favor in planning public low-cost housing in poor countries, expanding an initially minimal unit as their needs require and means permit.

(4) *Portability.* Depending on the type and the degree of refinement of the finish, the *barraco* can be removed with little loss from one location to another. This portability is an important consideration in situations, as in Brasília's squatments, of doubtful or insecure land tenure, or of a fluid labor market.

The Brasília in-migrant, arriving with little capital, can construct a very small, primitive *barraco* in a few hours or days, and immediately set forth on his main task, earning money in one way or another. He can then expand, move, or otherwise modify his *barraco* as he makes money, expands his business (in the case of commercial buildings), or as his family arrives. In the interim the *barraco* provides him with protection from the elements, a place to sleep and to guard his property.

Though the apartment houses of the Pilot Plan superblocks are posed almost as if on display—indeed, they are part of the fare offered to the visitor on guided tours and souvenir postcards—and the *barracos* of the Social Security Invasion and other settlements in Brasília are more diffidently screened from the eyes of the casual observer, the *barraco* is as creative a response to the conditions of lower-class existence in Brasília as the apartment house is to middle-class life. And like the *barracos* that make up their community, many other elements in the way of life of the dwellers in the Social Security Invasion reflect their status as full, if unequal, participants in the social systems of the new capital, of Brazil, and of the global society.

II. The Beginnings of Squatting

> You've got a palace to live in,
> I've got just a shack and love, ai, ai . . .
> It's the fear of turning poor that terrorizes.
>
> (O senhor tem palacete p'ra morar/Eu só tenho
> um barracão e um amor, ai, ai . . ./Ah, Doutor,
> ah, Doutor,/Eu sei que o mêdo de ficar pobre
> apavora.)
> —Carnival song.

We have already observed that the pressure on the authorities posed by the actual and potential growth of squatter settlements was instrumental in their repeated acceptance of urban settlements which deviated from the original intentions of Lúcio Costa's plan, which provided the superblock apartment buildings of the Pilot Plan as the modal form of dwelling for all sectors of the population except for the uppermost elite.

To a degree the intensity of the "squatter problem" reflected the overwhelming priority given to the readying of the new capital for the inauguration ceremony of April 21, 1960. Of course, this very priority, the monumental conception of the city, and the emphasis on automotive circulation in a society where the overwhelming majority of people cannot even aspire to owning a car reflect the concentration of political and economic power in the hands of a minority elite. The rise of the squatments in Brasília was not merely the consequence of momentary neglect brought about by intense concentration on a crash program of construction.

The notion that squatting is intimately related to the structural characteristics of the national social system is reinforced by the frequency of squatting in other Brazilian cities and throughout the underdeveloped world, and by the persistence of the squatting phenomenon in Brasília through political administrations with widely divergent styles, professed ideologies, and declared policies in regard to the new capital.

For many members of the lower strata of Brasília's population, squatting was simply the only possibility, for they were blessed neither with political influence nor with the acquired rights of civil servants, and lacked the money to resolve their problem in the tiny private real estate market. These people either had no choice at all, or their alternative was that of obtaining a legalized lot in a distant satellite town such as Gama, known to some as Brasília's "Siberia," where they would be distant from the labor market, from the main source of medical assistance for the indigent —the so-called District Hospital—and from the commercial and street life of the city.

Hence the frequent decision to "invade" (invadir) or squat. Some of the areas where squatting occured were (1) the outer rim of the South Wing of the Pilot Plan, both toward the lake (where one of the squatments acquired the name "Japan" [Japão] because of its proximity to the embassy of that country), and to the west, past W-3 Avenue, and even in some abandoned superblock areas; and (2) in the Pilot Plan's North Wing, between the University of Brasília, isolated by a goodly patch of cerrado, and the Residential North Wing, one of the few built-up areas in this part of the Pilot Plan. (3) Other squatments arose in the forest reserve area along the road from the Industrial and Supply Center to the satellite town of Sobradinho, along the road to the Paranoá Dam. (4) A few commercial shacks appeared wherever a construction site was active or a group of apartment blocks was built at some distance from more substantial commerce. These latter "invasions' were not always organized, for often they consisted of as few as one or two shacks. Some commercial shacks were built very small, and a few on wheels, since often they would move because of official pressure or the completion or paralysis of the construction jobs on which they fed.

(5) The largest squatment, however, was the Social Security Invasion. This began as a tolerated zone of shacks within the perimeter of the Social Security Hospital, inhabited at first by hospital employees. In the days before the inauguration of the new capital, practices of this kind were

The Congress.

Esplanade of Ministries.

View of south wing, Pilot Plan.

The Plateau Palace.

The bus station, lower level.

View of a superblock, south wing.

Bank of Brazil apartments, south wing.

Standard row house off W-3 Avenue.

*"JK" walk-up
superblock building.*

Commercial block, W-3 Avenue.

Commercial block, Free Town.

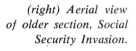
(above) Aerial view of greater Free Town.

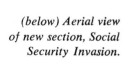
(right) Aerial view of older section, Social Security Invasion.

(below) Aerial view of new section, Social Security Invasion.

*(above) Social Security
in the rainy season.*

A shack (barraco)
undergoing expansion.

*Waiting to take
water from a public
tap in the Social
Security Invasion.*

*A street in the Social
Security Invasion.*

Squatters ...

taking the truck ...

to work.

often tolerated because of the lack of any alternative and the riveting of official attention on the construction timetable. As a result, even in this period the population probably was not confined to hospital employees. The sale of shacks was frequent, and continued to be so right up to 1967 —for only severe police methods could have prevented it. With the extinction of Vila Amaurí by the rising waters of Lake Paranoá in the weeks prior to the inauguration, a number of shacks were moved to the area behind the hospital, in spite of the expectation in the highest echelon of the administration that the moves would be to Taguatinga, the approved site at that time for such transfers.

From this early beginning, the Social Security Invasion was an official orphan. No government agency would take responsibility for it. It has none of the features that make attractive material for Brazilian political or administrative figures. There is little opportunity for patronage, as in public education, police, the courts, or almost any other service, nor does the treatment of the problem, short of the decision to build public housing, offer the prospect of large public expenditures whose distribution to contractors can pay or create obligations. Unlike public works, moreover, the administrative treatment of a squatment is not likely to project a civil servant positively in the public eye as a doer, a dynamic figure; but adverse publicity associating a politician with what the press and the middle class regard as an eyesore could damage a career. In some other cities, such as Rio de Janeiro, electoral politics—under a system of proportional representation—provides a motivation for some official interest in the local squatments (*favelas*), whose residents trade off their main asset— population—in the form of votes, for official favors and protection (*cobertura*) of de facto land tenure and technically unlawful use of water and electricity. Brasília, however, has never had a local election; it depends, like Washington, D.C. in the United States, on the Federal authorities for basic political decisions; so even the protection afforded by electoral clientelism is largely denied to the Social Security Invasion and its residents.

Official action in the early sixties was limited to a negative policy designed to prevent the uncontrolled expansion of the Invasion. The construction of new shacks and the repair or expansion of the old ones was prohibited, a prohibition enforced by inspectors (*fiscais*) maintained by the Prefecture. In some cases where violators of this order were discovered they found their houses damaged or were removed summarily to the satellite city of Gama. In one case, where a special order was obtained from a higher authority to permit the repair and expansion of a shack, the job had to be done in one day—presumably to limit the damage to the prestige of the general prohibition still in effect—and the neighbors were mobilized in a shared work program similar to the *mutirão* common in the agricultural sector of the Brazilian Northeast (Galvão 1959).

An attempt actually to remove the invasion was made in 1963 by the Prefecture, in response to an appeal by the athletic club which held nominal title to an area occupied by some of the *barracos* (shacks). Without warning, a fleet of trucks was mobilized—fifty of them, according to the account of one resident—and the shacks were quickly dismounted and removed to Gama, which, as we have seen, was an exceedingly unpopular place to move.

As soon as the first *barracos* were moved, resistance to further moves quickly began. At the very first, agents of the Prefecture had insisted that the squatters themselves move their shacks, but the inability or unwillingnss of the squatters to cooperate led to stronger measures. To the argument that they were "invaders" on the lands legally belonging to the club, the squatters responded that the land had no master, since "God made it, and didn't give it to the rich or to the poor."

It was after the actual moves had begun that the first meetings and rallies took place. The squatters sent a delegation to the Mayor, whose members insisted on a personal interview. When this was finally granted, the insistence of the delegates prevailed, and he acceded to the request that the move to Gama be canceled. Instead, an area only a few hundred meters away from the club lands, virgin *cerrado* directly behind the hospital and overlooking the Côrrego Vicente Pires, was set aside for those whose shacks were actually located within the athletic club's property. Even by 1968, incidentally, the athletic club had failed to complete its building on the site, which did, however, remain fenced and devoid of squatters.

The Prefecture provided carpenters to take apart and aid in reconstructing the shacks, as well as trucks to remove them. Each resident was given a measured lot ten meters in front by fifteen meters, with the proviso that a meter on either side be left open to provide protection against fires, which in the Free Town had proved to be frequent and devastating. The giving of the land was not a permanent cession in any legal sense, however, but merely a temporary assignment. The change in attitude by the government was due presumably to fear of an incident which would reflect on the populist and labor credentials of the government of the time; in the face of the declaration by some squatters that to remove them to Gama the authorities would have to run tractors over them, the cession of virgin *cerrado* of immediate use to no one seemed more prudent.

The most recently constructed shacks on the athletic club land were the first to be moved. One woman recounts that she slept under a table for several days until she was able to get out of her predicament by paying a young man to clear away the *cerrado* and put her shack back together again.

These concessions by the Prefecture were soon followed by a breakdown of the previous restrictions on new construction and repair of existing structures. The shacks which had been removed were repaired and expanded, and people from invasions in the Pilot Plan, often under police pressure to move, began moving to the Social Security Invasion. While not so close to the Pilot Plan as the other squatments were, the Social Security site had three advantages: (1) the proximity of the Free Town, (2) the force of numbers, and (3) relatively abundant transportation. The Free Town, when combined with the nearby agglomerations, was, as we have seen, the third largest urban concentration in the Federal District. As a market and warehousing center, it also was the base for much occasional employment and petty commerce. A worker, unemployed or on his day off, could walk to a warehouse and buy a sack of oranges or a crate of vegetables, cheeses, or other products, and resell them for a small profit. The daily market provided an opportunity for small trading in produce also. Even for those not dependent upon such petty commerce, the active market (*feira*) and commercial zone were an attraction in Brasília, a city of dispersed and largely inefficient retail business.

Because of its size, the Social Security Invasion also provided more security of tenure than the small squatments in the Pilot Plan, which was the priority area for new construction, and therefore the area where attempts to remove squatters were most likely to occur. The owners of the land or the middle-class neighbors of the squatters could at any time exert pressure for their removal, and in small numbers the squatters possessed little with which to fight back. The cost of removing them would not be prohibitive, a place could always be found for a small number of people, and the potential resistance could not pose a sufficient threat of public scandal or physical effectiveness to give pause to officialdom. At Social Security, however, none of these factors held. No major construction was planned in the area, most of the land was public, and the only neighbors were a few gas stations. The Free Town's businessmen, in fact, welcomed the growth of Social Security as a source of customers for building materials and retail items in general. And the size of the squatment meant that an attempt to remove all of it would be very costly, would require considerable space, and, unless the move met with the approval of the residents, would possibly lead to mass resistance, a resistance which had every chance of success as long as the Federal government was populist, laborite (*trabalhista*), and included elements interested in "popular mobilization" against their political adversaries.

Finally, in addition to the access to the labor market represented by the Free Town, the Social Security Invasion was ideally located in regard to the bus routes and the routes taken by the trucks which some construction companies provided for their employees; or even not out of the way for those who used bicycles or shoe leather to get to work.

All these factors meant that when the Prefecture in effect acquiesced in the continuance of the Social Security Invasion, abandoning the effort to remove even a part of it, it began to grow. Much of this growth occurred at night, when the inspectors were not active. Soon there were shacks from the Brasília–Anápolis–São Paulo highway all the way to the height on which the Social Security Hospital and the original starting point of the Invasion were situated, as well as further and further inward—upward and away from the highways.

The proximity of the newer area of the invasion to the highway provoked another characteristic reaction. In the opinion of the press and some elements of the administration, the presence of such unattractive dwellings so close to important interstate auto routes took prestige away from the new capital. Just as during the same period, in Rio de Janeiro, the government selected for removal those *favelas* most obvious on the route from the city center to the South Zone neighborhoods (Copacabana, Ipanema, Leblon, etc.), mecca for tourists and the higher social strata, in Brasília the sudden appearance of large-scale squatting in full view of even casual passersby led to a reaction. The agents of the removal this time were the Forest Police (presumably because the area was meant to be a part of Brasília's future green-belt).

The police tactic was to remove the roofing material from the shacks, which would make them uninhabitable during the rainy season, at least for enough time for the trucks to come and haul them away. The extreme poverty of some of the most recent arrivals in this sector and the arbitrary attitude of the police added fuel to the fires of resistance. Many squatters from outside the immediate area of conflict feared that if the police could successfully remove a small number of shacks, there would be massive general removals in the future.

This time the conflict soon erupted into violence. After a few preliminary verbal altercations, the police began to lay it on with nightsticks, while the residents retaliated with rocks, brooms, hoe handles, or whatever they could find. One man who was a leading figure in this episode was arrested and accused of being an "agitator." When the police took him, he called out to his wife, who was in the crowd. A police officer objected, but he insisted that he, and no one else, gave orders to his wife, whom he ordered (along with their children) to climb into the Black Maria along with him. As a result, he recounts, he was not beaten in the police station, as is alleged to often happen to poor people who are arrested in Brazil.

In the midst of this fighting, the police beat a hasty retreat, and called for reinforcements in the form of long open trucks with two rows of benches, facing the street, mounted on them. These trucks can move rapidly into a disturbance, and the police can jump off the trucks and into action much more rapidly than from a bus or an ordinary truck. While the reinforcements were on their way, however, an appeal was made by some of the squatters to a federal deputy (who is now in exile).

Now in this period of Brazilian history a group of deputies sought to advance their names and positions by mobilizing popular support for reformist causes, and since they formed one of the bases of the government's parliamentary support, they were often able to influence events. In the case under discussion, the arrested leader was soon receiving apologies from the police, and his name was broadcast over the radio as a hero rather than an "agitator."

The removal of the squatters near the highway, however, was reinitiated, but it was carried out in a peaceful manner under the supervision of the Brazilian Army, and instead of Gama, the squatters were taken to another area of the Social Security Invasion. Once again, an incident had a counterproductive effect, from the point of view of the eradication of the settlement; official concessions to the squatters after an abortive attempt at removal implied consent to the permanence of the agglomeration as a whole.

The last days of the Goulart administration were marked by a polarization of political forces in the nation that increased daily. In the early weeks of 1964, there was a movement, centered in the Free Town, known as "Good Will" (*Bôa Vontade*), whose demand was the elevation of unemployed workers, hired on a short-term basis by the Sanitation Department, to the status of public employees—a position having such security and prestige as to make it a goal for many Brazilians of almost all the social strata. This movement led to some violence, including a small riot at the building housing the office of the Regional Administrator (Subprefect) of the Free Town. According to some accounts, the movement was encouraged by figures in the Federal Administration.[1]

On April 1, 1964, the Goulart government fell to a military coup supported by many right-wing and centrist civilian political figures. Among the consequences of this coup for Brasília was a period of relative governmental stability as opposed to the frequent shifts of personnel and policies during the Goulart administration. And in spite of their proclaimed anti-

---

1. This movement appears to have had no relationship to the movement of the same name led by Alziro Zarur.

pathy toward Brasília and Kubitschek, who was deprived of his political rights after the coup, the new rulers of the country finally embarked on a drive (far more restrained than Kubitschek's efforts, to be sure) to complete the new capital.

This drive involved the preparation and application of a series of administrative measures (see section VII below). Among these was the policy adopted in regard to the problem of squatting, especially in the area covered by the Pilot Plan. The problem was made more acute by the fact that the satellite towns, originally established in response to the problem of squatting, had begun to reach their planned capacity. In Taguatinga and Sobradinho, all the planned lots had been allocated, while the urban plans for distant Planaltina and Braslândia had not been completed. Only Gama, of the nearby and newly founded satellite towns, was not full.

Though not a squatter settlement in the strictest sense, it was Vila Planalto, an area which remained on high ground after the flooding of Vila Amaurí, that was the site of the first large-scale removal attempt in the Pilot Plan. The attempt was unsuccessful. One version has it that the removal was never carried out fully; another is that cleared portions of the area began to be repopulated soon after being cleared. In any event, the area continued to be heavily populated.

It was the residents of this area (with the exception of those in officially sanctioned encampments, who were permitted to remain) who were taken to Vila São João in Gama, soon baptized Vila Vampiro (Vampire Town), from whence many moved, some back to Vila Planalto and others to Social Security, unwilling as they were to face the desolation, lack of amenity, and difficult transportation characteristic of the area the government had chosen for them.

As a result of this experience, when the Prefecture turned its attention to the total removal of the Pilot Plan's squatments, a special Invasion Removal Commission (*Comissão de Remoção das Invasões do Plano Pilôto*) was created in the Mayor's office to deal with this problem (DOU May 10, 1965: Decree 406). This commission included a representative of the police and the official Social Service Foundation.

The foundation was assigned the job of making a series of sample surveys to determine the applicability of the National Housing Plan (see section VII), first to the squatters and later in other areas of the Federal District. These surveys, carried out by the Planning Staff within the foundation, provided a general view of the situation in a number of areas. The criterion used by the staff for the identification of a squatment or "invasion" (*invasão*) was the following:

Any and every construction in an unforseen location in the Federal District, without the authorization of the competent authorities, is considered an "invasion." If this authorization was given, it will be considered an "encampment" (*acampamento*), which should have an administrator charged with, among other things, not permitting squatting in the area.

There are cases in which constructions, having originated as encampments, have become "invasions" due to the absence of an administrator, as in the case of [the invasions] Sanitation (*Limpeza Publica*) and Do-Re-Mi . . . (FSS 1965*a*).

Only some of the residents of these settlements were potentially capable of paying the monthly cost of a minimal house that would conform to official standards, even when financed over a thirty-year period.

Based upon their surveys, the Foundation's planners came to the conclusion that from 24,000 to 25,000 units would be needed to eliminate what they classified as "subhabitations" from the Federal District, based upon the 1965 population and assuming no new in-migration. From this estimate, we can calculate that a good 100,000 people lived in such "subhabitations." This amounts to more than a third of the total population as estimated from the same sources used by the foundation (PDF-SEC 1965). A "subhabitation" was defined as one with at least three of the following seven features:

(A) Rough construction in wood or other material of low
     resistance (wattle-and-daub, abode, etc.).
(B) Precarious sanitary installation . . .
(C) Roofing with improper material or tiles in a poor
     state of repair.
(D) Earthen floor.
(E) Absence of light [presumably electric].
(F) Lack of piped water.
(G) Lack of space for lodging of the residents
     with consequent crowding (*promiscuidade*) and precarious
     hygiene (FSS 1965*b*).

The estimate of over twenty-five thousand families in these conditions was subdivided as follows:

(A) Invasions [presumably in the Pilot Plan only]:
     5,000 families.
(B) Satellite towns (fixed lots and with streets opened—
     ownership legal or in process, or ceded or rented, or living
     with others in the same shack): 14,500 families. For the
     Satellite Town of the Pioneer Nucleus [Free Town] the
     plan provides 1,424 lots for 5,000 families now living
     there; the provision is for the removal of 3,500 families.
(C) Rural zone: 3,500 families.
(D) Encampments: no estimate (FSS 1965*b*).

Some families in "subhabitations" earned as much as five times the legal minimum wage, but most earned much less: "it is believed that 25 per cent have a monthly family income of *less than* the minimum wage." Very low income families must have been present in much higher proportion than 25 percent in the squatter settlements of the Pilot Plan. These settlements nevertheless had priority under the National Housing Plan and the local scale of priorities.

It was clear that the housing plan as constituted could not possibly provide for all of the squatters. The Prefecture, however, was under pressure from two sources. Constant complaints about squatters were received from the middle-class residents of the Pilot Plan and in the local paper, the *Correio Braziliense* (part of the conservative Associated Dailies chain —*Diários Associados*). The squatments not only marred the appearance of the city, but created a feeling of insecurity among some residents of the superblocks. In a few cases the invasions did house prostitutes and petty criminals, providing fuel for fevered middle-class imaginations. The other source of pressure on the Prefecture was the simple realization that the continued toleration of the invasions would permit their expansion and create a de facto situation which with every passing year would become more and more difficult to correct. Although arguments could have been raised which would justify the legalization or toleration of the invasions, these were probably given scant consideration, for many in the administration were under the influence of the idea of the sanctity of the Costa plan, the symbolism of the new capital, and class prejudice against the "ugly" settlements.

Yet as we have seen, available information indicated that many of the squatters could not qualify for the low-cost housing program. In fact, this was true of the majority; in addition to those below the minimum wage level, there were many who earned just the minimum, and together these groups made up a majority. Unemployment was widespread and odd jobs (*biscates*) were the main source of income for many. People in these economic categories had been transferred from Vila Planalto to Gama and bcame squatters again; in addition, although some lots in Gama continued to be available, the number was not sufficient for all the squatters who were to be removed.

The consequence was the decision to transfer many of the Pilot Plan squatters to the Social Security Invasion. This decision was taken as a temporary expedient; even in recognizing its necessity, the officials refused to consider it a definitive solution or to make a permanent and legally recognized change in the city plan in favor of the Social Security Invasion. The result was merely to concentrate the squatting phenomenon geographically and postpone any further treatment of it for decision by the next group of administrators to take office. Within the government the loudest protests came from the professional social workers. And no group or agency was willing to assume administrative responsibility for anything more than the transfer of the invaders and the allotment of space for the reerection of their shacks. To emphasize to the residents themselves the temporary nature of their land tenure, public services of almost every variety were denied them, and as each family was moved it was informed in no uncertain terms that it was *not* getting a permanent lot (*ganhando um lote*).

The squatters were moved on trucks, some owned and some rented by NOVACAP. At one time, four trucks and sixteen men were involved in the procedure. The squatters were notified in advance of the move, although they were given no choice but to go where they were sent. When the day for a move arrived, carpenters and manual laborers from NOVA-CAP demolished the shack, and put the boards and building materials on the truck, along with whatever movable property the family in question possessed. A police escort accompanied the team, in order to protect it in the event the family resisted the removal. In some cases this resistance was strong. One leader of an Afro-Brazilian cult whose shack was located in an isolated site along a highway was able to mobilize in his support high officials of various ministries, who interceded to try to block the action. Since the move was the consequence of complaints by a nearby farm-owner that fear of his unwanted neighbor prevented him from leaving his family alone at home, the chief of the Invasion Removal Commission resisted the pressures and carried out the move.

The truck containing the household effects and the boards and roof tiles from the shack would proceed at high speed to the Social Security Invasion, where a Social Service Foundation office, housed in a small shack, was the first stop. Here the foundation's representative made a record of the name, number of dependents, identity documents, and the like, of the head of the household. Any civil document—identity card, birth certificate, elector's registration card, social security employment record, or veteran's identification—was accepted. Many squatters had no documents at all. The record made at this time enabled the post to keep an approximate accounting of the number of new residents and their condition, and is to be used in the future in the event that any new programs set up for the housing of squatters require the establishment of priorities. In addition to those transferred by the Invasion Removal Commission, others were assigned places for their shacks on presentation of a note from a Social Service Foundation community center, from the head of the Invasion Removal Commission, or from the Subprefect of the Free Town.

Actual assignments of lots and the laying out of new streets were in the hands of two men, one of them illiterate, under the supervision of a NOVACAP foreman. None of these men was formally trained in urban planning, social work, or surveying. They laid out a gridwork of streets crossing one another at right angles. As can be seen from aerial photographs (see illus. 13 and 14), taken in late 1966, most of the streets were laid out in this perpendicular fashion, with the exception of some streets in the oldest part of the invasion near the hospital, where the process of settlement was not officially sponsored and in fact partially clandestine. These NOVACAP employees were instructed to make an effort to limit the spatial expansion of the invasion by filling in all of the areas where gaps and empty lots made it possible to squeeze in a few more shacks. A number of alleys were created in this fashion, exceptions to the generally ample width of the streets, which permitted one-way and in some cases two-way vehicular traffic. Only a few squatters with larger-than-normal lots were able to prevent a reduction of their de facto property; one, who exercised a certain informal leadership in the invasion, was able to preserve a large area given over to a garden planted with manioc and sugar cane, perhaps basing his claim on the special problems he had as the father of twenty-seven living, legitimate children! His wife has given birth to thirty-two children, of whom twenty-seven are alive (*Journal do Brasil* November 23, 1967; and *O. Cruzeiro* December 9, 1967: 136–137).

As the removals continued, an official policy resulted in the appearance of a certain de facto zoning within the Social Security Invasion itself. A number of prostitutes had operated out of shacks in the *cerrados* of empty superblock lots in the Pilot Plan, and engaged in streetwalking on a stretch of W-3 Avenue. When the decision was made to remove them, the problems they might create if simply transferred to the family areas of the Social Security Invasion led the Invasion Removal Commission to order their transfer to a special area of the Social Security Invasion. Another nearby area was reserved for unmarried men, on the ground that their sexual propensities might also create problems for the families. The result of this procedure was the growth of a typical low-end red-light district or "ZBM" (from *zona de baixo meretrício*). Frequent crimes of violence, the flow of *cachaça* (sugar cane liquor), and the presence of *demi-monde* types known in Brazil as "marginals" (*marginais*), created a lurid notoriety for this area, known as Vulture Hill (*Morro do Urubú*) although it is neither a hill nor has vultures. In the minds of the middle class, this area's reputation soon was extended to the Social Security Invasion as a whole.

The press contributed to this reputation by publishing routine police notices such as the following:

CANKER OF MARGINALS IN SOCIAL SECURITY INVASION

According to statistical data, the majority of cases of disorders, distur-
bances, fights, stabbings and other incidents of this type, take place in the
Social Security Invasion, an authentic canker of marginals and women of
ill fame, replete with bars which, lighted by kerosene lamps, stay open all
night, serving only *cachaça,* the only merchandise they have for sale.
The invasion referred to, in the jurisdiction of the 11th Police District, is
completely unpoliced. . . .

Among the incidents which occurred yesterday in the Social Security Invasion, is one in which figures as the victim José Arimatéia Pereira (unmarried, 21 years) who in the interior of a bar, where he was drinking
accompanied by a woman, was attacked with a dagger by a stranger, who
fled. Wounded in the throat, the victim was sent to the Emergency Ward
of the District Hospital (*Correio Braziliense* December 10. 1966).

The Vulture Hill area, like the rest of the Social Security Invasion, was
the chosen area for segregation of certain social phenomena which existed
elsewhere in the city and would undoubtedly crop up again even if the
Invasion were to be removed or eliminated. Gama and Planaltina had
areas of prostitution, the former of the same low variety as in Social Security. The higher-class version of the same phenomenon was concentrated on the Brasília–Belo Horizonte highway just outside the Federal
District in the municipality of Luziânia, where flourished bordellos thinly
disguised as nightclubs with names such as "Venice," "Seven Waterfalls,"
and "A Thousand Nights and a Night." Their location insures that these
places will be frequented only by those with access to cars or able to pay
a stiff taxi fare; but the wealth of the clients does not prevent the same
sort of violence as occurs on Vulture Hill. In this particular, also, Brasília
follows the general rule for Brazilian cities: the establishment of red-light
districts in separate, specified areas, differentiated according to the class
of the clientele (see Louzeiro 1965).

III. The Official Quandary over Squatting

The growth of the Social Security Invasion and Vila Tenório, separated
only by Vicente Pires creek and the narrow strip of gardens along it, stimulated by the authorities as a makeshift solution to some of their immediate
administrative problems, soon came to be regarded by officials as a problem in itself, calling for political decisions at the Prefecture level. In the
absence of any official preventive action, the settlements continued to expand without the benefit either of legal sanction or of most of the amenities of urban life. No agency was responsible for the *administration* of the
settlements, nor would any accept this responsibility. The creation of a
new organ would in itself represent a political decision on the fate of the

settlements. Even the Invasion Removal Commission and the Subprefecture of the Free Town, respectively responsible for the expansion of Social Security and Vila Tenório, assumed responsibility only for removal and the cession of lots to the squatters, and in the case of Vila Tenório, for the installation of a small water network.

This policy amounted to something more than mere neglect; for the authorities were well aware of the problem and its potential worsening. The government was unwilling openly to facilitate the consolidation of the invasions. As a result, it systematically denied to the residents of the two settlements the public services it was installing as best it could in the satellite towns. The one exception was two wooden primary schools built in the Social Security Invasion.

Even without public services, however, the settlements obviously would, with time, become more and more rooted, cohesive, and harder to remove.

It was this realization that provided the justification for a conference called by the Secretary for Social Services in the last days of the Castelo Branco administration, in March 1967. As a result of the change in the Presidency, this period also was the end of the administration of Federal District Mayor Plínio Catanhede. The conference, held in the luxurious Hotel Nacional without the presence of a single resident of the Social Security Invasion (with the doubtful exception of the author, who at the time was a temporary denizen of the area), was entitled "Policy for Integration of a Marginalized Population" (*Política de Integração de uma População Marginalizada*). Present were representatives of more than twenty governmental entities. The conference had as its stated objectives:

> To become familiar with and to analyze experi-
> ments of promotion of marginalized populations, carried
> out in the Federal District and in other places in the
> nation.
> To become familiar with the particular character-
> istics of the marginalized populations, in the Federal
> District, along with the mechanisms which generate them.
> To point out guidelines for a policy of integra-
> tion of marginalized populations, dealing especially
> with the Social Security Invasion (SSS 1967: 4).

Both the press and many of those present at the conference had serious doubts about the conference as a vehicle for decisions on the policy to be taken toward the Social Security Invasion. The criticisms centered around the argument that it was futile to discuss a problem which would require fundamentally political decisions, at a time when the new Prefect and his appointees had not yet been selected, and around the accusation, publicly voiced at the conclave, that the conclave was a vehicle for the political self-promotion of its initiator, Social Services Secretary Darcy Mesquita da Silva. The counterargument was raised that the "technical people" (*técnicos*) would survive the change in government and that the exchange of views and the exposure given to the problem were justified (*Correio Braziliense* March 9, 1967).

The official plans exposed at the seminar centered around two programs, although many other aspects of the problem were touched upon. The first was the popular housing plan executed by SHIS (ex-SHEB). The second involved a form of deurbanization, the carrying out of a rural colonization plan in the priority agrarian reform zone which had been created in the Federal District and its environs. There were several drawbacks to both plans, however, and doubts as to whether, even if both were carried out, they would actually eliminate the squatment, the goal generally agreed upon by the participants in the conference.

As we have seen, the SHIS plan could not provide housing for the lowest stratum of the population on a financially sound basis. This impossibility was precisely what motivated the transfer of squatters from the Pilot Plan squatments to Social Security in the first place. Second, the areas then proposed for new SHIS houses were outside the orbit of the Free Town; for some residents, at least, the new location would be less convenient to the labor market and more expensive in terms of commuting than Social Security.

Rural settlement also has a number of drawbacks, the most serious of which was perhaps the policy of the Agrarian Reform Institute (IBRA— *Instituto Brasileiro de Reforma Agrária*) of carrying out programs in obedience to the highest standard of technical norms possible, with the result that the programs amounted to little more than pilot projects which unless simplified and expanded could not materially contribute to the elimination of as large a settlement as Social Security, which had some 4,000 dwellings at the time of the seminar. Going by the book is a classic tactic for not carrying out a policy while seeming to endorse it—the fate of Brazilian agrarian reform to date. The figures mentioned by IBRA people were about 400 families to be settled in the colony of Alexandre de Gusmão—itself a former (rural) invasion, with the candidates for land already on the site. A considerable segment of the residents of the Social Security Invasion were unwilling to trade their situation, albeit uncomfortable, for a rural life which on the basis of most Brazilian experience was likely to be far more difficult than life in the shantytown. Rural colonization, in fact, required a cultural background in farming and the presence of a family group. The type of land tenure envisaged implied a marked sexual division of labor, so that bachelors were ineligible from the start.

Even if these programs could definitively eliminate the Social Security Invasion, the prevention of further squatting pressures would require measures to limit the internal migration of lower-class Brazilians to Brasília, especially since the opportunities envisaged would be exceptional in Brazil. Only a very powerful and efficient authoritarian government could limit in-migration (as the Union of South Africa, or the People's Republic of China). The alternative would be a national policy of creating alternative destinations for migrants that would be more attractice to the migrants than the new capital, which itself in the past had served as an alternative to São Paulo and Paraná as a migrant destination. It is imaginable that programs such as agricultural colonization along the Belém–Brasília highway, exploitation of the considerable mineral deposits of northern Goiás, or development programs in the Araguáia Valley might reduce the migratory influx in Brasília, along with industrialization programs in the Northeast itself, stimulated by government investments and tax incentives.

However, except for some extent for the last of these, there is not much prospect for large-scale development efforts along these lines in the present political and economic climate in Brazil, where government investment has been sharply curtailed in favor of foreign investors and others who have favored extractive industries and consumer production. The housing project solution would have the additional effect of increasing the demand for construction workers, which would also stimulate in-migration.

This kind of attraction is fraught with danger, because most local administrators believe that Brasília's construction industry cannot employ indefinitely all of the workers currently working in the building trades. Civil construction in Brasília is almost entirely dependent on government works, and these are largely dedicated to the completion of the city's infrastructure and to the office buildings and residences required for the transfer of the federal bureaucracy. This process is bound to be limited in extent, and sooner or later a decline in construction employment is likely to result, this time not from the ill will of the authorities but from the nature of the city and the lack of a regional plan of investments, colonization, and industrialization to absorb the migrants.

This prospect, indeed, is one of the specters hovering over the popular housing program of the Brasília government. Insofar as the program really supplies housing to the lower strata—largely tied to the construction industry—it is likely to have its economic soundness threatened by the unemployment of the residents.

Few participants in the conference favored maintaining the Social Security Invasion in its present location, or providing an area where migrants and others would be allowed to build houses of whatever material they could arrange. Brasília, possessing relatively flat terrain and abundant undeveloped land, would seem to be an area where this kind of development could be permitted with results leading to a gradual improvement in time, according to the overall economic situation.

The participants of the conference, however, rejected the prospect of the permanence of the Social Security Invasion or other similar settlements on the urban perimeter of the Federal District. One important reason is pride in the modernity symbolized by Brasília, and the feeling that the presence of shantytowns was incompatible with that modernity and with the special role of Brasília as the capital of the country. We have already seen that the location of the Social Security Invasion on the main road access routes to the capital is particularly galling to those who think in this manner.

Another factor is that the permanence of the Social Security Invasion, much closer to the Pilot Plan than are the satellite towns, might tend to attract people away from these towns, which to a certain extent suffer from the effects of distance and the imperfections of the public transportation system. The satellite towns, though their growth was in part the result of emergency measures, are an experiment of some importance in the avoidance of urban sprawl and in the advantages of decentralization, the Social Security Invasion, on the other hand, is close enough to the Pilot Plan to eventually threaten, if not its engulfment, at least the creation of a ring or semicircle of low-quality housing around the modern center of Brasília.

Finally, the rejection of the permanence of Social Security was based upon what might be called the "humanitarian-technical" argument. The technical personnel seemed to view the settlement as a challenge to their capacities and their power to effect change, on the one hand, and as a manifestation of social pathology, and consequent human suffering on the other. High rates of infant mortality, illiteracy, crime, and family instability were cited as aspects of this condition, and a process of "marginalization" or social disorganization is supposed to take place in some cases, under the influence of the squatment environment. Not to do away with the Social Security Invasion would seem, to those imbued with this viewpoint, temporization with these evils. In part, no doubt, this picture reflects an essentially middle-class view of the invasion and its residents. It also reflects an implicit belief that the solutions proposed—notably the provision of "better" houses—would be fundamental to eliminating those phenomena viewed as pathological. These assumptions are at best debatable.

Although the social service organs of the government in Brasília had adopted the concept of "community development" and had even gone so far as to create a special training entity to put this concept into practice, the social workers involved doubted that the Social Security Invasion would be a good place to try out a community development program, since the prevailing conviction in the government was that it ought to be done away with. The community organizers feared that any official program, especially any program contributing to the material or psychological consolidation of the settlement, would contribute to the growth of the settlement, stimulate the demand for its fixation, and generate more effective resistance to its future removal.

The tendencies present at the conference continued to dominate the new administration which took office in accompaniment to the national President, Marshal Artur da Costa e Silva. The new Prefect of the Federal District, Wadjô da Costa Gomide, and his Secretary of Social Services, Domingos Malheiros, both were former directors of SHIS, the popular housing program in the Federal District.

By June 1967, the Prefecture announced plans for a new development of popular houses "with the objective of eradicating the largest *favela* in the Federal District," that is, the Social Security Invasion. This new settlement would eventually be composed of 7,000 units; the first stage, targeted for completion in June 1968, called for the construction of 4,284 units, for which the National Housing Bank had furnished NCr$22,000,-000 (about U.S.$8,150,000). These houses were to be allocated among three categories of applicants: 2,200 for those living in shacks, with preference to residents of Social Security and Vila Tenório; 1,100 for civil servants; and 984 for commercial and industrial employees. The dwellings would be financed up to fifteen years, with a compulsory deposit similar to a down payment of 15 percent for the civil servants and 30 percent for the workers in the private sector. The second stage of the program projects the construction of an additional 4,176 units, for a total of 8,460. Presumably 1,460 of these units would not fall into the category of "popular" housing (CB June 7, 1967). SHIS also planned to build at least one hundred popular houses in Planaltina and some apartments in the Pilot Plan for Prefecture employees. Emphasis was to be placed upon the use of prefabrication techniques so as to reduce the demand for labor created by the project, and possible resultant in-migration.

The new development was to be located in the Industry and Supply Sector, not far from the present location of the Social Security Invasion, though far enough to remove it from the orbit of the Free Town. Access to the Pilot Plan would be more direct. One factor in the plans, no doubt, was the hope for an increase in industrial employment centered on the Sector, and the resulting avoidance of commutation problems, the Achilles heel of a settlement like Gama, for example.

What remains to be seen is whether this project, even if executed according to plan—and the work on the first stage is already under way—can contribute decisively to the elimination of the Social Security Invasion and Vila Tenório. The 2,200 houses destined for the residents of these settlements obviously will not be sufficient: Social Security had 4,050 houses in early 1967, and by mid-year these had increased to 4,700. Vila Tenório had about half that number. Even with no further increases, about 5,000 shacks would be left over after the execution of the first stage of the new program according to plan. Assigning all the units to be built in the second stage to the eradication of the two invasions would leave 1,000 shacks there still to be dealt with.

And there is another obstacle: the financial incapacity and unwillingness of the residents of the Social Security Invasion—which no doubt extends to Vila Tenório as well—to participate in the National Housing Plan. For participation the requirement is an income equal to 1.5 times the minimum wage in the city of Rio de Janeiro (slightly higher than in Brasília). According to the Social Service Foundation, 74.1 percent of the family heads in the Social Security Invasion and 67.3 percent of the family groups had monthly incomes of NCr$125.99 or less (about U.S.$47), or less than 1.5 times the then-prevailing minimum wage (FSS 1967: 5). In other words, the 2,200 houses to be constructed in the new "Industrial Town" in the first stage of SHIS's program would just about exhaust the number of those able to satisfy the financial requirements. Yet it is probable that many of these people would be unwilling to move. The general feeling is that the SHIS house is very small (it is a "core house" [casa embrião] designed for future expansion), that it is impossible for a worker to pay the rent—or installments—and that the correction for inflation implies a constant increase in the total amount owed on the house, even as the payments continue. Restrictions on multiple uses of the house also reduce its attractiveness. The Social Service Foundation itself reports that more than half the residents of Social Security would prefer to stay where they are (FSS 1967: 17). Of those who would prefer to move, only 4.1 percent cite "better housing" as a reason.

Another program initiated by the Prefecture, this time only for NOVA-CAP workers, is a financed self-help housing scheme, under which those workers professionally qualified would execute—cooperatively—(mutirão is the Brazilian expression) their own houses. According to reports, this program is attracting considerable interest, and even office workers —who usually, in Brazil, consider manual labor beneath them—complain that they are not included in the program but are too low in the civil service hierarchy to buy apartments (Jornal do Brasil September 8, 1967). They complain that while the workers will be living in three-room houses they will continue in wooden encampments. This program, how-

ever, is on a very small scale, like some attempted in Taguatinga and
Gama by the U.S. Peace Corps volunteers, who often find the detailed
bureaucratic requirements for approval of the plans an insurmountable
obstacle.

IV. The Internal Structure of the Squatment

The general impression we obtained during our stay in the Social Security
Invasion was of a community that is relatively weak in terms of formal
organizations, political and voluntary, both compared to North American
communities and to other squatments personally known to us and reported in the literature. On the other hand, Social Security seems to be
quite rich in informal networks, circles of friends, and situational leadership.

It is this informal quality of internal social organization that accounts
for the impressionistic quality of the present report. A sprawling settlement, growing daily, inhabited by 20,000 people, the Social Security Invasion is extremely difficult to get a handle on ethnographically—and the
task is made even more difficult by the paucity of formal institutions other
than municipal and federal agencies imposed from without. Furthermore,
as indicated previously, the primary research focus was historical and
concerned with the origins of the squatment and the development of
Brasília's settlement pattern as a whole. The present section, then, sum-
marizes the results of informal interaction and interviewing, and a great
deal of observation, concentrated but not confined to the immediate vicinity of our house.

The lack of formal organization in Social Security is striking, especially
when the squatment is compared to many in Rio de Janeiro, where such
groups as residents' associations and samba schools abound, and Lima,
where the great strength of voluntary associations is a watchword.

A number of factors may account for this situation. The squatment, for
one thing, is very young, while in Rio some settlements at least have a
three- and even four-generational depth. Certain kinds of internal diversification in squatments takes time to develop. For example, the large
favela Jacarèzinho in Rio de Janeiro manifests a range of occupational
types far greater than Social Security, including a quite active group of
entrepreneurs, who are constructing reinforced concrete buildings, expanded businesses, and the like. Similar diversification in organizational
forms may likewise take years to develop.

Furthermore, even under the military regime installed by the coup of
1964, Rio de Janeiro has held periodic elections for state legislative posts
and the governorship. While military tutelage has reduced the ideological

diversity of the campaigns along with their intensity and import for the population, elections are sufficiently contested to permit the system of electoral clientage to function. This system permits the limited funneling of resources from the governmental structure into squatments in exchange for votes, and provides incentives for the development of internal leadership in the squatments, which may be able to deliver, or promise to deliver, electoral support to the candidates. In Social Security, there have been no such processes at work, since Brasília is effectively disenfranchised, like Washington, D.C., voting only in Presidential elections when they were direct. Now that they are indirect, there are no elections in Brasília at all.

The military regime installed in 1964, furthermore, while straining to maintain the formal legal system at least formally intact, has carried out a campaign for the elimination of "corruption and subversion." This campaign was initially directed primarily at the remnants of the Vargas political machine and the regime of João Goulart, and at the radical nationalist and socialist left. Later it extended to the elimination from politics, for all practical purposes, of all groupings and political leaders capable of gaining a measure of real popular support. For example, Carlos Lacerda, former governor of Guanabara (Rio de Janeiro city), a vocal opponent of Goulart and early supporter of the coup, has effectively been deprived of any influence or political opportunities.

The result of this atmosphere has been to chill any initiatives from below, in the labor movement and in such areas as land reform and possible squatter demands. Anyone in a squatment who assumed a position of formal leadership or attempted to mobilize a formal grouping would run the risk of imprisonment and worse. Even in periods of relaxed repression, such efforts would be unlikely to develop, since in fact the record has been one of periodic tightening and loosening of official pressure. Squatters are well aware of the situation. Frequently, albeit cautiously, given my nationality, they voiced discontent with the regime for its treatment of the poor. Many squatters were well pleased with the death of former Marshall-President Castelo Branco. Yet they are cynical about the political system and the viability of real political action from below. This caution and cynicism extends from the political sphere to other areas of organization which, in Brazil, soon would be likely to develop political implications.

A final factor accounting for the lack of formal organization is the proliferation of informal networks and bonds. This proliferation characterizes Brazilian society generally (Leeds 1964). While a formal bureaucracy exists and has great power concentrated in its hands, the effectiveness or not of recourse to these formal structures depends frequently upon ties of family, clientage, and political alliance or friendship. Lower-class people are either excluded from these opportunities or integrated into this informal system in a subordinate fashion, as far as the bureaucratic structure is concerned. In other areas, however, personal ties continue to dominate social interaction and organization. These ties permit a flexibility that does not exist, for lower-class people, in formal organizations, which if exclusively lower-class in composition, as would be the case in Social Security, offer risk without reward.

While almost entirely lower-class in composition, the Social Security Invasion is internally differentiated in a number of respects. Notably, the geographical areas within the squatment are diverse in their structure and composition. The broad area where we had our house is the oldest in the squatment, as can be seen in illustration 13. Compared with illustration 14, the older area has narrower streets and a less symmetrical pattern. This difference may be partly accounted for by the lay of the land, but it is fundamentally due to the fact that the newer area is being laid out under official auspices.

In the older area, the houses are closer together and have smaller yards, but they are generally of better quality, because periodic investment has gone on over the years, and the residents are, as a rule, better established economically. This distinction between the old (lower) and the new (upper) areas in Social Security corresponds to a distinction common to rural Brazilian communities between areas "*lá em cima*" (up there) and "*lá em baixo*" (down there). This distinction does not necessarily reflect stratification; indeed, even in Social Security the association with class or status differences is quite weak. Its function is probably closer to that of the moiety (two out-marrying group) systems found among many tropical forest Indian tribes—reinforcing communal ties and providing a focus for cooperation and emulation (Harris 1971: 320). Modern Brazilian units of this kind are not, of course, out-marrying in any but (conceivably) a statistical sense.

In addition to the old-new, up-down distinction, the Vulture Hill area in the upper section is a segregated enclave where prostitution is an occupational specialty and where individuals especially prone to the use of alcohol, marijuana, and to violent behavior congregate.

While overall Social Security is a lower-class community, there are important internal stratificational differences. Economic specialties are discussed in greater detail in the next chapter. Here we will confine ourselves to their associational and status implications. The wealthiest denizens of the area are the merchants, although not all of the merchants are prosperous even by Social Security standards. Some of them, however, have built up considerable inventories. Some of the economic considerations involving success as a merchant are discussed in a following chapter. One of the social prerequisites for expanding a business beyond a small "Mom and Pop" store is a large family. While merchants may employ nonrelatives, it is generally the case that employees will include a number of sons and daughters, in-laws, or other close relatives. The employment of relatives may be viewed as something close to a duty if the resources are available; by the same token, the employed relative tends to regard a higher degree of reliability on the job as his or her obligation as well. The purely contractual obligation between an employer and a nonkin employee is not nearly so strong a guarantee as the ideological imperative of kin solidarity.

The merchant group also differs from others in the community in that male authority tends to be stronger, since the husband is generally present in the store for most of the day, and the store is generally attached to the place of residence. This practice is not only economical, but serves as protection against theft, and permits the utilization of the labor of minors, and women without special child-care arrangements. Furthermore, the location of stores in the home permits the utilization of certain goods for both domestic and commercial purposes. For example, a kerosene refrigerator permits the sale of cold beverages, and also allows the storage of a small domestic supply of food. A television set attracts customers to a bar, but may also be watched by the family. Even the use of electricity from a local diesel generator may only be justified, given the level of income, by the potential it has for attracting business.

Merchants generally have a fairly fixed clientele, due to credit arrangements, solidarity of people from given states, kinship, and personal friendship. Stores may provide a focus for the exchange of gossip and for informal "street-corner" groupings.

Next to merchants, the economically better-off squatters include skilled workers and un- or semiskilled workers with permanent jobs, such as those in the civil service. There are considerable wage differentials between a skilled worker and an unskilled worker, as much as 200–300 percent. Furthermore, the possession of a skill or "profession" is a source of considerable pride. Frequently such workers as carpenters will use their skills on their day off either around the house or for friends in an informal reciprocal labor-sharing arrangement or in exchange for token payments. Impressionistically, skilled workers tend to associate with one another; there is even a degree of solidarity among workers who share a common skill.

The civil service enjoys a mixed status. On the one hand, civil service jobs, virtually guaranteeing lifetime employment, and generally functioning with a six-hour day, are considered highly desirable. I was frequently approached to obtain such positions for squatment residents, who believed that my governmental connections would permit me to help. On the other hand, there is a certain cynicism even among squatters about the probity and efficiency of the civil service. The general prestige of civil service work derives mainly, it seems, from the conomic security it affords.

The great bulk of squatters, however, do not derive much status from their work, which is intermittent, insecure, and poorly remunerated, whether it be construction work at the minimum wage, ambulant commerce, or maintenance work of various kinds. While hardly a source of shame, such work does not serve to differentiate a man from his fellows.

Women's work for money, such as seamstress work, provides economic rewards and may provide a basis for challenging male authority within the home. It does not have obvious major status implications, except to the limited degree that a reputation for competence does increase one's status among a circle of women.

Household composition in Social Security reflects a basic nuclear family organization. The ideal and the statistically most frequent pattern is a household composed of husband, wife, and children. Exceptions from this rule generally involve the absence of the husband, or the addition of one or two single, close relatives—an unmarried sister, an aged parent, etc. In particular, households containing more than one married couple, or two women with minor children, are quite rare. The assignment of cooking, laundry, child care, and housecleaning to women is quite strict, and almost invariably the lines of authority in this sphere are unambiguously clear. Houses are owned by individuals or by a couple, and ownership of the house and domestic authority are combined.

While adequate statistical data are not available, it is my impression that male-absent households are not overwhelmingly common. There is certainly not much evidence that anything approaching a matrifocal pattern exists; it is much less in evidence than, for example, along the Bahian coast. This difference, I believe, is primarily a result of the fact that migration is predominantly a male or a family affair. Women tend to follow husbands or other male relatives; on the Bahian coast, on the other hand, the women are left behind. Nevertheless, I would expect the pattern of unstable employment at low wages for males to give rise, in the long run, to the classic so-called matrifocal pattern (Liebow 1967; Harris 1971: 498–503).

A similarly tentative conclusion seems warranted with respect to increased generational conflict in many households. This conclusion is highly tentative, but it points toward some reduction in parental authority over children who have reached an age where they are capable of earning money of their own, compared, for example, to rural areas where a premium is placed upon family cooperation in agricultural labor and in the ownership of land. In Social Security, however, the pattern does not seem to be one of violent conflict between generations, as is often the case in conflicts over authority between husbands and wives. Rather there is a grudging accommodation to the changing pattern.

Nuclear family organization characterizes most domestic tasks and residence patterns. Larger social groupings, however, are activated to fulfill other, more limited kinds of social functions. Notably, the inadequate social security apparatus available through the governmental bureaucracy is supplemented by kin- and nonkin-composed informal networks based upon reciprocal aid of various types. Thus it is usual for visiting, presents of food, assistance in child care and in major household repairs, and, where possible, in minor commercial dealings and dealings with the bureaucracy, to be carried out by groups of relatives, some resident in Social Security, and frequently in the various satellite towns and Cruzeiro. In the event of sickness or emergency, in particular, several households of relatives are an important asset.

Where such networks are not present or are relatively weak, it is usual for people to attempt to improvise substitute reciprocal cooperative networks. One powerful ideological tool for creating such relationships is regionalism. In the neoteric society of Brasília, the state or city of origin of migrants is an important part of social identity.

Common origins in Brazil really do account for average social and cultural differences of considerable magnitude, although aside from regional economic inequality I do not believe these differences are as great as those in the United States. In any event, the common identity of people from Ceará or Piauí, or from the Triangle region of Minas, provides a basis for close friendship and cooperation, and provides an escutcheon of honor to be defended, and a set of stereotypes to be applied in various situations. Thus, for example, to be from Goiás in Brasília is to be the butt of jokes referring to one's backwardness and ignorance of big city ways, to be from Ceará is to be regarded as crafty, and so forth. Regional cuisine, gossip, politics, and occasionally religious cults reinforce this solidarity. The possibility of utilizing the developing interurban bus network in Brazil for visiting one's place of origin tends to reinforce this regional calculus of identity.

Two minority forms of religious organization also fulfill similar functions, as well as provide for emotional release and ideological guidance. These are evangelical Protestantism and the complex of African, Indian, and spiritualist elements known in Brasília as *umbanda*. Of the two, it is Protestantism that denotes the sharpest separation from the lifeways and identity of the average squatter. A series of prohibitions are laid upon the devout practitioner of Protestantism in Brazil, especially the Pentecostal and evangelical varieties most popular among the lower class. These prohibitions extend to dress (long skirts) and grooming (women may not cut their hair), sports (football is prohibited), drinking (forbidden), and entertainment (no movies). An appearance of probity and sobriety is cultivated, and the churches, typically congregationally controlled, provide an enveloping series of activities and demands which thoroughly involve their memberships.

While their declared function is religious, it appears that the Protestant churches particularly attract individuals who are in some form of psychological or material need which they cannot fulfill through kin ties. Frequently these needs are material, and the practice of charity, largely confined to the congregations, permits them to attract members. The close solidarity of church members, much like that among relatives generally, extends to buying patterns, employment, political favoritism, and the like.

It is with less confidence that the same can be reported of the umbandist cults, of which there are several in the squatment. Apparently these do attract devotees of considerable dedication, but frequently such temples are built around a single leader who is available to peripheral members or nonmembers for consultation in times of crisis. In Brasília at least, their organizational and ideological structure is less formal and more diverse than is the case with Protestantism. There are exceptions, however. To the west of Brasília there is a spiritualist utopian community, the *Cidade Eclética* (Eclectic City), of considerable affluence, under the leadership of a prophet named Yokanaam. This city seems to be modestly wealthy and its buses may frequently be seen bringing pilgrims from the Free Town and elsewhere in the Federal District to services in the Eclectic City.

Catholicism, on the other hand, is not well organized. There is a chapel where mass is said on Sundays by a priest from the Free Town, but there is not an active organization of the Catholic Church functioning in the Free Town, and while the vast majority of squatters profess Catholicism and engage in at least the major life-crisis rituals (baptism, marriage, and extreme unction in particular), for most it appears that Catholicism is nominal, a kind of residual religious background. For many, the private cult of saints is a more functional aspect of the religion than the ecclesiastically instituted rituals and practice.

The foregoing does not suggest the absence of relations of friendship and neighborliness unassisted by ideological devices of kinship, religious fraternity, or common geographical origin. These exist, particularly among young men, for whom "street-corner" groups and pick-up football clubs are often quite important. It is also common to find neighbors talking in the evening in front of the house or in a store, or collaborating in various tasks. For women, the water barrels, privately owned but usually grouped in one place for several houses, or the water spigots on the main street, provide a major focus for social interaction. But friendship, even among neighbors, is selective. Frequent disputes arise, notably over the activities of children, competition between poultry and vegetable gardens, and the use of water. Often these disputes remain fundamentally unresolved and continue for years, generally dividing groups of neighbors along loyalty lines. On less frequent occasions, the police *delegado* (a combination police chief and magistrate) in the Free Town is called upon to resolve the disputes. As a rule, however, even a recourse to minor violence does not lead to the intervention of the police, which is generally regarded as shameful and dangerous.

It is only in situations requiring the mobilization of larger numbers of people than are involved in any individual group mentioned above that what I have referred to as "situational leadership" is activated. The kinds of situations involve, typically, the need for a major public work, or some important threat to the land tenure of the squatters. Thus, for instance, when a woman fell into the gully produced by the runoff from the squatment (illus. 15), a group of neighbors was mobilized to appeal to the authorities to have the gully filled in. The leaders in this effort were the woman's husband and another woman, a Bahian, with a strong personality and a fairly wide circle of friends, whose house, significantly, was located near a major water tap, and who had no children. Certain individuals have been active on more than one occasion in exercising this kind of informal leadership, but others are active once and no more. Protection of informants forbids the detailing of certain incidents.

Not all instances of informal leadership, however, involve pressure upon or defiance of the authorities. On other occasions, prestigious members of the community have initiated such projects as the construction of the Catholic chapel, largely by self-help, and the foundation of the Interplanetary School, a private but officially subsidized institution. Generally these individuals have fairly dominant personalities, strong groups of family and/ or personal supporters, and are economically freer than the average squatter to spend time and effort on their activities, either because of lack of children or because they or their husbands have relatively high incomes. A certain sophistication and ideological predisposition to activism of some sort are also no doubt prerequisites for this kind of activity.

I have already indicated some of the reasons for the lack of more formalized structures of organization, in the political and other spheres, in the Social Security Invasion. In addition it should be noted that the development of information and situational responses to crises or acutely felt needs reflects the weakness, or nonexistence, during the period in question, of strong labor and/or lower-class political organizations. The labor unions were almost entirely under the control of the Ministry of Labor, and even the left-wing parties were fundamentally enmeshed in the political patronage systems. The relative structurelessness of social organization in the squatment is also a response to this situation. Different structures appear in a given conjuncture to deal with a given situation in the most appropriate manner, at minimum risk and minimum cost in effort to the leaders and participants. Some segments of the black power movement in the United States, at a higher rhetorical level, functioned in a similar manner (Gerlach and Hine 1970).

CHAPTER V

The Squatment and Labor Supply

I. In-Migration

> When I saw myself alone,
> I saw I understood nothing:
> Neither why I was going,
> Nor the dreams I was dreaming;
> I only smelled the leather
> Of the suitcase I was carrying,
> Which even though it was lined
> Stank and smelled bad.
>
> Aside from this, I continued,
> Crossing, following the road,
> Neither crying nor smiling,
> Alone, to the capital.
> —Popular song (Gil and Veloso 1968).[1]

In Brazil a migratory stream flows from the lower to the upper pole of the national economy. This takes the form of a net migratory loss in rural areas and small cities, especially in Minas Gerais, Bahia, and the Northeast, and a net gain for the more southerly, technologically advanced parts of the country, and (to a lesser extent) for regional metropolises such as Fortaleza in Ceará, Recife in Pernambuco, and Salvador in Bahia. Migration may involve a series of moves by individuals from place to place over a period of years or even generations, but its net effect favors such places as Greater Rio de Janeiro city, Greater São Paulo city, and the frontier areas of northern Paraná.

From time to time the intensity and direction of the migratory stream

1. E quando eu me vi sòzinho./Vi que não entendia nada/Nem de porque eu ia indo,/Nem dos sonhos que eu sonhava;/Sentia apenas que a mala/De couro que eu carregava,/Embora estando forrada,/Fedia, cheirava mal./Fora isto, ia indo,/Atravessando, seguindo,/Nem chorando, nem sorrindo,/Sòzinho para a capital.

varies in response to environmental and economic factors. Drought conditions in the Northeast, for instance, accelerate out-migration. Declining terms of trade for agricultural export products, or shifts from labor-intensive to capital-intensive land use (for example, from vegetable crops to cattle-raising), also stimulate migration. On the other hand, increased labor demand in a region, such as arose from the pre-World War I rubber boom in the Amazon Valley, the expanding coffee frontier in Paraná, or the growth of the import-substitution industries in São Paulo, attracts migrants.

Migration to urban areas is far in excess of what could be justified merely by demand for industrial employment. A large population of unemployed persons does depress the wage level, and there is considerable demand for service workers, steady and intermittent, as a prop to the lifestyle of the middle and upper classes. From the point of view of the impoverished rural migrant, however, even intermittent or menial employment at low wages is an improvement over conditions in the rural sector. Thus, for instance, a migrant from Espírito Santo recounts that he arrived in Anápolis by train with his wife and two children, dressed in white homespun, with all his earthly possessions in a cloth sack. The only work he could find was in the rice harvest, at NCr$1 per day. To sweat under the hot sun for this sum (less than forty cents), he said, was not for him. The more so since the rice harvest does not last the year round—far, far better to try his luck in the capital, where the police soon directed him to Social Security. Such social services as are available are also concentrated in the cities, increasing the appeal of in-migration.

In Brasília's early days, large government expenditures in an area of virtually nonexistent labor supply stimulated a large and increasing influx of migrants. Official entities as well as the communications media contributed to the attraction of some of the migrants to the new capital. Reports former NOVACAP director Ernesto Silva: "INIC, in compliance with its obligations, in every corner of Brazil pointed out the path to Brasília and facilitated transportation" (*Correio Braziliense* June 4, 1967). INIC is an acronym for the National Immigration and Colonization Institute (*Instituto Nacional de Imigração e Colonização*). While statistics only partly confirm the image, the typical migrant in Brasília is often referred to as a *pau-de-arara,* literally, a "parrot perch." This term refers to migrants from the Northeast region, who travel at times on the backs of trucks, riding on improvised wooden benches, protected from the elements by a large waxed canvas. The term *pau-de-arara* is extended from the trucks' superstructure to the passengers. In São Paulo, migrants are termed *baianos* (Bahians), and are the butt of stereotype jokes characterizing them as ignorant and backward. Examples: What's a Bahian escalator? A banana peel. What's a sheath for a Bahian knife? A São Paulo belly.

According to a special census taken in 1959 in what is now the Federal District, ". . . of 64,000 inhabitants, nearly 57,000, or approximately 90 percent, were migrants; the reciprocal relation would indicate, then, that of 100 inhabitants of the future Brazilian Capital, only 10 were born in her territory" (IBGE 1959: 40). Only about 2 percent of these were born outside Brazil, demonstrating that the population of the area had increased in the period almost exclusively as a result of internal migrations.

Arriving at valid conclusions about the details of migration from census material is a complex task, but this census does provide a picture of the situation *in the year previous to the formal inauguration* of the capital. Summation of the census categories Western Northeast (*Nordeste Ocidental*), Eastern Northeast (*Nordeste Oriental*), and Northern East (*Leste Setentrional*) provides a measure of the dominance in the migratory stream of the greater Northeast (Maranhão through Bahia), arriving at a figure of 43.0 percent of migrants born in this area, followed by the Southern East (*Leste Meridional*) and Center-West (*Centro-Oeste*) with 23.6 percent each. In the former region Minas Gerais accounts for most of this figure, in the latter Goiás for virtually all of it. Minas and Goiás, of course, are contiguous to the Federal District.

Various surveys taken later in the Social Security Invasion show an even greater proportion of migrants from the Northeast and Bahia. Survey results in table VI show that from something more than half to over two-thirds of the household heads were born in the *greater* Northeast (the category Northeast in the table excludes Bahia). Minas Gerais, the large

TABLE VI
Birthplaces of Residents of the Social Security Invasion, Percent

| State or region | Household heads | | | Dependents |
	1965	1966	1967	1967
Northeast	50.3	36.7	44.7[1]	20.5[1]
Bahia	17.1	18.4	15.1	9.4
Minas Gerais	20.4	26.5	19.4	18.0
Goiás	7.9	16.3	10.8	12.4
Federal District	—	—	—	27.1
Guanabara	0.9	—	—	—
Others	3.4	2.0	9.7[1]	7.7[1]
TOTAL	100.0	99.9	99.7[2]	95.1[2]

Sources: FSS 1965*d*: 11; FSS 1967: 10; sampling of FSS registry in Social Security Invasion

1. Some states given as part of the Northeast category in this chart for other years seem to have been included in Others in this survey, because individually their totals were very small.
2. While the total is given in the source as 100.0 per cent, the addition of the figures provided checks out to the figure given.

contiguous state, provides from one-fifth to one-quarter of the total, and Goiás virtually all of the remainder. This reflects the predominance of lower-class migrants from the Northeast and Center-West; Guanabara, São Paulo, and the Extreme South, the more prosperous region of Brazil, provide largely technical, professional, and civil service types, and very few workers of the sort who gravitate toward the squatment. Hence the miniscule contribution of the more developed states to the Social Security Invasion.

The conclusions shift a bit if we consider the last place of residence before the move to Brasília (*procedência*). In the 1959 census, dominance in this category passed to the Center-West region, especially to Goiás. The region came to account for 38.6 percent of the migrants, and the Northeast (including Bahia) for only 27.3 percent, while the Southern East continues practically unchanged from the place-of-birth results, showing 23.1 percent. The South, including industrial São Paulo, accounts for only 6.7 percent of migrants *born* there, but for 10.0 percent of migrants *last residing* there (IBGE 1959: 41–45). Thus we have a basis for surmising that a large group of migrants did not leave their birthplaces to come directly to Brasília, but that many—principally from the Northeast—had migrated previously to Goiás and São Paulo, later re-emigrating to the site of the new capital.

This surmise is confirmed by table VII, which shows the results of surveys confined to the Social Security Invasion. While differing considerably among themselves, the various surveys do show consistent differences

TABLE VII
Last Place of Residence before Brasília, for Social Security Invasion Household Heads, Percent

State or region	1965	1966	1967
Northeast	43.2	30.6	24.2[2]
Bahia	14.3	8.2	9.9
Minas Gerais	18.9	16.4	11.8
Goiás	13.4	38.8	22.8
São Paulo	3.5	—— [1]	8.9
Guanabara	0.6	—— [1]	7.4
Others	2.3	6.1[1]	14.1[2]
TOTAL	96.2[3]	100.1	99.1[3]

Sources: FSS 1965*d*: 11; FSS 1967: 10; sampling of FSS registry in Social
    Security Invasion.

1. São Paulo and Guanabara included in Others.
2. Some Northeast states included in Others.
3. While in the source the Total is given as 100.00 percent, the addition of the figures provided checks out to the figure given here.

from table VI, which deals with the place of birth of the same respondents. The generally higher figures for Minas Gerais, Goiás, São Paulo, and (in the 1967 survey) Guanabara suggest that these were stopping-off places or places of temporary residence for many of the migrants who eventually wound up in the Social Security Invasion.

And in fact 29.3 percent of the migrants to the new capital in this period, according to the 1959 census, came indirectly, that is from a State other than their state of birth. This is true notably of those from Bahia and Sergipe, 53.2 percent of whom were indirect migrants. The West-Northeast (Maranhão and Piauí) and East-Northeast (from Ceará through Alagoas) also show high percentages of indirect migrants, 37.1 and 34.2 percent respectively (IBGE 1959: 46). As the census analyst points out: "The rates of indirect migration are in strict correlation with the geographic distance from the region of birth . . . [The rates] tend to go down, the shorter the distance between the birthplace and the territory of Brasília" IBGE 1959: 47). It appears that the principal intermediate points for the migrants are Goiás, São Paulo, and Minas Gerais. According to the analyst, however, Minas, as a region of demographic exportation, would not attract such a movement of immigration; it is suggested that the result may be attributable to the fact that "Minas Gerais is the necessary route of migrations of Northeasterners and Bahians towards Brasília (and where, in the course of events, a part of the migrants might stop over, to provide themselves with the resources necessary to continuance of the trip)" (IBGE 1959: 47).

It should also be noted, that a majority of the migrants from every region of the country, cite as "urban" their previous place of residence; less than 20 percent declare a rural place as their previous residence.

This is true of the Social Security squatters, also; 59.8 percent were born in urban areas (*cidade*), and 63.5 percent raised in them, as compared to 40.2 percent born in rural areas (*roça*) and 36.5 percent raised in them. By the time the last place of residence was reached, however, much rural-urban migration had taken place; 84.2 percent lived in an urban place just before coming to Brasília, and only 15.8 percent in a rural one (FSS 1967: 11). Such figures cast doubt upon the simplistic characterization of the squatment as a rural enclave or even as a place where the culture shock and disorientation supposedly attendant upon an abrupt move from country to city dominate the social landscape.

The census analyst points out that these results were due in part to the official and popularly accepted definition of a city in juridical rather than sociological terms, so that some "urban" responses probably refer to places more properly called rural. The proportion of those coming from "rural" places rises above one-third only in the greater Northeast, amounting to as much as 47.7 percent in Ceará, 34.6 percent in Bahia, and 34.1 percent in Pernambuco. Concludes the census analyst:

Brasília is acting as one of those metropolitan centers which exercise attraction, principally, on the populations of the urbanized areas of secondary importance. The local labor market, similar in nature to that of the great metropolitan centers of the country, would justify the parallelism in regard to the migratory origin of her population (IBGE 1959:49).

The tendency to attribute urban growth exclusively to a rural exodus is, then, simplistic. There undoubtedly is an overall trend to a higher proportion of urbanites in the national population, but this trend, it appears, reflects population movements far more complex than a simple transfer of masses of people from farms and plantations directly to urban shantytowns.

There are, however, cases where changes in the agrarian interests of the landholding rural capitalists, reflecting among other things the fluctuations of the world economy, lead to rapid and even forced evacuation of the rural lower strata. As Caio Prado Jr. (1966: 71–73) points out, this change is most often a result of the expansion of nonlabor-intensive cattle-raising at the expense of landless cultivators. One case reported in the Brasília daily *Correio Braziliense* (October 2, 1966) concerns a group of families abducted at gunpoint from a nearby rural area in Goiás and unceremoniously dumped in the streets of one of Brasília's satellite towns.

Another man, today a resident of Social Security, told me he left Rio Grande do Norte in the Northeast, where he was a farmer, for an area in Northern Goiás where a state-sponsored colonization project was taking place, which enjoyed the favor of the state government in the form of expenditures for road construction, loans, and so on. In the new area the man operated a horse-car for hauling construction materials. His prosperity thus depended upon the continued growth of the colony. However, large landholding interests opposed to the colonization project gained the ascendancy after the fall, through Federal intervention, of Goiás governor Mauro Borges. Through harassment, and control of tax and police functions, these interests not only prevented the growth of the colony, but forced many people to leave. This man came to Brasília. Somewhat older than most migrants, he had difficulty in obtaining work, and he was afraid to drive a horse-cart along the steeply embanked and relatively heavily trafficked highways of the capital. Through relatives and friends from his native Rio Grande do Norte, however, he did obtain work in construction. His wife bought a sewing machine on the instalment plan and took in work as a seamstress, and the two girls went to public school; the older has a fair chance of being graduated from middle school (*ginásio*).

Least content is the husband who dislikes the trip to work, by truck or public bus, and finds the heavy work difficult. As we were about to leave, however, he found a lighter job as caretaker in some temporary buildings in the Pilot Plan, and no longer speaks of going elsewhere, which pleases his wife and daughters.

Unlike these cases, however, migration is usually from the rural areas to smaller cities, and from these cities to the various poles of attraction in the great metropolitan centers.

In the period of the construction drive, there was a snowball effect. In the beginning, the migrants came largely from Goiás, Minas Gerais, and São Paulo, relatively near the site. The northeasterners (including Bahians) came in greater numbers later. At the time of the Experimental Census of May 17, 1959, for instance, a majority of the residents had arrived within the previous year, and 24.5 percent within the previous three months (IBGE 1959: 151 ff). Table II shows that the population more than doubled between the 1959 and 1960 censuses, an increase almost entirely attributable to migration.

The attraction exercised by the new capital was mostly economic, either in the form of a relatively strong demand for wage labor, or a general atmosphere favoring the efforts of the adventurous and the industrious. For the commercially ambitious, the latter was of course the case.

One man, today a storekeeper, recounts that he had headed for São Paulo from Pernambuco. When he disembarked in São Paulo, a trucker offered him a ride to Brasília. He accepted the invitation. With little money, he chanced upon a drunken Bahian in the street, who offered him a handcart and a load of oranges for the equivalent of U.S.$10. When the Bahian sobered up, he repented of the sale, but to no avail. Selling the oranges, which, like everything else, went rapidly in those days, the budding entrepreneur used virtually all the proceeds to buy more. Gradually increasing his capital, he was soon buying whole truckloads of fruit coming up from São Paulo. He had nowhere to store them, but eventually the manager of a bank branch arranged some space for him. This same manager offered him a job as watchman, but he refused, preferring to continue his commercial career.

Soon the budding businessman branched out into the notions business, and purchased an old truck. It was shortly afterwards that the truck was smashed in an accident. A few days later, while watching a movie, he learned that the hotel where his merchandise was stored was burning (all the temporary buildings were of wood) but returned too late to save most of the goods, consumed in the flames. So he started over again. Today his position is far more modest than at the height of his career.

However embroidered the story above may be, it reflects the widespread conviction that the commercial road to success was open during the preinauguration period in Brasília, and many who arrived later lament that they delayed so long.

Brasília's daily paper, the *Correio Braziliense,* occasionally runs a series entitled "They Make the Progress of the City," a paean to precisely this sort of petit-bourgeois Horatio Algerism. For example:

Work, perseverance, will power and an uncommon fighting spirit, which led him to overcome always the adverse moments which appeared before him, define, in general, the personality of Eduardo Pedroso Perez, retail and wholesale meat dealer, established here [in the satellite city of Taguatinga] with the "Copacabana Slaughterhouse and Freezing Plant" (CB, Dec. 4, 1966).

Few, very few, can say they collaborated as much for the progress of this city as José Tertuliano Tavares . . . "When I arrived . . . I tried to settle in the Pioneer Nucleus [Free City]. Business there was fabulous. And as I said, I always aspired to enter into business . . . I installed my commercial establishment, the Casa Joterta, in the same place it is to be found today. I slept in the store, on a hay mattress, on the ground, in a room formed by an improvised screen.

" 'This guy is nuts,' people I knew told each other. And I say today, if I hadn't assumed so many responsibilities, I would have gone back to São Paulo. I was obliged to stick with the ship. The city was completely primitive . . . There were no banks, no . . . credit. You had to take the risk of selling on time without the least security . . . But, thank the Lord, in the end it came out all right" (CB October 20, 1966).

Among the women who also make the progress of the city, Maria Mercedes Granjeiro deserves, without a doubt, a place of distinction . . . Dona Mercedes . . . came to Taguatinga with her husband Jose Granjeiro, a Cearense from Milagres, determined and disposed to conquer, with the opportunities she foresaw in the city whose vertiginous growth surprised even the most optimistic. "I'm nearly always at the head of the firm's business, which today includes three butcheries, our job being to furnish meat to nearly fifteen retailers" (CB September 30, 1966).

Many informants did not report such calculated economic motivations. Often they refered to more personal kinds of factors, such as disputes with relatives, boredom, a lust for adventure, and the like. In these cases, the economic opportunities available in Brasília merely attracted the migrant there rather than somewhere else. To be sure, the migrant's report of his own motivation is not conclusive for understanding the migration process. Complaints of boredom, or the prevalence of interpersonal disputes, may reflect stresses upon a class, a community, or a region as a whole, stresses which have a differential impact upon individuals. A propensity to move with little hesitation, in the case of Northeasterners, may be an adaptive response to the intermittent and unpredictable occurrence of droughts in their region.

An example of the interpersonal "trigger" for migration is the case of a girl who left her home in northern Goiás after a dispute with her step-father. She came to the new capital from northern Goiás with two brothers and a paternal aunt. Her moves since her arrival in 1957 are of a type common in the life stories of lower-class people in Brasília. On arrival, they stayed in the workers' barracks on the site of the National Hotel in the Pilot Plan, but a few days later moved to a shack in Social Security. A few months later her brother got married, sold his shack in Social Security, and the family moved to a shack he bought in a squatment near the Industrial Sector. The Prefecture soon insisted on the removal of the "invasion" there and moved the shacks to Gama. Although the residents of this small squatment did not protest the move, they were very discontent, first because they received no help in rebuilding their shacks, and because, as she told me, "Gama was a terrible place, there was no work," and "poor people need to work." She went out there, looking for clothes to wash, or work as a domestic, but could not find it.

So her brother sold the shack in Gama and they moved to another squatment near Cruzeiro. All they had was a large piece of canvas. They arrived at about 8 P.M., knowing no one, and attached the canvas to a tree and made a tent, and improvised a small stove. Their purpose in going to Cruzeiro was to be near a construction site, which was active at this time, and set up a business selling food and coffee to the workers. Unfortunately, however, they lacked the money to begin. Her brothers were able to get work as house painters, but still they stayed two months and a half under the canvas, which was full of holes and constantly had to be repaired with pitch.

In the same period her aunt found a job for her working in a bar, from which she was able to accumulate enough money to buy a small one-room shack in the same area, and later bought enough lumber to expand the shack, and then divide the expanded area into two additional rooms. This is a good example of the adaptability of the shack as opposed to more permanent and higher prestige types of house.

Soon, in fact, due to the constant fights and drunkenness in the area, they decided to move the entire shack to another part of the same invasion, which they did, by placing it on a horse-cart. Her aunt and the aunt's son then moved to a construction site in the North Wing to sell coffee and food, and then to still another site, by order of the Prefecture. At the latter site the aunt's son remained in order to sell fish, while the aunt returned to Cruzeiro, where she decided to build a shack of her own, from used lumber she bought from a construction company.

Soon, however, the girl's brother, with whom she was living, decided to live with another woman in the shack, a woman the girl disliked intensely, so she returned to Social Security to live with her married brother, who by this time had returned there. Now she works as a domestic by day and returns to her brother's shack to sleep.

This case is an example of the use of squatting in the search for work in a fluctuating labor market with shifting geographical focus—especially characteristic of the construction industry, dominant in Brasília. The shack is not only a means of locating oneself near the sources of employment and of subsidiary sources of income (such as small retail business locations), but is a means of accumulating at least a small amount of capital, which can be fairly readily turned into cash if the need arises.

More skilled workers tend to have less unstable histories in terms of place of residence in Brasília, as do people with more stable family status than an unmarried girl. Thus a carpenter from Bahia and his wife report only one move once they reached the new capital, though they, like many others, had moved more than once before reaching Brasília. This woman and her husband moved from a small town in rural Bahia to Salvador, the capital, because in the country there was nothing but subsistence agriculture on other people's land. In Salvador he worked as a carpenter and lived in a house provided by the employer, a cement factory owner. After three years, however, he was laid off because the construction job was finished, and he was forced to live by means of odd jobs and to pay a fairly high rent, to which he had to allot practically all he earned.

It was then that they left the state of Bahia looking for better things. They came in an open truck (*pau de arara*), sleeping in the open along the way, in the rain, the truck getting stuck in the mud constantly. Often they had to walk for long distances alongside the truck to avoid forcing it deeper into the mud. It was "the greatest sacrifice in their life" (*o maior sacrifício da vida*), but, "Brasília's fame went far; they told us the wages were better."

As soon as they arrived and managed to build a shack in Social Security, they were robbed. One day they went off to the Lake by bus to fish, and the bus they were coming back in broke down on the road (a common occurrence). When they arrived, late at night, their shack had been broken into, and some money and the man's tool chest had been taken. Now in Brasília construction workers are expected to provide their own tools; on arriving, job-seekers are asked, "Where are the tools?" and those who can't produce them don't get work.

As a result, the woman of the house ("who is childless") went to work in middle-class houses (*na casa das madame*) to get together the money to buy more tools.

Work was hard to get anyway in this period, when Jânio Quadros stopped all the construction projects, ". . . and everybody was eating food given by the government, confronting the longest lines in the world to get a little plate of food and families at home hoping a little would be left over to bring to the families and the children."

Later, however, things improved, the husband got a steady job as a carpenter, a job he has retained ever since. He has since worked long enough to be entitled to a considerable indemnity under Brazilian labor law in the event that he is fired, which would enable him to open a business or buy a house. Accumulation of this much seniority is unusual in Brasília, where frequent firings and rehirings are the rule for all but the most highly skilled workers, who are in short supply.

The shack this couple had was in the area of Social Security claimed by an athletic club (see Chapter III, section VI), which began to measure the area for a playing field and to insist that the residents move out. They refused, and organized a delegation of more than two hundred people, hired a truck, and went to protest to the Mayor. His secretary received them, heard them out, and ordered a halt to the work, which had already begun in the part of the area where there were no shacks, the dust and noise of the machines being used to intimidate the residents. A week later the secretary appeared on the site and asked if the people were willing to move to Gama, but they refused on the grounds that it was too far and the bus service was miserable. So they were relocated in the part of the Social Security Invasion near the present Main Street (*Avenida Principal*) (see illus. 13). The playing field and clubhouse, incidentally, were never finished.

In the relocation process, only the trucks were provided. The *cerrado* vegetation was not removed, nor were the shacks put up. The couple, like others, was forced to stay in the open air, under the hot sun. Their house was ". . . under a table. The government here is unjust to the people, the poor people, who live thrown around like garbage, first they throw you one way and then another." Half the roof tiles were broken in the removal process:

They come, with rudeness (*estupidez*), come in, don't want to know if a person has the money to buy the material; for them a poor man is nobody, they do what they please. Whoever you are, it's your problem (*quem quiser que se vire*), they don't want to know if you have a child, they're here to take it away, they're not in business to ask your age or anything.

Finally they hired someone to clear the area and her husband reconstructed the shack. In this period people from other areas came in the dead of night to move their shacks into Social Security, since it was still technically illegal. These were people from the Pilot Plan who were being pressured by the police to move. These new squatters preferred the Social

Security Invasion, still technically illegal, to Gama or homelessness.

For this couple, the move to Main Avenue was the last. They miss Bahia, and talk of it with longing, like many migrants to Brasília, who talk as if they wanted to return home. But, as the woman of this household says:

I don't like it here but I'm obliged to stay, I like Bahia better but I have to stay here because in Bahia you can't make it (*nao dá*). It's a rich state but they make it poor . . . He [the husband] doesn't want to go back, because we live from what he earns, and there it's very little, here the wages are better. We live under four sticks of wood. We're subject to being taken off to one place and then another.

Nevertheless they have remained where they are for five years, and if their discontent and sense of the injustice in the social system are transparent in their comments, it would nevertheless probably be fair to say that they have improved their lot.

Couples did not always come together. Another woman, who was born in a small town in Maranhão but spent most of her life in Teresina, the capital of Piauí, was preceded by her husband, a tailor by profession. He felt he made little in Teresina and came to Brasília in 1960, at the height of the construction boom, to see if he could do better. He came, also, because a group of friends were all anxious to come, and their excitement was contagious and affected him as well. He liked it and did well, and decided to stay. At first, he lived with a friend in a Free Town boardinghouse, but soon they built a small shack in Social Security. His wife and two children came a year later, to surprise him, by plane (he had come by bus). Since they had corresponded, they knew where he was, and stayed with him and his friend in the shack for three years.

This shack was located in the area belonging to the Social Security Hospital, whose director did not seem to object to shacks in this period, even if the residents were not employees of the institution. At this time, the husband was working as a tailor on his own account; as his wife says,

It's good to have a profession because if you become unemployed you can make a go of it (*quebrar o galho*), but he doesn't like to work at his profession, he'd rather have a good job.

When he got here there was a flood of money, he didn't bother about it, he didn't make an effort to get a steady job, since he thought that [prosperity] of JK's time would go on forever. When the thing began to go back, it was too late. He passed a Civil Service exam but he didn't take the job because the pay was small.

The husband likes Brasília, and even though relatives have arranged employment for him back in Teresina, he refuses to leave, if leaving means returning to a lower position.

They expanded their shack, in spite of the rules of the period prohibiting any repairs, after obtaining special permission from the Prefecture, after the wife appealed to the official in charge that ". . . it was inhuman, I had children exposed to the elements, anybody could come in and steal other people's clothes." A group of friends and neighbors cooperated with the improvement, since the repairs had to be done in a single day. The owners of the house provided the food and bought the material in a warehouse in the Free Town.

Two years ago, the hospital began complaining about the presence of shacks belonging to people who were not employed by the IAPI, the agency controlling the hospital. Even though they never directly were asked to move, the couple decided it would be prudent to move the shack outside the fence. The hospital administration provided a carpenter, the family moved in with neighbors for three days, and the move was completed to a site a few hundred yards outside the fence.

II. The Squatment as a Labor Reserve

Central to the lives of Social Security Invasion residents is their position as employees and potential employees in the urban money economy. Low wages and a high rate of unemployment and underemployment (reliance on odd jobs, petty commerce, and the like) are a part of the pattern of integration of these people into the economic system, but they do not contradict the fact of such integration. Far from implying marginality to the system, they are the conditions of integration of these people into it.

The fundamental resource the squatters possess in order to obtain the necessities of life is their ability to work for wages. The small amount of domestic production that is carried out is insignificant in relation to the returns from employment from wages and petty commerce. Without the cash that people get from wage work and commerce, this domestic production, which amounts to the planting of small gardens in the backyards of the houses, sewing by women, and maintenance and repair work on furniture and the shacks by men, would be inadequate to sustain life.

Construction Employment

Tables VIII and IX show that various sources are in substantial agreement on the predominance of employment in the construction industry as the source of income for household heads in the Social Security Invasion, in spite of the divergent categories employed in the three instruments. In each case, the largest single category is that of laborer, and in every case, laborers and construction workers of other types account for over one-third of the household heads. The figure of 55.1 percent given

in the registry samples in 1966 suggests that many of the people listed as
"Other or none" for 1965 and 1967 are in fact in various occupations
connected with construction, since in the 1966 sample it was possible to
interpret every individual reply in this regard, and the result is a significantly higher total for the construction sector, and a lower one for "Other
or none." This conclusion is also confirmed by the fact that table IX, taken
from the same survey as the 1965 figures in table VIII, lists 43.8 percent
of household heads as in the construction industry, although the sum of
individual professions so connected is only 33.6 percent, or 10.2 percent
less.

These survey results correspond to the results of nonstatistical observations and interviewing in the Social Security Invasion, where the construction industry is central both to present employment and to people's expectations about their sources of future employment.

This is not to say, however, that the numerical predominance of jobs
in the construction industry corresponds to the prestige ranking of the
sectors. Here the construction industry probably ranks lowest, except for

TABLE VIII

Present Occupation of Household Heads in the Social Security Invasion,
Percent, According to Various Sources

Occupation	1965[1]	1966[2]	1967[3]
Carpenter	5.5	—	5.4
Laborer (servente)	18.4	30.6	27.9
Mason (pedreiro)	5.8	—	6.8
Other construction	3.9[4]	—	—
Construction in general	—	24.5	—
Subtotal: Construction,			
incl. laborers	(33.6)	(55.1)	(40.1)
Commerce	5.9	10.2	8.3
Domestic and laundry	7.1	20.4	8.6
Driver (motorista)	4.5	5.1	4.0
Farmer	1.0	—	2.9
Odd jobs (biscates)	14.3	—	3.4
Other or none	33.6[5]	8.2	32.7[5]
TOTAL	100.0	100.0	100.0

1. FSS 1965d: 16.
2. My own sampling of the (incomplete) registry maintained in the Social Security Invasion post of the Social Service Foundation, which is biased against
longer-term residents and those who have bought shacks from them without reg-
istering the purchase.
3. FSS 1967:7, a sample survey.
4. Includes cabinetmakers, painters and plumbers.
5. Includes some construction trades.

agriculture and domestic work, while civil service employment is highly regarded. This researcher was frequently importuned, subtly or otherwise, to act as patron or sponsor for invasion residents who desired civil service jobs, even menial ones such as washroom attendant. The principal factors in this desire for civil service employment are undoubtedly job security, which is very high in this sector, and the short hours generally prevailing (a 30-hour week is the rule, as opposed to a 44-hour week or more in industry and commerce).

As I have indicated, the primacy of the construction industry as a source of employment in Brasília dates back to the pre-1960 construction drive. It was this drive and the resultant demand for labor which

TABLE IX

Sector of Employment of Household Heads in the Social Security Invasion, Percent, 1965

Sector	Percent
Commerce	9.7
Construction industry	43.8
Other industry	0.8
Civil service[1]	15.0
Service	20.3
Agriculture	2.2
None	8.2
TOTAL	100.0

Source: FSS 1965d: 17.

1. Including Prefecture, NOVACAP, and Foundations.

TABLE X

Year of Arrival in Brasília of Household Heads in Social Security Invasion, Percent

Year of arrival	Percent of household heads
Before 1960	25.2
1960	21.0
1961	12.5
1962	12.5
1963	7.4
1964	7.4
1965	6.6
1966	7.4
TOTAL	100.0

Source: FSS 1967: 13.

created the "pull" factor in the lower-class in-migration, and to some extent the availability of this kind of work still motivates the continued flow of migrants into the new capital. Table X shows that most Social Security Invasion household heads migrated to Brasília in 1960 or before.

Undoubtedly the principal factor in this decline in in-migration was the virtual paralysis of construction activity ordered by Jânio Quadros when he took office in 1961. Had this policy been fully maintained for a period of years it might have led to a decline or at least a stabilization of the size of the lower-class population. Because of the widespread unemployment in the aftermath of Quadros's order, hunger was rife in the period. The Social Security Food Service (SAPS) maintained a restaurant at the NOVACAP encampment, and as one woman present at the time put it, "a lot of people only survived because of SAPS." Men waited on line in the hot sun for their lunch, to which they were entitled as bearers of a document certifying them as contributors to the Social Security Institutes, and they did their best to get leftovers for their families. Jânio Quadros is still an unpopular figure in Brasília. This same woman calls him "an evil man who caused a lot of suffering here." Many men left Brasília in search of work elsewhere in this period, on damsites and elsewhere, returning to their families in the new capital when times got better.

Since Quadros remained in office for only a few months, however, and all of his successors have to some degree stimulated construction activity in Brasília, the construction industry has remained a major source of employment, and in the Social Security Invasion the largest source.

Employment is a somewhat different experience for unskilled laborers and those possessing skills which are at a premium, such as carpentry. The presence of large numbers of unemployed and underemployed workers makes possible a constant rotation in the ranks of unskilled laborers in the construction industry, which is a means of avoiding the hiring of workers on a permanent basis, since in Brazil an indemnity calculated on the basis of the number of months or years of employment must be paid to workers who are fired. Many workers are fired at the end of their three-month "trial period," since the employer can easily find new employees, and avoid the dangers of acquiring a long-term obligation in an industry that depends on the vagaries of political decisions. Under recent legislation, a Time of Employment Guarantee Fund (*Fundo de Garantia de Tempo de Serviço*) was set up as an optional alternative to the old form of indemnity. As of the time of the research it was too early to assess its effects. As of June 10, 1965, 43.0 percent of household heads were unemployed (FSS 1965d: 18).

Skilled workers, on the other hand, are an asset, and one finds many of them have worked in the same job for years. They also generally earn a premium of 50 or 100 percent over the minimum wage offered to the laborers. Stability of employment and the prospect of receiving a large indemnity is often referred to by these workers as a factor in their plans. The indemnity is often used as capital for the purchase of a house or the opening of a small commercial enterprise.

However, such ambitions are beyond the daily reality facing the vast majority of the residents of the Social Security Invasion, who must subsist on infinitesimal incomes. In February 1967, for instance, the modal income per month of families in the squatment was between NCr$42 and NCr$84 (about U.S.$15 and U.S.$31). Two-thirds of all squatment *families* had incomes *under* NCr$126 (about U.S.$47) per month, and only 3.7 percent had incomes exceeding NCr$252 (about U.S.$93) monthly. On the basis of an average four members per household, which is probably too low (see FSS 1965d: 20), two-thirds of the residents of the squatment have annual incomes per capita of *less than* U.S.$141 annually, and modal income per capita is *below* U.S.$100 annually; and about 15 percent of the squatters must subsist on family incomes below U.S.$16 per month (FSS 1967: 5). It should be noted in this regard that this is a cash economy, in which the role of subsistence agriculture in providing food is at best minor. Yet even with these incomes more than four-fifths of the household heads disclaim any intention of going back where they came from, and nearly 90 percent say they are happier in Brasília than where they came from, and more than half cite labor conditions as the reason for their preference! (FSS 1967: 14–15).

Other Economic Roles

While tables V and VI should provide sufficient warning against an exaggerated emphasis on commerce as a principal source of income for squatment dwellers, commercial enterprise makes its mark as (*a*) an important feature of the squatment landscape, (*b*) the point at which distribution of goods to the family level takes place on a daily basis, and (*c*) as a principal source of income for many and a supplemental source for others.

Of the more than 250 commercial establishments located within the Social Security Invasion, more than 90 percent are "bars" (*bares*) and small grocery or general stores. These are the poorest and smallest of the stores in all but one or two cases.

Next to the home, the bar may well be the most common Brazilian scene, combining architectural and behavioral regularities of impressive frequency. Statistically bars are far more common than churches, schools, or military bases.

Unlike the North American bar, however, the Brazilian one is generally not the exclusive preserve of male adults, nor is it a place where imbibers of alcoholic beverages are segregated from other people. It combines the functions of a social club, a petty retail store, and a snack shop with the sale of liquor by the drink, along with soft drinks, coffee, and sometimes milkshakes (*vitaminas*). While bars may vary in their reputation and in the predominance of one or another of their various functions, they are thoroughly respectable places in many instances, having little in common with the North American saloon.

The typical bar in the Social Security Invasion is a shack not distinguished by any special features, except that a room facing on the street is divided from the rest of the house, and there is a counter, usually with glass-enclosed cases on top of part of it. Soft drinks, beer, *cachaça* (sugarcane liquor), cigars and cigarettes, candy, cakes and biscuits of various kinds (*doces*) as well as salt-flavored snacks, coffee, aspirin, and similar medicines comprise some of the most common products distributed in small quantities at these stores. Most of these products are prominently displayed, although generally kept safely behind the counter. The more prosperous of these stores have a kerosene refrigerator to keep the beverages cold. Such a machine sells for some NCr$700 (about U.S.$260): for the poorest bars this may represent several times the total invested capital.

Grocery stores are also common, and are similarly physically attached to the residence of the owner. These, however, deal in the standard staple foods which are consumed by the squatters, who favor the local merchants with their purchases when they are in need of small quantities or when they need credit. Among these commodities are salt, matches, cooking oil, beans, onions, rice, manioc flour (*farinha*), soap, coffee, and sugar. Less basic, though also common, are powdered milk, tomatoes, fresh manioc (*aipim* or *macaxera*), squash, bread, corn flour, cabbage, eggs, and canned goods including tomato paste, luncheon meat, and fruit. Fresh vegetables other than those mentioned are rare in the local grocery stores in the squatment, and are unknown even by name to many, especially those from the Northeast. Prices for most items are cheaper than those in the Pilot Plan and comparable to those in the Free Town, though quality is often poorer, and there is considerable variation in price from store to store.

The fundamental requisite for success in the building of a retail grocery operation is the granting of credit. A merchant who is unwilling to grant credit will usually find his clientele limited to neighbors and passersby who will make minor purchases as a matter of convenience. The granting of credit, however, is a risky business and requires considerable psychological acumen. One prerequisite is literacy, since a record book in which credit customers' purchases are recorded is maintained. Typically, people requesting credit will assert that they are employed, but that the employer has defaulted on payment, or has delayed it until he in turn receives payment for services rendered (often to the government, in the case of construction companies). These claims are undoubtedly usually true. Credit is generally granted for as much as NCr$60 or NCr$70, but rarely for more, unless payment on account is made.

Delays in payment are not the only reason for people to request credit, of course. Many are chronically incapable of making ends meet on their small earnings, and must live on credit at the end of each month in order to eat. On certain days of the month, for instance, the supermarket for NOVACAP employees in the Pilot Plan is filled with people waiting to buy sacks of beans and rice and other food items on credit against later deductions from their paychecks. Even larger crowds appear when the Federal Savings Bank (*Caixa Economica Federal*) opens applications from civil servants for small loans against future salaries.

The ability of a grocery store owner to grant credit probably also depends upon his ability to obtain credit, especially from his suppliers. Most of these are located in the Free Town and Vila Tenório, and it seems plausible to me that the credit system provides the basis for chains of dependency similar to those already described in the political sphere. However, I do not have reliable information on this point. There are also instances where it was reported that grocers in the squatment were obtaining stolen goods, soap for example, for resale; tax evasion is certainly widespread. Owing both to the sensitivity of the topics and to the fact that I did not actively pursue the details of retail commerce, conclusions on these points remain speculative and anecdotal.

In addition to bars and grocery stores, common types of stores are drugstores, butcher shops, and notion stores. There is one very large branch of a building materials house from the Free Town located on the main street of the invasion, one automobile mechanic at the entrance to this street specialized in the rebuilding of ancient cars and trucks, and several bicycle repair shops. A single store on the main street deals in furniture and appliances on the installment plan.

In general, however, purchases of cloth, clothes, tools, appliances, and other such items are made in the Free Town, and to a lesser extent in Taguatinga and the Pilot Plan. In spite of the prevailing low incomes, weekends see fairly frequent taxi trips from the Free Town to Social Security, by people returning from shopping trips. For large deliveries, there are also horse-carts for hire in the Free Town. It is also common for people to walk to the Free Town and Vila Tenório, generally to shop.

For women, the principal source of employment is domestic labor.

This work is most frequently engaged in by young women who have not yet married, and are able to live in the Pilot Plan homes of middle-class families. Typically they receive room, board, one day off a week, and a small salary of from U.S.$10 to U.S.$20 monthly. The work is rarely specialized, and includes cleaning, child care, and cooking. For a young unmarried woman the main advantage of this work, in addition to the financial reward, is the freedom from the authority of parents whose notions about what is appropriate behavior for young girls may be somewhat less than cosmopolitan, and who may expect a young girl to perform for free the same sort of tasks she is paid for in her employer's house.

Girls from the ages of ten to about sixteen are sometimes informally adopted by middle-class families, but they do not receive treatment identical to the natural-born children. They are expected to accept an inferior status in the household, and to perform domestic tasks at no pay. The arrangement does not usually require a complete break with the girl's own parents.

Day labor at domestic tasks is also common, though much less so than live-in arrangements. Usually the women involved are specialists, for example, laundresses, and their productivity is higher than that of live-in servants. Pay is about NCr$6 per day, which on a monthly basis is the equivalent of what many male workers are able to earn.

Many women also produce various kinds of artifacts, often decorative ones, for sale to neighbors or use in the home. Like many handicraft items in the squatment (including the *barracos* themselves), a good proportion of these items involves the reworking of industrial products: frying pans and pots made from old cans, decorative animals made from used light bulbs, and so on. The income from these items is very small, however.

Dressmaking, on the other hand, represents a very common and relatively lucrative enterprise, and it is relatively easy to begin, since an employed relative can purchase a sewing machine on the installment plan.

For a woman, extra income from petty commerce, the production and sale of small artifacts, or a small business as a dressmaker not only provides additional means of subsistence for herself and her family, but enables her to adopt a less submissive and more independent position vis-à-vis her husband. There is frequent tension in many families over these sources of income and over the relative status of husband and wife, often expressed through mutual accusations of infidelity. In one case, quite typical of many others, a woman was beaten by her husband every time she returned from an adult literacy class. At the same time she was busy setting up and expanding her dressmaking business, which she ran from her home, in order to accumulate money to leave her husband and move to Rio de Janeiro. He would accuse her of infidelity, and she claimed to have found him with lipstick—a kind she said only black women use—on his shirt when he returned late at night. He made her nauseous, she said, when he came back and made sexual advances; she could only think of him as infected with gonorrhea.

Occupational multiplicity is typical of Brazilian society on all levels (see, for example, Leeds 1964). This is probably one reason for the very inconsistent figures in table VIII for the category of odd jobs (*biscates*). Not only is the definition of the term unclear, but the *biscate* and the *bico* (supplemental job or source of income) are common among people who are temporarily unemployed or who wish to supplement their incomes from regular jobs, as well as being, for some, an exclusive source of funds.

Types of odd jobs may vary. There are many people who may be interpreted as being engaged in service occupations whose activity is intermittent and who so might be put into the category of *biscateiros*. Several empty lots in the Pilot Plan boast crude signs which advertise the services of plumbers, electricians, and repairmen who are prepared to offer their services to the passersby. These men are of widely varying competence, and their capital usually consists of a small satchel of tools. In general this kind of odd-job work is not very easy to come by, since the supply of workers is seemingly much greater than the demand.

This type of work, however, calls in question the stereotype of urban un- and underemployment in Latin America. Whereas labor-intensive methods are increasingly the rule in the manufacturing sector of the economy, whose technology is imported from the industrialized countries, the maintenance function has not been corporately organized to nearly the same extent. One wonders about the fate of much of the Brazilian economy, did not small entrepreneurs and *biscateiros* fill the maintenance niches left open by the larger enterprises and the state.[2]

Slightly different is the pattern of ambulant commerce, usually of a petty variety. This takes forms such as the sale of oranges, which are usually peeled by an ingenious hand-cranked machine, small wrapped pieces of guava paste and caramel (*doce de leite*), ices, popcorn, or (less frequently) products such as cheese and fresh vegetables. The capital involved varies, but is usually small. Such activity involves wholesale purchases in the Free Town, and the transport of the merchandise, usually on a public bus, but sometimes by bicycle or on foot, to the point of sale, which can be a bus stop, a public square, the entryway of a public building, or a busy street. Hawkers (*camelôs*) of items such as ballpoint pens, umbrellas, plastic toys, and sunglasses are abundant on certain stretches of W-3 Avenue, in the Free Town, and on Little Church Street (*Rua da*

2. I am grateful to Anthony Leeds for helping to clarify this point.

Igrejinha), an important shopping street in the Pilot Plan.

In the Social Security Invasion itself there is some petty street commerce, notably the sale of ice pops (*picolés*), a specialty of young boys, and notions and cheap toys.

There are also door-to-door salesmen (*mascates*) who operate in the Social Security Invasion, selling on credit items such as blouses, plastic doilies, men's pants, and women's shoes. Some of these men, many of whom are of Arab extraction, use bicycles, while others carry their suitcases of merchandise. Typically they receive a down payment sufficient to cover the wholesale cost of purchases, so that default on further payments will not cause them catastrophic losses. In most cases their prices are much higher than in retail stores in the Free Town. The offer of credit for relatively small purchases, as well as the attraction of their merchandise at the point of sale, accounts for their modest success.

The granting of credit often depends upon the salesman's knowledge of the customer and her reputation. In one instance, a girl bought an item from a salesman and had disappeared by the time he came around for a payment. Since her neighbor, who was a long-time customer, had introduced her, the neighbor was embarrassed and resentful because of her behavior. The neighbor did not, however, offer to pay for the merchandise. In general, deadbeat behavior of this kind is looked down upon. This researcher has observed a similar valuation of prompt payment in a village in northern Bahia, and it is also reported for the sugar plantation zone of Puerto Rico (Mintz 1951). In each case, a good reputation for payment of debts is an important defense in the face of the intermittent pattern of income and employment.

These economic activities all relate the squatment directly or indirectly to the larger political economy. The basic asset they provide is a large, nearby supply of low-wage labor, for the industrial segment of the economy (in Brasília the fluctuating construction industry) and for the service sector which contributes vitally to the preservation of the middle-class lifestyle. At little expense to the government or to the middle class, the squatment provides a close-in, but not threateningly close-in, area for residence of this segment of the society. And the squatment is carefully hidden to avoid detraction from the politically and touristically valuable image of Brasília as an ultramodern, well-planned capital. The abundant petty commerce in the squatment is connected to the wholesale distributors in the Free Town, and contributes to the maintenance of the settlement's population, as well as providing for the distribution of the prevailing poverty to a larger population by disguising the low rate of productive employment.

Thus the kind of work often deprecated as disguised unemployment or as unproductive work in the tertiary sector has a number of social functions. From the point of view of the workers, even employed workers, such work provides a supplementary source of income which is important in the face of the prevailing low wages and the chronic inflation which afflicts Brazil. It also is a cushion in the event that a worker is laid off or fired, or in the even more frequent event that his paycheck is delayed due to the chicanery of employers or the failure of the government agencies that sponsor construction projects to pay their bills on time. In terms of the settlement pattern, the proximity of the Social Security Invasion to the Free Town, where opportunities for part-time work and petty commerce abound, and to lines of transportation to the Pilot Plan, another place where such work may be engaged in, relates quite as much to these types of work as to the primary occupations, in the civil service, construction, or other fields.

From the point of view of the employers, the availability of odd jobs and similar opportunities makes possible the presence of a large number of people who are potential employees, thus limiting pressure for wage increases or for the benefits accruing to those who are signed on as permanent employees. Just as in the case of the welfare system in the United States, the supplemental sources of income make it possible to fix a population which is seasonally or intermittently useful as a source of workers. The need for labor in Brasília's politically conditioned construction industry is, of course, a fluctuating one. These means of subsistence also provide for a population which, in the absence of such means, might become politically dangerous to the established order. So the tacit toleration and even support provided by government and private industry to the Social Security Invasion, to be further discussed in the next section, is far from irrational. It is pathological only insofar as the system as a whole might be regarded as pathological. The squatment is marginal in terms of its relatively small share of the social product and political power, not in terms of its relevance to the social and economic system as a whole.

III. Maintenance of the Squatment as a Labor Reserve

To sustain this supply of labor at minimum cost, it is convenient for employers and government, whose interests are in this respect largely intertwined, to provide certain services to the workers and their families. These services fail to alleviate the gross inequalities between the classes. Indeed, by making life in the squatment a little easier, such practices contribute to the maintenance of social peace, while the layout and location of the Social Security Invasion are such as to reduce to a minimum its potential for a successful challenge to the established order.

A key to understanding of this pattern is observation of a six-day-a-week scene at the bus stop near the upper (Brasília–Belo Horizonte highway) entrance to the invasion.

While a majority of the many people who wait there take the public buses, many await the arrival of large trucks, which belong to construction companies and are used to bring the workers to the construction sites (see figs. 19, 20 and 21). Since the trucks usually stop first at other satellite towns, generally they arrive full. Only two companies provide trucks leaving directly from the Social Security Invasion.

At the stop, various groups, employed by different companies, await the arrival of the trucks, but they are intermingled and only separate from the crowd when their truck approaches. Generally the workers maintain an equal spacing, and do not carry on conversations. They maintain rigid postures and even a certain blank or angry expression.

When the truck belonging to a particular company approaches, more movement and murmuring begins as the group composed of those who are going to take the truck separates from the crowd and moves forward although they do not know exactly where their truck is going to come to a halt—they always move forward (toward the truck, which is coming up-hill).

Usually these trucks are open, but above them there is a canvas-covered wood frame, tentlike in appearance, covering the front half or two-thirds of the back of the truck. A ladder on the back of the truck facilitates climbing in.

When a truck comes to a halt, there is a scramble for position. The trucks are already crowded, but at the Invasion we observed as many as forty workers, self-proclaimed "peons" or "pawns" (*peões*), climb into a single truck.

Since the canvas superstructure in the front does not admit any air, and the disorientation of riding in the dark as the truck speeds around curves

TABLE XI
Means of Transportation to Work of Household Heads in the Social Security Invasion, 1967

Means of transportation	Percent
Public buses	44.4
Employer's vehicle	30.6
Walking	15.7
Bicycle	6.3
Others	3.0
TOTAL	100.0

Source: FSS 1967: 8.

is unpleasant, there is a struggle to get a position in the open area of the truck, a scramble to climb up. Some members of the group assist their coworkers, and each one, as he reaches the top, receives the customary pat on the back, a truncated version of the Brazilian *abraço* or greeting hug. The weaker ones and the latecomers, however, must ride in the front under the canvas.

In the evening, when the trucks return, the descent from truck is made with great enthusiasm and many of the workers are smiling. The stop is much shorter, and if one does not descend quickly from the vehicle he is liable to end up in Gama.

According to workers who ride in the trucks, the experience is distinctly unpleasant. They report fear, since accidents are frequent. The overloaded, top-heavy trucks, driven at excessive speeds, overturn easily. This fear is increased if one is inside the canvas area, since, it seems, the sharpness of curves is exaggerated if one lacks visual cues, and there are fewer places, inside, to hang on.

When we went out early in the morning to observe the scene, and took a number of photographs, many of the workers thought we were muck-raking journalists bent on exposing the inequities and dangers of this mode of transportation.[3]

The truck or other means of transportation provided by employers is the means of transportation of about a third of the household heads in the invasion, as shown in table XI. Undoubtedly the financial importance of this free transportation to the average worker is considerable. Assuming that only one bus is required, transportation to and from work would amount to nearly 10 percent of the minimum wage in Brasília; to many locations two buses must be taken.

This free transportation is of considerable importance to our argument that squatting is an integral (and not marginal, pathological, etc.) part of the political economy of the new capital. It has several characteristics which, as we shall see later, are far from unique: (*a*) It contributes something to the squatter involved that cannot be exchanged or sold. (*b*) The cost to the squatter of providing a substitute at his own expense would be high (in the case of a bus ride, as we have seen, nearly 10 percent of his wages). (*c*) The marginal cost to the employer, who needs the trucks anyway, is minimal, amounting to fuel for the route covered and, theoretically at least, added depreciation. (*d*) Free transportation contributes to the persistence of the squatment at the present site and to the provision of a steady stream of workers at the employer's construction site. To a degree, this pattern holds for the subsidized public transportation provided by the

3. Most of the data on commuting by truck was written up by Dilene M. Epstein (1967).

Brasília Collective Transport Ltd. (TCB—*Transportes Coletivos de Brasília Ltda.*), whose losses are financed out of taxes and inflation. Elimination of such transportation services might have consequences such as expanded squatting at construction sites, which are mostly in the Pilot Plan area, or a smaller or less steady flow of workers.

Examined from the "emic" point of view that concentrates on the material reality of behavior whether or not it contradicts the verbally communicated sense of meaning and fitness of the actors (Harris 1968: 557), free transportation, like the official promotion of the transfer of squatters from the Pilot Plan to the Social Security Invasion discussed in Chapter III, is a major contribution to the observed deviation of the settlement pattern of Brasília from the Costa plan. In the face of low wages and great distances, it contributes to the promotion of the economic well-being of the construction industry and to the political position of the officials connected with the construction programs. It also contributes to the economic survival of the workers at a level of satisfaction which, while low, is higher for a vast majority than that previously experienced.

The contribution of the construction industry to the housing of workers shares with free transportation the features discussed on the previous page. A common source of raw materials for the *barracos* (shacks, see Chapter IV, section III) in the Social Security Invasion is the discarded wood used as molds for the reinforced concrete apartment houses of the Pilot Plan. This is of very little value to the construction companies, since it is difficult to reuse and not profitable to sell; at the same time, the building materials for a shack, if bought new, are prohibitively expensive for a squatter. A man who rebuilt a comparatively small shack in 1967 reported paying over NCr$600 for materials, amounting to several months' wages for the typical squatter. Depending on the desirability of the location (proximity to water and—for commercial purposes—main pedestrian routes), a shack would sell for NCr$500 to NCr$2,000. So the gift of lumber is of little moment to the giver and of considerable worth to the receiver. At the same time it provides a functional requisite for the continued fixation of the needed large number of workers in the city: housing. At times the gift of lumber is complemented with transport of the material to the site; at other times the worker must hire a truck for the job.

In most areas, the relations between government agencies and the squatment show a similar pattern: minimal services are supplied, to the extent necessary to provide for the continuance of the community and to avoid social disruption, but the official bodies avoid taking responsibility for the settlement beyond this minimum.

Water supply is a case in point. There are three sources of water for most residents of the Invasion: (*a*) private wells; (*b*) public taps on a few streets, including Main Street; and (c) deliveries by tank trucks. Something less than one-sixth of the shacks have wells (*cisternas*), which are generally located in the backyards of the houses and may go down as much as fifty feet, although they are dug by hand. Few people use this water for drinking, since three-quarters of the houses do have pit latrines which undoubtedly contaminate the water. In addition, the water is usually muddy and quite unattractive. People who have such wells will usually lend water to neighbors. In the latter part of the dry season, August and September, the wells often run dry.

More common are the empty gasoline drums which are almost universally used as storage vessels for water, which is delivered weekly in most cases by tank trucks belonging to various agencies of the Prefecture, along regular routes. These tanks are obtained from gas stations, and they cost about NCr$30. They must be cleaned, and repainted from time to time to extend their active life. Many people use wooden or other covers on their tanks, which are grouped on a single side of each street every fifty yards or so, to facilitate delivery.

These tanks occasionally are the source of disputes between neighbors. One woman aroused the hostility of her neighbors because her children and grandchildren used the barrels as a play area and defecated near them from time to time. She was forced to move the barrels across the street, but the men who delivered the water complained, because this made their task more difficult. Finally, after much invective and intervention of the police, she moved her barrels to another cluster some fifty yards away.

More fortunate are those who live near a public tap. During the Goulart administration, a group of informal leaders from the area prevailed upon the Prefecture to lay a small one-inch water line along the Main Street. This connected with the water supply of the Free Town and Vila Tenório, which comes, unpurified, from the upper reaches of Vicente Pires creek. The motive for this supply was ostensibly to supply the schools which are located on this thoroughfare. Nominally this continues to be their function, but a much larger proportion of the water is undoubtedly consumed at the half-dozen public taps which draw on this pipeline. Throughout the daylight hours there are lines of people, mostly women and children, collecting water from these taps, especially in the lower reaches of the system where the water pressure is higher. In the dry season, the taps are in use even in the early hours before dawn.

The usual vehicle for transporting water is the five-gallon kerosene can, frequently adapted by removal of the top and the installation of a wooden handle. Pails are also used at times. Some women carry the cans on their heads, but many others use their hands or homemade carts and wheelbarrows.

There are many small boys who bring water from the taps to their own homes and earn small sums by bringing it to the homes of others. On occasion boys under ten will bathe naked under the tap.

One merchant, whose store is located on Main Street, improvised an ingenious method of supplying water to his own house without carrying it. He cut a tap into the main line, and when he wishes to fill his barrels, he attaches a flexible garden hose to it and fills them.[4] This practice was a source of envious and angry comments by his neighbors, because at one time he had a public tap in front of his store but had not permitted anyone to use it, and had bullied several children who tried, throwing their pails on the ground. This action led to angry words with the children's father. The people say, "God's the one who gives the water, and it belongs to everyone." This merchant contends that the children who come to take the water are disorderly and bad for business. In this particular case, some people complained to the Water and Sewers Department, and an inspector finally required the merchant to make some changes in his system and to use it only at night, because it was supposedly responsible for a drop in water pressure at the schools.

This water, incidentally, may be one source of the widespread gastrointestinal infections in the squatment, especially, though not exclusively, among the children (and anthropologists). Reports the *Correio Braziliense* of the water supply:

Hundreds of shacks in the "invasion" of the Vicente Pires creek, in addition to various pig farms, are threatening the population of the Free Town, since it is this stream which supplies that satellite town with water, without any treatment.

In its headwaters, tens of people bathe, do laundry, and empty every sort of waste. The majority of the invaders cultivate small crops of corn, manioc, papaya, tomato, lettuce, etc. . . . The vast majority of the invaders is made up of poor people and lives in the most complete lack of hygiene, in crowded, rustic shacks.

Among the residents are sick people, the case of a young girl being known who suffers from Hansen's disease [leprosy] and bathes there. In addition, the creek is a substitute for toilets, which do not exist in the shacks of the "invasion."

It is this water which the population of the Free Town [and the Social Security Invasion] uses . . . (June 10, 1967).

A later story reports that the Health Secretariat recommends the boiling of the water in the Free Town, which, unlike that of Taguatinga, Sobradinho, and the Pilot Plan, cannot be drunk without danger (June 13, 1967).

A lesser source of water is a natural spring which comes from a hillside near the entrance to the squatment on Main Street, which is used mainly

4. Walter Szczepanek (personal communication) reports a similar practice in a squatment in Caracas, Venezuela.

for washing clothes, although on occasion one can see women carrying the water on their heads in spite of the steep hill leading from the spring. The spring was linked to some old pipe obtained from the nearby hospital at the instance of an old lady, who organized a group of neighbors to do the job, and construct a platform where washing is done with the water. Now this woman also claims a special right to the water, a claim disputed by others who argue that water, supplied by God, belongs to everyone equally.

During our stay, trenches were dug at one extremity of the squatment for additional pipes and taps, but most of these were abandoned and silted up; pipe finally was laid only along a single street. According to informants in the government, this abortive effort was a result of indecision as to whether there would be serious attempts to eliminate the squatment in the near future. The installation of such seemingly permanent services as water would tend to undermine any attempt at removal of the squatment.

Similar considerations, as well as simple economics, underlay the failure to provide such services as garbage collection, sewage, and electricity. The latter two are financed by special charges to homeowners or to the managements of apartment houses. Most squatters would be unable to pay for them; as a result, they are not provided and the people must make do with substitutes.

Garbage is burned, buried, or thrown in the street or down the deep gully that cuts into Main Street. Dogs and chickens scavenge, but what residents report as an official prohibition on pigs, in order to prevent the spread of parasites, seems to be largely effective. We only knew of one pig in the squatment. Rats are common.

Sewage is largely disposed of in home-dug pits in the backyards, which may account for the luxuriance of many of the gardens, as well as the high incidence of gastrointestinal disease. When a pit of this kind is full, people simply cover it up and dig another.

Most people use kerosene lamps, both homemade ones made from cans and small bottles, and the commercial variety; candles are also used. Transistor radios run on batteries and treadle-operated sewing machines are common. A small minority of people (about 5 percent) purchase electricity from small diesel-powered generators which run from dusk to about 10:30 P.M. daily. Wires from these private establishments crisscross the squatment. Generally they are hooked to light bulbs, radios, and, in a few instances, television sets. The operators charge monthly rates (in advance) based on the number of watts of equipment a person has installed. For three light bulbs we had to pay almost U.S.$4 monthly. Many of the customers are merchants who hope the lights will attract customers in the evening.

As well as being suited to the provision of a steady stream of laborers at low wages for the construction industry and other menial roles, the location of the squatment is suited to the rapid repression of any effort its residents, stimulated by their economic deprivation and political power-lessness, might make to challenge the status quo through riot or rebellion. We have seen in Chapter II that one of the expressed motivations for the transfer of the capital from Rio de Janeiro was a desire to remove the functioning of the central government from the pressure of the problems, and the potential for socially motivated disorder, of the old capital. Now one of the features of the Brasília plan is that the geography of the new city does not favor disorder of any kind, and provides, even more than the boulevards of Paris, a military situation that could be easily controlled by a small, trained, and well-armed military force. This is tacitly recog-nized by people in Brasília who are concerned with such matters, both those responsible for and those desiring to disrupt the present social order.

Whereas in Rio de Janeiro a reservoir of at least potential rioters or rebels is to be found in the squatter settlements, some on hilltop sites and dominating major strategic points in the city (major nodes in the trans-portation and communication networks and near middle- and upper-class neighborhoods), Brasília's squatments possess no such potential. After the 1964 coup, the relocation program eliminated such potential as had existed previously, concentrating the squatter population in the Social Se-curity Invasion. While this squatment does lie at the confluence of two major interurban routes, excellent and secure bypasses exist, and the lay-out of the squatment makes it easy to control entry and exit with a few police detachments. The orderly and broad street layout provides a con-trast to the narrow and winding streets, alleys, and stairways of most Rio squatments.

Little direct evidence is available on the place of conscious military security considerations in the formulation of official policy with respect to squatting as such. The prominence of these matters in the outlook of the military establishment is evident, however. Consider the following, from the *Correio Braziliense* of May 26, 1967:

Two thousand men from the 11th Military Region, the Guard Battalion, the Army Police, and the 6th . . . Battalion from Ipameri, since yesterday are carrying out war and guerrilla maneuvers in the Sobradinho–Planaltina region.

At the same time there is being developed an action of Civic-Social char-acter with help for the population of that region, consisting in the provision of food, bridge- and road-building, houses in addition to other teaching [*sic*] . . .

There is evidence that the efficacy of removal as an anticrime security measure was considered. The presence of *demi-monde* elements in some of the Pilot Plan squatments was cited by middle-class petitioners whose pressure was confessedly one factor in the official decision to implement the relocation program.

It should be noted that the University of Brasília, which precedent in various Latin American countries might suggest as an even more likely candidate than the squatter areas as a source of political agitation, riot, and rebellion, is isolated in its campus, surrounded by *cerrados*, to an even greater extent than the Social Security Invasion. In spite of a (possibly deserved) reputation for political radicalism, the University has never been a source of major disorders, and has with little difficulty been surrounded and occupied by the military on various occasions.

It might be argued that the relative success of the mass resistance by squatters to attempts to remove them from locations in the Social Security Invasion is evidence against the geographic argument presented here. It is arguable, however, that under the special conditions prevailing in the Goulart Administration it was the official desire to appear as champions of the workingman and the publicity that threatened to undermine this image that were most effective. Yet in each case, the specific area which was intended to be cleared, was cleared; concessions dealt with the place to which the workers were to be transferred, not with the fact of the removal itself.

These geographical conditions and the presence of large numbers of federal troops in the capital, whose number is increased in step with the transfer of other governmental agencies, have perhaps obviated the need for any day-to-day police activity in the squatment on "national security" (that is, political) grounds. Indeed, while a shack was built in the squatment to serve as a police post, it was rarely occupied. Two policemen were dispatched to provide support for the removal of squatters from the Pilot Plan and other areas to the Social Security Invasion, but there were, for instance, no foot patrolmen or motor vehicles regularly assigned to the area.

Not always is there, on the other hand, reluctance on the part of squatters to involve the police in local disputes. The police post in the Free Town is frequently called upon to intervene in disputes between neighbors or in family quarrels. The usual result is a lecture by the *delegado,* or at worst being held overnight in jail. The squatters consider this somewhat dishonorable; as one woman said to us, in pejorative reference to a neighbor who had been run in for petty theft, "My ass never polished a station-house bench."

On the other hand, a woman who was being beaten unmercifully by her husband berated her neighbors for having called in the police, when, as a result, the husband was carted off to jail.

Police intervention is common in the Vulture Hill region, where prostitution, fights, marijuana (*maconha*), and public intoxication are common, as well as the hiding of criminals. Generally these activities have been tolerated, and occasion a steady stream of vehicular traffic toward the area, especially on weekend nights. From time to time, however, the police declare war on the district, with great fanfare in the press. Closings of bars, police raids, and motorized patroling increase. On one occasion officers of the military police, accompanied by an entire truckload of troops, appeared outside our house asking where Vulture Hill was located. They were not sure of its location, but they had decided that they would investigate the possibilities.

Since public notice of arrests and crimes of violence seem to recur, no matter how many times the area is "cleaned out," it is easy to become somewhat cynical about extinguishing in Brasília a type of zone of activity that exists consistently everywhere there are urban societies which maintain patterns of lasting and severe social inequality. Segregating such phenomena and providing occasional evidence of the preponderance of police power would seem to be an efficient and relatively inexpensive technique of social control.

CHAPTER VI

Brasília in Context

Many current treatments of urban poverty both inside and outside the United States, as well as of rural communities in the colonial and semi-colonial countries, focus their principal investigative energies and explanatory attention upon internal characteristics of individual social isolates, whether these be individuals, rural communities, families, neighborhoods, or neighborhood segments. While all the entities which are the subject of discourse in the social sciences are ultimately derived from observation and recording of the behaviors, verbal and nonverbal, emitted by individuals in localized settings, and the examination of localized social systems (communities and others) has been and no doubt will continue to be a major source of insight into human social behavior, in this historical epoch no explanation of poverty and underdevelopment can be derived exclusively from research which fails to take into account the general features of the national and global social systems. In an urban setting, the urban social system as a whole must be taken into account as well.

From a historical viewpoint, many features of the Brazilian regional and local ecological systems, social stratification, economy, and ideology (including such areas as literature, the arts, social science, and fashion) developed in ways intimately connected to Brazil's position as a satellite to a succession of international metropolitan powers, a position from which Brazil produced successively such commodities as sugar, minerals, cacao, natural rubber, coffee, sisal, and iron ore. The influence of the export-oriented plantation system, for example, on Brazilian social structure, national character, and ideology is a case in point (Freyre 1946).

It might be argued that in contemporary Brazil the growth of industrial production in the Paraíba Valley and elsewhere has diminished the integration of Brazil into the global society, but examination of the international auspices of much of this industrialization (Black 1968; Frank 1964; Gordon 1961; Locker 1968; Vinhas de Queiroz 1965) suggests that the form of Brazilian integration into the international political economy has changed more than its subordinate position. Examination of such

171

items as the brand names of common products, trends influenced by the mass media, and intellectual fads suggests, that the derivative character of many important aspects of Brazilian culture has not diminished either, in spite of recurrent campaigns and movements, especially among intellectuals, in that direction.

None of the above is intended to be a denigration of the worth of the Brazilian people or a dismissal of its many creations and achievements, above all in the area of popular culture. The international stratification system has produced analogous results throughout Latin America, Asia, and Africa, and may be promoting a similar pattern in Western Europe as well (Servan-Schreiber 1968). Vidich and Bensman (1958) observe that relative powerlessness and lack of autonomy seem to characterize a small North American community also. In all these cases, understanding the situation in its many ramifications is a necessary (though far from sufficient) condition for carrying out changes which might permit the rise of a higher degree of creativity and richness of cultural expression in the area studied.

It is thus reasonable to assume the utility of examining the lower socioeconomic strata in terms of the full range of social stratification, and the dependent members of metropolis-satellite relations in terms of the full system of dominant and dependent parties. The contrary emphasis upon the internal characteristics of dependent social units, with but scant reference to the matrix in which they are located, tends to produce a view of their situation which attributes their position (poverty in the case of individuals and families, underdevelopment in the case of regions and nation-states) to their own characteristics, especially their values, beliefs, and psychological motivations. These characteristics, from a systemic, historical point of view, can be looked at as the products, rather than the causes, of the differential enjoyment of wealth, power, and social prestige. It is precisely this nonsystemic outlook, often ahistorical as well, which has dominated much contemporary North American social science research in the countries of Asia, Africa and Latin America. What Martin Nicolaus says of sociology may be extended to other academic disciplines as well: ". . . the eyes of sociologists, with few but honorable (or: honorable but few) exceptions, have been turned downwards, and their palms upwards" (Nicolaus 1968). That is to say, while they are recipients of funds and institutional status derived from those at the upper pole of the stratification system, they focus their attention on the characteristics of the people on the bottom, and the information produced, like most of the other goods of the society, is more readily available to those with wealth and power than to those without.

This downward-looking view also characterizes popular views of squat-

ting held by North Americans, who usually think of it in terms of the
favelas of Rio de Janeiro. As with much of Asia, Africa, and Latin
America, Brazilian squatter settlements are thought of either as symbols
of the abject misery, backwardness, and lack of enlightenment of the
country, or, contrariwise, as the exotic abodes of poor but fun-loving
devotees of the samba, Afro-Brazilian cults, and restrained eroticism.

These views are also common in Brazil, and are reflected in popular
lyrics:

> Ugly, it isn't pretty,
> The favela exists but asks to be done away with.

> (Feio, não é bonito,/O morro existe mas pede para
> se acabar.)

And *Chão de Estrêlas* (*Stars on the Floor*) by Orestes Barbosa, one of
the most famous Brazilian popular songs:

> The door to our shack didn't even have a latch,
> But the moon, shining through the holes in the
>   zinc roof,
> Sprinkled stars on the floor.
> You stepped on the stars, oblivious,
> Never knowing that happiness in this life
> Is a woman, the moonlight and a guitar.

> (A porta do barraco era sem trinco,/Mas a lua
> furando nosso zinco,/Salpicava de estrêlas
> nosso chão./Tu pisavas nos astros distraída,/
> Sem saber que a ventura desta vida/E a cabrocha,
> o luar, e o violão.)

While these views seem to derive from ignorance born from snobbish
superiority or romanticism, they have their parallels in two schools of
thought entertained by social science professionals, both of which provide
partially erroneous and partially correct factual accounts and explanations
of the phenomenon of urban squatting in Brazil and elsewhere in the
Third World (more accurately, the subordinate half of the First World).
The errors of both schools, to a degree, are the result of a failure to consider squatting in relation to the larger social structure of which its practitioners are only a part.

The first school was discussed in some detail in the first chapter. While
there are many differences of emphasis and phraseology, a short synthesis
would state that these writers look upon squatting as the pathological pole
of a fundamental urban dualism. For some it is the locus of disease, crime,

anomie, and political instability; for others, rurality is its salient feature, on occasion the basis for denominating squatments as the homes of sub- or microcultures. Various forms of pure or impure psychological determinism look upon the failure of squatters to adopt the life-style of bankers, generals, or even clerks as a consequence of a failure to develop a need for achievement (a concept elucidated in McClelland 1961); or it is attributed to early acquisition of a perhaps originally economically based but ultimately self-perpetuating "culture of poverty."

The contrary view emphasizes the adaptive and even conservative characteristics of urban squatting, and grew up as empirical studies by sophisticated observers began to show the error contained in many of the generalizations and explanations provided by the pathologist-dualist school discussed above. These writers (see, e.g., Mangin 1963, 1964, 1965, 1967; and Turner 1963, 1966) emphasize the adaptive characteristics of squatter settlements and their evolution, which often leads them past initial challenges to their land tenure to a high degree of stability as urban neighborhoods. Often these authors defend the squatters against exaggerated imputations of criminality and other forms of social deviance, which they show to be lower in squatments than in the central-city slum (Rotondo and others 1963; Goldrich and others 1966). Some writers emphasize that except on the issue of land tenure, squatters tend to be politically centrist or even conservative (Bourricard 1964; Halperin 1965; Peattie 1966). Like many anthropologists, these "optimists" identify with their informants and look askance at uncritical schemes to "eradicate" squatting, establish public housing, and "reform" squatters (Safa 1964), and emphasize the relative satisfaction of the migrants with the squatment as opposed to his place of origin, especially when that is rural (Herrick 1965; Germani 1961).

Each of these perspectives contains some elements of value. Although its proponents are often politically conservative, the pathologist-dualist viewpoint is based upon the blatant economic and social inequality which pervades every phase of urban life in those cities where squatting is observed, often made painfully apparent to the outsider by the close juxtaposition of shabby squatter settlements and luxury apartments, as in Rio de Janeiro, or by contrast with such ultramodern architecture as dominates the center of Brasília. The more optimistic adaptationist view is founded ultimately upon the observation that in society people usually have motivations in some sense rational for the strategies and practices they adopt, and proximately based upon ethnographic fieldwork (often of high quality) that finds the reasons. As we have seen in Brasília, squatting is often a good strategy (or the best available) for people in certain social situations, to the point where public housing cannot compete with it as a solution to the housing problems of the urban poor. This is so with respect to the atmosphere of social life, terms of payment (in public housing, usually inflexible), location (generally inconvenient), and rules (which often fail to make allowance for such fundamentals as occupational multiplicity).

A general criticism of the first school, stated in the first chapter and borne out by the study of squatting in Brasília, is that it takes the special features of squatting to constitute, or to result from, a failure on the part of squatters to become integrated into urban society, when in fact it is not a failure to integrate but the *form* taken by their integration which is at stake, and ultimately responsible for the contrast between squatment and luxury apartment.

The main criticism to be raised against the optimist viewpoint that squatting is adaptive, or functional, for its practitioners and society as a whole, is that in demonstrating that squatting is a viable strategy of survival or even of upward mobility it tends to deemphasize the fact that squatters remain at or near the bottom of a highly polarized urban social structure; they are upward mobile but rarely climb very far. While their perception of the value of squatting and of its characteristics is different, the optimists, like the pathologist-dualists, tend to lose sight of squatting in relation to society as a whole. It is precisely upon this relation that I have focused in the present study.

The generalized, systemic emphasis of this study runs counter to much, though far from all, of the recent production of North American anthropology. This emphasis to a degree did prevent the gathering of much data in certain standard ethnographic categories such as religion, that would no doubt be of considerable literary and scientific interest. If to some extent I have sacrificed to the generality and scope of the subject matter a more refined, specific, and thorough use of the tools perfected by distant and immediate anthropological predecessors, I can only reply that it was my conviction that in this case I should apply to academic anthoropology the words Paul Baran addressed to his fellow economists: "It would certainly seem desirable to break with the time-honored tradition of academic economics of sacrificing the relevance of subject-matter to the elegance of analytical method; it is better to deal imperfectly with what is important than to attain virtuoso skill in the treatment of what does not matter" (Baran 1957: 22).

In the case of Brasília, there may be found on the level of the national and international stratification systems patterns of interests, practices, and ideology which determined many of the features of the architectural plan and its execution, including the following: (*a*) the monumentalist emphasis on dramatic architecture and broad vistas; (*b*) the favoring of automotive circulation in spite of the fact that cars remain a luxury for the vast majority of the Brazilian population; (c) only cursory attention being paid to the needs and desires of the first residents (the construction workers) and to the lower-class residents in general; (d) the nondevelopmental, static, or skeletal character of the plan, expressed as a final output rather than a process of growth which at all stages would involve human lives; (e) the necessity, given prevailing political practice in Brazil, of finishing the city according to plan within a three-year period (Kubitschek's Presidential mandate) if it was not to be later abandoned; (f) the centralized character of the planning and execution processes themselves, with no provision for consultation or participation by any but upper-level technical and political personnel. Moreover, the central fact of in-migration, its scope and direction, arose and persisted as a consequence of the polarization of Brazilian society between the internal metropolis of São Paulo and the regional satellites in the Northeast and Center-West, between city and country. Like the Mezzogiorno in Italy, Mozambique in Southern Africa, the Andes in Peru, and Puerto Rico in the United States, these satellites have become breeding areas that supply in-migrant laborers to more prosperous areas for the filling of the least prestigious and most poorly rewarded economic and social roles.

There were further motivations, in the case of Brasília, for emphasizing data reflecting on the total urban, national, and international context, rather than on an isolate such as the Social Security Invasion, one or a number of families, or voluntary associations. The first of these is that much of the worldwide interest in Brasília stems from the hope that in the "planned" nature of the city and in the specific features of the plan may be found lessons which may be applied to the desperate urban crises affecting both the developed and underdeveloped capitalist countries and to some degree at least the East bloc countries as well. To understand the deviations from the plan and its utilities and defects requires some examination of the features of the plan and the process by which it was (partly) put into effect and changed in practice. The city-wide character of these areas of concern is exemplified by the fact that it was the construction of the planned center—the government buildings and superblocks—which provided, in the form of effective demand for labor, the *raison d'etre* for the massive in-migration and the establishment of the Free Town, Vila Amaurí, and other peripheral settlements.

The squatments and to a considerable extent the satellite towns serve as reserves, at little cost to the employers, where large numbers of workers may be maintained; proximity to lines of transportation permits their access to the work sites; high unemployment rates depress wages; domestic service and commercial work are available to diminish the effects of (and potential reactions against) this unemployment and ease the burdens of the middle and upper classes; official pressure permits the squatting to be confined to areas of low visibility to the outsider and at a distance from the middle-class zones sufficient to reduce casual contact between the classes; and the location, terrain, and settlement pattern are such as to facilitate military and police measures to repress or contain riot and rebellion should they arise. At the same time, the formal official condemnation of squatting as an evil to be eradicated permits the capital to maintain its symbolic "developmentist" associations in the eyes of the middle class.

On the other hand, from the viewpoint of the in-migrants, the relatively high economic rewards they were and are able to obtain in Brasília as opposed to the Northeast, especially its rural sector, and in the rural sector of the Center-West—reflecting, as has been stated, the polarization characteristic of most large capitalist countries—as well as the generally higher level of public services (education, health, social security), make the situation appear to be one of upward mobility. Squatting, by eliminating the need for payment of rent and property taxes, enhances their economic position, and in particular provides a form of security in an unstable labor market characterized by frequent firings, retarded paychecks (due in part to the dependence of the construction industry on political decisions), and other insecurities. The physical form of the shack permits it to be expanded in accord with the changes in family size and unanticipated receipts of funds. It may also be used as a business asset: a store, a sewing business, a rented store, or as a source of capital through its sale should the owner decide to move elsewhere.

The worldwide spread of squatting also gives the lie to the frequent elitist assumptions of social scientists. While at least in Brasília squatting did not provide a base for political mobilization in the sense of formal organization and ideological development, the whole experience suggests an active, creative response by lower-class people to their situation. While relatively powerless and short of resources, the squatters in Brasília are not fatalist or unmotivated putty whose fate depends exclusively upon the whim or wisdom of an elite. The squatter, as well as the university-trained planner and the politician, is an actor in the making of history—even if his or her activity follows the prescriptions of no preconceived ideology.

As for the question of what lessons the Brasília experience offers to those who would deal with the urban problems of many countries throughout the world, one implication of this study is that the construction of Brasília has fallen short of many of its declared goals. Further, the values and practices of planners themselves (and of those who select, approve, and determine the manner of execution of the plans) are subject to influences which prevent certain aspects of social life from being taken fully into account in the planning process. Notably, the standards of urban form and amenity to which the planners pay lip service are derived from the reality of Europe and North America, while scant attention is paid to the implications of the economic status, lifeways, and day-to-day existence of the majority of the population of the country, let alone to finding out the desires of the lower class. These biases reflect the urban, professional status of the planners, their position as servants of the ruling minority in a highly stratified society, and the semicolonial position of Brazil as a whole.

On these grounds, given the differential distribution of wealth and power between the developed and underdeveloped countries and the higher and lower social strata in the latter countries, and the associated ideology as they affect the methods (such as the public workers complex) and goals (monumentalist, symbolic, elite-oriented) of city-building, it is doubtful that the manipulation of bricks, mortar, and asphalt, according to the implicit social criteria mentioned above and explicit esthetic and engineering criteria, is likely significantly to increase the social homogeneity, demographic stability, or general welfare of the majority of urbanites. Planning in practice, under these conditions, remains fundamentally a prop to the life-style of the upper minority. While the question is beyond the bounds of the present inquiry, there are grounds for making analogous statements about planning in the United States as well.

Let it be understood that the conclusion of the study is not that the Brasília project was a failure or that Lúcio Costa and his associates should be condemned. Fulfillment of their highest pretensions was impossible; indeed, one suspects that some of the pretensions were rhetorical.

Brasília is an old idea, a dream brought to rapid fruition in the space of a single Presidential term. Following the political eclipse of her promoter, Brasília nevertheless continued to exist and to grow throughout the extended period of political conflict that prevailed under Presidents Jânio Quadros and João Goulart, and the resolution of that conflict with the military rule of Marshall-President Humberto Castelo Branco and his successor, Artur da Costa e Silva.

What Brasília is not and does not seem likely to become is a city which would transcend the frustrations of urban life in the underdeveloped world, no longer manifesting the typical contrast between the skyscraper and the shack, the broad avenues of the downtown and the dank alleys of the squatments and suburbs.

For, just as we have contended that the rise and persistence of the squatter settlements in Brasília are a manifestation of the structural characteristics of Brazilian society, so also we suggest that squatting is not amenable to eradication by any administrative or financial measures within the reach of those responsible for the government of the new capital, for so long as the basic structure of the society persists. Resettlement schemes will run up against the economic, political, and social imbalance between city and country, deeply ingrained in practice and in popular expectations. It would be simply quixotic to suppose that any large numbers of urbanites (even squatters) would consent to return to the economic exploitation, isolation, and lack of social services that characterize rural Brazil under present conditions. Furthermore, any resettlement scheme, however well planned on paper, is subject to the uncertainties of administrative discontinuity; its chances of surviving a Presidential mandate are small. Even the most optimistic proponents of rural resettlement admit that stringent restrictions on the type of people who would be selected for subsidy and loans would be required.

The same is true, albeit to a lesser extent, of rehousing schemes, which have been tried on a fairly large scale in Brasília. Indeed, the tacit official acceptance of the growth of the Social Security Invasion (made manifest by the transfers of families to that area on official orders, in official vehicles) reflects an admission that at the income levels of many families, a pay-as-you-go plan, no matter how modest the house and long-term the payments, is impossible. Any decline in the rhythm of construction in Brasília, indeed, is likely to lead to widespread unemployment and defaulting on payments. It is possible to give housing away, of course, but to do so on a small scale is to make inevitable the exercise of political favoritism in the selection of recipients, and to fail to resolve the problem posed by those not so favored. Distribution of housing on a large scale would possibly lead to further in-migration (given the polarization of Brazilian society by regions and between city and country), and a renewed unemployment problem.

To mobilize the funds needed for a rehousing program on a *national* basis, combined with regional and rural development programs sufficient to stem or even reverse the migratory tides, would of course amount to a massive reorganization of national priorities, implying a shift in the power structure of the nation. Even if such a shift were forthcoming, it is highly doubtful that housing as such would receive a higher priority than such items as education, public health, and capital investment in production in industry and agriculture. Cuban development planning, for example, has given housing and urban development a very low priority.

The current emphasis on housing programs reflects, first, the continued viability of the public works complex. Association with brick-and-mortar projects has continued to be a sure route to higher political position. Such projects do not compete with private economic interests, but on the contrary, make possible the provision of major rewards, through government expenditure, to some private companies. And in a period characterized by economic stagnation, declining real wages, and political repression, it constitutes an "impact" project serving to suggest that the political groups in power do in fact have an interest in the well-being of the poor.

Only time will tell whether this symbolism is more effective with the middle class and the construction industry or with the squatters themselves, to whom, I believe, many things are more urgent than housing as such: the size of their paychecks, the price of food and clothing, educational opportunity for their children, the availability of medical care, and security of tenure where they have constructed their shacks. The pay-as-you-go housing scheme reduces the funds available for subsistence, since it requires a sizable monthly payment and often doubles the price of the journey to work. By requiring years of regular monthly payments in an uncertain labor market, rehousing also decreases, rather than increases, the squatters' sense of security. So it is possible that the political "impact" of housing schemes will not be what their proponents hope.

This is not to suggest that I have any evidence that the squatters of Brasília are a likely source of active political opposition to the established order in the near future (Epstein 1969, 1970). There is a widespread conception that the dark world of the slums and squatter settlements breeds bitter men whose long knives will one day slit the throat of an outdated and oppressive social order. The imagery is evocative and appeals in different ways to left and right alike.

Riots, legal-political maneuvers, and community organizing efforts in the squatter settlements of Latin America have not fulfilled the fondest dire predictions, which suggest that a capital-intensive import-substitution industrialization produces a relatively small and privileged proletariat (Quijano 1968), but generates a much more massive rural-urban migratory flow. The flow is further stimulated by the concentration of welfare services in the cities and by the changing cultural ecology of the countryside itself (e.g., the replacement of subsistence farming by commercial stock-raising). These migrants overshadow the traditional proletariat in social and political weight, and yet are thrown into "marginal" status and neighborhoods. Once the initial charms of city life wear off, the argument runs, these people will be ready to revolt. The French West Indian revolutionary Frantz Fanon, for example, saw this "urban lumpenproletariat" as a potentially revolutionary group (Worsley 1969: 39–40).

In Brasília, of course, industrialization in the manufacturing sense is insignificant, although it is the Paraíba Valley industrialization that made a Brasília possible. Furthermore, we have already seen the defects of the concept of marginalization. In addition, squatting has a number of integrative aspects which tend to envelop the squatter. These include electoral politics and political patronage, where elections are held. A remarkable parallelism in terminology exists; for example, Brazilian Portuguese *cabo eleitoral,* "ward heeler," literally "electoral corporal," corresponds to prerevolutionry Cuban Spanish *sargento electoral,* "electoral sergeant." These systems tie the most active elements of squatter populations directly into the official political system, with at least a token payoff. In attenuated form, even where elections are not present, bureaucratic blandishments and official privileges may be made available to the informal leadership of a squatter settlement in return for a cooperative attitude.

In many squatments, widespread voluntary associations develop. Certain types recur in most cities: hometown clubs, evangelical churches, athletic clubs, residents' associations; others are more localized, though they have parallels elsewhere, for example, the samba schools of Rio de Janeiro. In Brasília, the churches are the most evident of these groups, as far as formal organization is concerned.

In many large cities, organized crime, especially gambling and other "crimes without victims," may integrate certain elements into the social system. While formally opposed to the state, crime of this kind depends upon the property system and benefits from the social distance, inequality, and barriers separating lower-class communities and the state apparatus. In Brasília this kind of crime was relatively undeveloped, and spatially segregated within the squatment. Yet just as loosely integrated traditional peasant societies could tolerate and informally regulate chronic social banditry, crime in contemporary urban societies is a fundamentally "businesslike" enterprise which does not threaten the fabric of the social order,[1] and may even provide a channel for the most discontented and aggressive young people, who might otherwise be drawn to activist movements.

When political disputes involving squatters do arise, they are usually concerned with land tenure. Such disputes can end either with the destruction of the community, reducing its political weight as a community to zero, or the transformation of the group of squatters into de facto or de jure homeowners. Thus successful squatter movements provide the cleverest of their participants with a payoff and a vested interest in the society.

For many squatters, in Brasília, migration has meant, subjectively and objectively, an improvement in their situation. While they are aware (and

1. The traffic in "hard" drugs (opiates and barbiturates) may be an exception to this generalization. Neither type was important in Brazil in the sixties.

more so than they are usually inclined to state to a North American or to members of the middle class) of their subordinate position in the society and often identify it as an injustice, their perception of improvement is, perhaps, one basis for their relative political quiescence. What is less certain is whether, as the rhythm of construction in Brasília diminishes, as it must, and only a minority of squatters obtain economic stability through government employment, the establishment of businesses, or work in the few industries of the new capital, the economically defeated and those who grow up in the city (and thus lack any sense of relative improvement) will remain so passive. This question is a crucial one throughout Latin America. While skepticism about the immediate potential for political unrest among Brasília's squatters persists, we can legitimately ask about ". . . the political possibilities inherent in massive rural migrations to cities without industrial employment . . . the political opportunties among the new generation of slum dwellers who were born and raised in the *barriadas* [squatments] and who do not accept the marginal changes accompanying movement from a rural to an urban milieu . . ." (Petras 1969).

Whatever the future may bring, for the moment urban squatting remains an integral part of the social system of Brasília, Brazil, and the underdeveloped world in general. Far from being a mere survival of rural culture or an excrescence of local pathology, its causes go to the very roots of local, national, and global social structure and ideology. Given the realities of the system as a whole, squatting involves solutions to important immediate problems of both the lower class and the political and economic elite. Short of revolutionary changes in society at large, which do not seem to be an immediate prospect, squatting is thus likely to persist, in spite of pro forma attempts to eliminate it. Furthermore, squatting would have been well-nigh impossible to prevent, in some form, in the new capital.

Glossary

Words appear in the grammatical form used in the text. Place-names appear only if their literal meaning in Portuguese is of special interest. Extended verbatim expressions used once have been omitted. Literal meanings of idiomatic expressions appear in quotes.

abraço: hug, ritual greeting and leave-taking among male friends and relatives

acampamento: licensed construction camp

aipim: fresh sweet manioc (S. Brazil)

alagados: squatter settlements built over water in Salvador, Bahia

alvenaria: stucco construction

amasiado: in a consensual union

Asa da Morte: "Death Wing," pejorative slang term for *Asa Norte*, "North Wing"

auxílio: "aid," alms

baiano: Bahian, and in São Paulo, any Northeastern in-migrant

bairro: neighborhood

bandeira: "flag," exploratory expedition setting out from São Paulo in colonial times

bar: "bar," coffeeshop, corner store

barraco: shack, usually of wood, typical of squatter and lower-class housing

barriada: Spanish for squatter settlements of Lima, Peru

bicheiro: illegal lottery salesman

bico: "faucet," supplemental job or source of income

bidonville: French for squatter settlement

biscate: odd job

biscateiro: one who subsists on odd jobs

bloco: apartment building

Bôa Vontade: "Good Will," a social movement in the Free Town prior to the military coup of 1964; also the unconnected quasi-religious movement led by Alziro Zarur

bôbo: fool, cretin

cabeça de pôrco: "pig's head"; overcrowded slum rental housing; derives from a house of the same name in turn-of-the-century Rio de Janeiro

cabelo bom: "good hair," i.e., straight hair

cachaça: sugarcane liquor

camelo: hawker, street vendor

campo cerrado: "closed country," woodland savanna found in Brazil's Central Plateau *candango*: inmigrant construction worker in Brasília

carioca: native of Rio de Janeiro city

casa embriao: "embryo house," i.e., core house

castanha-do-pará: Brazil nut

castanho: brown

cerrado: see *campo cerrado*

cidades satélites: satellite towns

cidadezinha: "little city," a somewhat pejorative use of the diminutive

cisterna: water well

cobertura: "coverage," political protection or favors from above

contador: counter, accountant

coronel: "colonel," in rural areas a political boss and/or major landowner

coronelismo: rural political bossism

correção monetaria: adjustment of mortgages or other obligations according to the rate of inflation

cortiço: "beehive," overcrowded rental slum housing

delegado: police chief, usually a lawyer, with quasi-judicial function

desenvolvimentismo: "developmentism," the slogan of the Kubitschek government

direitos adquiridos: "acquired rights," e.g., of civil servants

distrito: "district," subdivision of a *municipio* or the seat of such a subdivision

dobradinha: bonus offered to civil servants who transferred to Brasília

doce: "sweet," any sugared food, such as candy, cakes, biscuits, etc.

doce de leite: caramel

empreguismo: "handing-over-ism," a leftist term implying submission to imperialist interests

esmola: alms

estabilidade: security of employment under Brazilian labor law

Estado Nôvo: "New State," the first Getulio Vargas government, especially after the authoritarian constitution of 1937

estupidez: rudeness

falta de verbas: "lack of funds," a common excuse for governmental inefficiency

farinha: flour, usually manioc flour

favela: squatter settlement, especially in Rio de Janeiro

fiscal, fiscais: inspector(s)

feira: open-air market, often held weekly

fôgo selvagem: a skin disease prevalent in rural Goiás

funcionário público: civil servant

ganhando um lote: obtaining a permanent lot

habite-se: official certificate of occupancy

igrejinha: "little church," an informal patronage-sharing unit grouped around a superordinate personage

Inconfidência Mineira: proindependence conspiracy of 1789, in Minas Gerais

indenização: indemnity, e.g., in the event of loss of a job after legal security of employment (*estabilidade*) has been achieved

indústria das secas: "drought industry," political patronage and graft derived from public works against the Northeast's frequent droughts

invadir: "invade," squat

invasão: "invasion," squatting, a squatter settlement

jeitinho: a subterfuge or "fix"

Juiz de Menores: Minors' judge

lá em cima, lá em haixo: "up there," "down there," a common spatial division in rural Brazilian towns

loteamento: real estate subdivision

Limpeza Pública: Sanitation, and the squatter settlement of the same name in Brasília

macaxera: fresh sweet manioc (N. Brazil)

maconha: marijuana

mandato: term of office of a public official, usually not renewable

mandato de reintegração de posse: a lawsuit to regain possession of property

marcha para oeste: "Westward March," the idea that settling the interior is the key to Brazilian economic development

marginal: in crime reporting, a low-life, a ne'er-do-well

marginalidade: marginality, the idea that a given group is outside the social system

Maria Fumaça: "Smoky Mary," an old-fashioned steam locomotive

mascate: door-to-door salesman

mocambo: squatter settlement (Recife)

morrendo de fome: starving

Morro do Urubu: "Vulture Hill," the red-light zone of Social Security

movimento: urban hustle and bustle

município: the basic unit of local government in Brazil, usually a city or small town and its immediate hinterland

mutirão: rural labor-sharing custom, common in the Northeast

obras: physical public works

oeste: west

pai dos pobres: "father of the poor," Getulio Vargas

panelinha: "little pot," an informal horizontal patronage-sharing unit

patrão: boss, patron; often a paternalistic figure in an asymmetrical but personalistic dyadic relationship, especially in rural areas

pau-de-arara: "parrot perch," a truck converted for passenger transportation; by extension, any Northeastern in-migrant in Southern Brazil

pelego: intermediary in the Ministry of Labor's clientele system

pensão: boardinghouse

peões: peons, pawns; lower-class men

picaretagem: writings or statements designed to garner favor with superiors or political patrons; "yes-man-ism"

picolé: icepop

Placas de Mercedes: "Mercedes Signs," an area of the Free Town marked by billboards nearby

político mineiro: "Minas Gerais politicians," noted for astuteness and opportunism

Prefeito: Mayor

promiscuidade: unsanitary overcrowding

procedência: prior place of residence; where a person came from *quebrar o galho*: "break the branch," solve the problem

roça: slash-and-burn or swidden cultivation, or a plot so cultivated; any rural area
rouba mas faz: "He steals but he builds," political slogan of São Paulo ex-Governor Adhemar de Barros

sede de municipio: seat of a *municipio*
sertão: countryside, especially the arid backlands of the Northeast
sigla: acronym
Sorbonne: slang for the Upper War College (Escola Superior de Guerra) in Rio
superquadra: superblock

técnicos: technical personnel, technocrats
tipógrafo: typography
topógrafo: topographer
trabalhista: "laborite," usually a supporter of the *Partido Trabalhista Brasileiro* (PTB), the Brazilian Labor Party, or an allied smaller party
tubinho: a simply cut dress, popular among lower-class women

unidade de vizinhança: neighborhood unit, within the Residential Axis of the Pilot Plan
urbanismo: city planning
urbanização: "urbanization," referring to the provision of public works and services, and the extension of legal status to an area
utilidade pública: "public utility," a legal status of property, often prior to expropriation

Vila Vampiro: "Vampire Town," slang for Vila São Joao in Gama
vinte-oito: "twenty-eight," the (28-story) Congressional office towers
vitamina: milkshake, usually made with avocado or other fruits

References Cited

ALEXANDER, CHRISTOPHER
    1966   A city is not a tree. Design 206: 46–55.

BARAN, PAUL A.
    1957   The political economy of growth. New York: Monthly Review Press.

BARAN, PAUL A., and PAUL M. SWEEZY
    1966   Monopoly capital: an essay on the American economic and social order. New York: Monthly Review Press.

BASTIDE, ROGER
    1964   Ethnologie des capitales latino-americaines. Caravelle 3: 73–84.

BELL, PETER
    1966   Public administration and development. *In* Robert Levine, ed., Brazil: field research guide in the social sciences. New York: Institute of Latin American Studies, Columbia University, 148–164.

BLACK, CYRIL EDWIN
    1966   The dynamics of modernization. New York: Harper and Row.

BLACK, EDIE ("EDB")
    1968   The Hanna industrial complex. NACLA Newsletter 2 (3): 1–5; 2 (4): 1–7; 2 (7): 1–7 (part 3 with Fred Goff).

BOEKE, J. H.
    1953   Economics and economic policy of dual societies. New York: Institute of Pacific Relations.

BONILLA, FRANK
    1962   The favelas of Rio: the rundown rural bairro in the city. Dissent 9: 383–386.

BOURRICARD, FRANÇOIS
    1964   Lima en la vida política peruana. America Latina, October-December.

CB—CORREIO BRAZILIENSE
    Daily newspaper, Brasília.
CALLADO, ANTONIO
    1960   Os industriais da sêca e os "Galileus" de Pernambuco. Rio:
            Editôra Civilização Brasileira.
CONJUNTURA ECONÔMICA: ECONOMICS AND BUSINESS IN BRAZIL
    1962   Public expenses—Brasília 9 (12): 47–53.
COSTA, LÚCIO
    1957   Relatório do Plano Pilôto. Revista brasileira dos municipios
            10: 41–44.
    1962   Sobre arquitetura. Porto Alegre: Faculdade de Arquitetura.
CRULS, LUIS
    1957   Planalto central do Brasil. Rio de Janeiro: Editora Jose
            Olímpio, Coleção Documentos Brasileiros 91 (reprint).
CRUZEIRO
    Weekly illustrated magazine. São Paulo.
DCN—DIARIO DO CONGRESSO NACIONAL
    Rio de Janeiro and Brasília: Imprensa Nacional (Brazil).
DOU—DIARIO OFICIAL DA UNIÃO
    Rio de Janeiro and Brasília: Imprensa Nacional (Brazil).
DASGUPTA, SAMIR
    1964   Underdevelopment and dualism—a note. Economic Devel-
            opment and Cultural Change 12 (2).
DELLA CAVA, RALPH
    1966   History: the Northeast. In Robert Levine, ed., Brazil: a field
            guide in the social sciences. New York: Institute of Latin
            American Studies, Columbia University, 97–119.
DOXIADIS, CONSTANTINOS
    1963   Architecture in transition. London: Hutchinson.
ELKAN, WALTER
    1963   The dualistic economy of the Rhodesias and Nyasaland.
            Economic Development and Cultural Change 11 (4).
ELLSWORTH, P. T.
    1962   The dual economy: a new approach. Economic Develop-
            ment and Cultural Change 10 (4).
EPSTEIN, DAVID G.
    1969   A revolutionary lumpenproletariat? Monthly Review 21.
    1970   Urban squatting and revolution. Paper presented to the Sym-
            posium on Urban Squatter Settlements, Annual Meeting of
            the American Anthropological Association, San Diego, No-
            vember 19–22.

EPSTEIN, DILENE M.
1967   Os caminhões. Brasília, typescript.
FSS—FUNDACÃO DO SERVICO SOCIAL (BRASÍLIA)
No date. Breves conclusões do levantamento da Vila Dimas. Brasília,
ditto.
1964   Estimativa do número de desempregados no Distrito Federal.
        Brasília.
1965a   Aspectos demográficos e sócio-econômicos das invasões do
        Plano Pilôto de Brasília. Brasília, mimeograph.
1965b   Estimativa de sub-habitações. Brasília, mimeograph.
1965c   Aspectos demográficos e sócio-econômicos da cidade-satélite
        de Planaltina—DF. Brasília, ditto.
1965d   Aspectos demográficos e sócio-econômicos da invasão do
        I.A.P.I.—DF. Brasília, ditto.
1965e   Aspectos demográficos e sócio-econômicos do Núcleo Ban-
        deirante: 5a Avenida. Brasília, ditto.
1965f   Aspectos demográficos e sócio-económicos do Setor "D"
        (Vila Matias) do Núcleo Satélite de Taguatinga—DF. Bra-
        sília, ditto.
1967   Alguns dados da Invasão do I.A.P.I. Brasília, mimeograph.
FAORO, RAIMUNDO
1958   Os donos do poder: formação do patronato político bras-
        ileiro. Pôrto Alegre: Editôra Glôbo.
FOSTER, GEORGE M.
1961   The dyadic contract: a model for the social structure of a
        Mexican peasant village. American Anthropologist 63:
        1173–1192.
FRANK, ANDREW GUNDER
1964   On the mechanisms of imperialism—the case of Brazil. Ann
        Arbor, Michigan: Radical Education Project.
1967a   Capitalism and underdevelopment in Latin America: histori-
        cal studies in Chile and Brazil. New York: Monthly Review
        Press.
1967b   Sociology of development and underdevelopment of sociol-
        ogy. Catalyst (summer): 20–73.
FURTADO, CELSO
1963   The economic growth of Brazil. Berkeley: University of
        California Press. Translation of Formação econômica do
        Brasil.
GALVAO, HELIO
1959   O mutirão no Nordeste. Rio de Janeiro: Serviço de Infor-

mação Agrícola, Ministério da Agricultura.

GEIGER, PEDRO PINCHAS

1963   Evolução da rêde urbana brasileira. Rio de Janeiro: Centro
        Brasileiro de Pesquisas Educacionais.

GERLACH, LUTHER, and VIRGINIA HINE

1970   The social organization of a movement of revolutionary
        change: case study, black power. *In* Norman Whitten and
        John Szwed, eds., Afro-American Anthropology. New York:
        Free Press, 385–402.

GERMANI, GINO

1961   Inquiry into the effects of urbanization in a working-class sec-
        tor of Buenos Aires. *In* Philip Hauser, ed., Urbanization in
        Latin America. New York: International Documents Service,
        206–233.

GIL, GILBERTO, and CAETANO VELOSO

1967   No dia que eu vim-me embora. *On recording* Tropicália. Rio
        de Janeiro: Philips (Companhia Brasileira de Discos).

GLUCKMAN, MAX, ed.

1964   Closed systems and open minds: the limits of naivety in social
        anthropology. Edinburgh: Oliver.

GOLDRICH, DANIEL, and others

1966   The political integration of lower-class urban settlements in
        Chile and Peru. Paper presented to the Annual Meeting of
        the American Political Science Association, New York City.

GOODMAN, PAUL, and PERCIVAL GOODMAN

1947   Communitas: means of livelihood and ways of life. New
        York: Vintage.

GORDON, LINCOLN

1962   United States manufacturing investment in Brazil: the impact
        of Brazilian government policies, 1946–1960. Boston: Divi-
        sion of Research, Graduate School of Business, Harvard Uni-
        versity.

GREENFIELD, SIDNEY

1966   Patronage networks, factions, political parties and national
        integration in contemporary Brazilian society. Paper pre-
        sented at the annual meeting of the American Anthropological
        Association, Pittsburgh, Pennsylvania, November 17–20.

GROSS, DANIEL R.

1969   Sisal and social stagnation in Northeastern Brazil. New York,
        mimeograph.

HALPERIN, ERNST

1965   The decline of communism in Latin America. Atlantic
        Monthly, May, 65–70.

HARRIS, MARVIN
1956 Town and country in Brazil. New York: Columbia University Press.
1971 Culture, man and nature. New York: Crowell.

HERRICK, BRUCE H.
1966 Urban migration and economic development in Chile. Cambridge, Mass.

HIGGINS, BENJAMIN
1956 The "dualistic theory" of underdeveloped areas. Economic Development and Cultural Change 4 (2).

HIRSCHMANN, ALBERT O.
1963 Journeys toward progress. New York: Twentieth Century Fund.

HOETINK, H.
1965 El nuevo evolucionismo. América Latina 8 (4): 26–42.

HOLFORD, WILLIAM
1957 Brasília, a new capital city for Brazil. The Architectural Review 122: 394–402.

IBGE—INSTITUTO BRASILEIRO DE GEOGRAFIA E ESTATÍSTICA
1958 Enciclopédia dos municípios brasileiros: vol. 36, Goiás.

IANNI, OTAVIO
1965 Estado e capitalismo: estrutura social e industrialização no Brasil. Rio de Janeiro: Editôra Civilização Brasileira.

IMPRENSA NACIONAL (BRAZIL)
1948 Constituições do Brasil acompanhadas das emendas constitucionais e projetos. Rio de Janeiro.
1962 Coleção de Leis. Rio de Janeiro and Brasília.

JACOBS, JANE
1961 The death and life of great American cities. New York: Random House.

JAMES, PRESTON E., and SPERIDIAO FAISSOL
1956 The problem of Brazil's capital city. Geographical Review 46 (3): 301–317.

JORNAL DO BRASIL
Daily newspaper. Rio de Janeiro.

KUBITSCHEK DE OLIVEIRA, JUSCELINO
1962 A marcha do amanhecer. São Paulo: Bestseller Importadora de Livros S.A.
1966 Latin America today. Tucson, Arizona: The University of Arizona Annie W. Riecker Memorial Lecture Series, 11.

KUPER, LEO, and others
1958 Durban: a study in racial ecology. New York: Columbia University Press.

LAMBERT, JACQUES
1959   Os dois brasis. Rio de Janeiro: Centro Brasileiro de Pesquisas
       Educacionais.
LEEDS, ANTHONY
1964   Brazilian careers and social structure: an evolutionary model
       and case history. American Anthropologist 66: 1321–1347.
1966   Locality power in relation to supra-local power institutions.
       Rio de Janeiro, mimeograph.
1968   The anthropology of cities: some methodological issues. In
       Elizabeth Eddy, ed., Urban anthropology: research perspec-
       tives and strategies. Southern Anthropological Society,
       Athens, Georgia.
LEEDS, ANTHONY, and ELIZABETH LEEDS
1967   Brazil and the myth of urban rurality: urban experience,
       work and values in "squatments" of Rio de Janeiro and Lima.
       Paper presented at the Conference on Work and Urbaniza-
       tion in Modernizing Societies, St. Thomas, Virgin Islands,
       November 2–4.
LEWIS, OSCAR
1966   The culture of poverty. Scientific American (Oct.) 19–25.
LIEBOW, ELLIOT
1967   Talley's corner. Boston: Little, Brown.
LOCKER, MICHAEL
1968   Overseas expansion and government contracting: the story
       of Kaiser's global empire. NACLA Newsletter 2 (2): 1–5.
LOUZEIRO, JOSE, ed.
1965   Assim marcha a família. Rio de Janeiro: Editôra Civilização
       Brasileira.
LUDWIG, ARMIN
1966   The planning and creation of Brasilia: toward a new and
       unique regional environment? In N. Baklanoff, ed., New
       Perspectives of Brazil. Nashville: Vanderbilt University Press,
       179–204.
LYNCH, KEVIN
1960   The image of the city. Cambridge, Mass.: MIT Press.
McCLELLAND, DAVID
1961   The achieving society. Princeton, New Jersey: Van Nostrand.
MANDELL, PAUL
       In preparation. The impact of Brasília upon agriculture in southern
              Goiás. Ph.D. dissertation, Columbia University.
MANGIN, WILLIAM P.
1963   Urbanization case history in Peru. Architectural Design. Au-
       gust.

1964   Sociological, cultural and political characteristics of some rural Indians and urban migrants in Peru. Wenner-Gren Symposium on Cross-Cultural Similarities in the Urbanization Process, mimeograph.

1965   The role of social organization in improving the environment. *In* Environmental determinants of community well-being. Pan American Health Organization.

1967   Latin American squatter settlements: a problem and a solution. Latin American Research Review 2 (3) 65–98.

MAO TSE-TUNG

1937   On contradiction. *Reprinted in* Anne Freemantle, ed., Mao Tse-Tung: an anthology of his writings. New York: Mentor (1954).

MARTINS RAMOS, J. B.

No date. Brasília: a nova capital do Brasil. São Paulo: Edições Zenit.

MEDAGLIA, FRANCISCO

1959   Juscelino Kubitschek, President of Brazil: the life of a self-made man. New York: Brazilian Government Trade Bureau.

MEIRA PENNA, J. O.

1958   Quando mudam as capitais. Rio de Janeiro: Instituto Brasileiro de geografia e estatística.

MINTZ, SIDNEY

1951   Canamelar, the contemporary culture of a rural Puerto Rican proletariat. Ph.D. dissertation, Columbia University.

MUMFORD, LEWIS

1961   The city in history. New York: Harcourt, Brace and World.

NIEMEYER, OSCAR

1961   Minha experiencia em Brasília. Rio de Janeiro: Editôra Vitoria.

OGLESBY, CARL

1968   Yankees vs. cowboys. Guardian (New York), April 13, April 20, and April 27.

ORICO, OSVALDO

1958   Brasil, capital Brasília. Rio de Janeiro: Instituto Brasileiro de Geografia e Estatistica.

PDF—SEC—PREFEITURA DO DISTRITO FEDERAL-SECRETARIA DE EDUCAÇÃO E CULTURA

1965   Censo escolar do Distrito Federal 1964: resultados provisorios. Brasília.

PARSONS, TALCOTT

1961   Introduction to "Culture and the Social System." *In* Talcott Parsons and others, eds., Theories of Society; foundations of modern sociological theory, vol. 2. Glencoe, Illinois: The

Free Press, 963–993.

PASTORE, JOSÉ

1968 Satisfaction among migrants to Brasília, Brazil: a sociological interpretation. Doctoral dissertation in rural sociology, University of Wisconsin, Madison.

1969 Brasília: a cidade e o homen. São Paulo: Cia Editôra Nacional.

PEARSE, ANDREW

1961 Some characteristics of urbanization in the city of Rio de Janeiro. *In* Philip Hauser, ed., Urbanization in Latin America. New York: International Documents Service, 191–205.

PEATTIE, LISA

1966 Social issues in housing. Cambridge, Mass.: Joint Center for Urban Studies, mimeograph.

PENDRELL, NAN

1967 Exploratory study of the etiology of squatting in Salvador. Ph.D. dissertation, Columbia University.

PETRAS, JAMES, and MAURICE ZEITLIN

1968 Latin America: reform or revolution? New York: Fawcett.

PFEIFER, GOTTFRIED

1964 Quelques remarques a propos de Brasília. Caravelle 3: 386–390.

PRADO JUNIOR, CAIO

1966 A revolução brasileira. São Paulo: Editôra Braziliense.

PYE, LUCIAN W.

1963 The political implications of urbanization and the development process. *In* Social problems of development and urbanization. Washington, D.C.: U.S. Government Printing Office. Volume VII of Science, technology and development, United States papers prepared for the United Nations Conference on the Application of Science and Technology for the Benefit of the Less Developed Areas, 84–89.

QUIJANO OBREGON, ANIBAL

1968 Tendencies in Peruvian development and class structure. *In* Petras and Zeitlin 1968, 289–328.

REDFIELD, ROBERT

1930 Tepoztlan, a Mexican village. Chicago: University of Chicago Press.

1941 The folk culture of Yucatán. Chicago: University of Chicago Press.

1955 The little community. Chicago: University of Chicago Press.

RIZZINI, CARLOS TOLEDO

1962 Preliminares acerca das formações vegetais e do reflorestamento no Brasil Central. Rio de Janeiro: Servico do Informação Agrícola, Ministério da Agricultura.

RODRIGUES, CARLOS, ed.
1967   Anuário de Brasília. Brasília: Souvenir Publicidade Ltda.

RODWIN, LLOYD
1965   Urban planning in developing countries. Washington, D.C.: Department of Housing and Urban Development.

ROSTOW, WALT WHITMAN
1960   The stages of economic growth. Cambridge, U.K.: The Cambridge University Press.

ROTONDO, HUMBERTO, and others
1963   Un estudio comparativo de la conducta antisocial de menores en areas urbanas y rurales. *In* Estúdios de psiquiatría social. Lima.

RUELLAN, FRANCIS
1947   Relatório preliminar da primeira expedição geográfica ao Planalto Central. Manuscript.
1948   Quelques problèmes de l'expédition chargée de trouver des sites pour la nouvelle capitale féderale des Etats-Unis du Brésil. Bulletin de l'Association des Geographes Français (Mai-Juin): 194–195.

SSS—SECRETARIA DOS SERVICOS SOCIAIS (DISTRITO FEDERAL)
1967   Política de integração de uma população marginalizada. Brasília, mimeograph.

SAFA, HELEN
1964   From shantytown to public housing: a comparison of family structure in two urban neighborhoods in Puerto Rico. Carribean Studies 4: 3–12.

SALMEN, LAWRENCE F.
1966   Report on Vilas Kennedy and Esperança. Rio de Janeiro, typescript.

SAMANEIGO, RAMIRO
1967   Meios de comunicação e migração em Brasília: relatório preliminar de pesquisa realizada. Brasília, Façuldade de Comunicação da Universidade de Brasília, mimeograph.

SANJEK, R.
1969   Radical Anthropology: values, theory and content. Anthropology UCLA 1 (2): 21–32.

SANTOS, MILTON
1964   Brasília, a nova capital brasileira. Caravelle 3: 369–385.

SEERS, DUDLEY, ed.
1964   Cuba, the economic and social revolution. Chapel Hill, North Carolina: University of North Carolina Press.

SEMINÁRIO SOBRE A POLÍTICA DE INTEGRAÇÃO DE UMA POPULAÇÃO
    MARGINALIZADA
    1967   Conclusões do seminário. Brasília, mimeograph.
SERVAN-SCHREIBER, JEAN-JACQUES
    1968   The American challenge. Translated by Ronald Steel. New
            York: Atheneum.
SILVEIRA, PEIXOTO DA
    1957   A nova capital: por quê, para onde e como mudar a Capital
            Federal. São Paulo: Pongetti.
SOARES, GLAUCIO ABY DILLON
    1968   The new industrialization and the Brazilian political system.
            In Petras and Zeitlin 1968: 186–201.
STAVENHAGEN, RODOLFO
    1968   Seven fallacies about Latin America. In Petras and Zeitlin
            1968: 13–31.
STEWARD, JULIAN H.
    1955   The theory of culture change. Urbana, Illinois: The Univer-
            sity of Illinois Press.
    1956   The people of Puerto Rico. Urbana, Illinois: The University
            of Illinois Press.
TURNBULL, COLIN M.
    1962   The forest people. London: Chatto and Windus.
TURNER, JOHN F. C.
    1963   Dwelling resources in South America. Architectural Design.
            August.
    1966   Asentamientos urbanos no regulados. Cuadernos de la Socie-
            dad Venezolana de Planificación, 36
USAID—UNITED STATES AGENCY FOR INTERNATIONAL
    DEVELOPMENT
    1966   Missions proposal for 1967—Congressional submission.
            Washington, D.C.
VIDICH, ARTHUR, and JOSEPH BENSMAN
    1958   Small town in mass society. Princeton, New Jersey: Prince-
            ton University Press.
VINHAS DE QUEIROZ, MAURÍCIO
    1965   Os grupos multibilionários. Revista do Instituto de Ciências
            Sociais (Rio de Janeiro) 2 (1): 47–78.
WAGLEY, CHARLES, ed.
    1952   Race and class in rural Brazil. Paris: UNESCO.
WAGLEY, CHARLES
    1960   The Brazilian revolution: social change since 1930. In Rich-

ard N. Adams and others, Social change in Latin America. New York: Harper.

WATANABE, TSUNEHIKO
1965   Economic aspects of dualism in the industrial development of Japan. Economic Development and Cultural Change 13 (3).

WHITTEN, NORMAN, and JOHN SZWED
1968   Negroes in the New World: anthropologists look at Afro-Americans. Trans-Action 5 (8): 49–56.

WORSLEY, PETER
1969   Frantz Fanon: evolution of a revolutionary: revolutionary theories. Monthly Review 21 (1): 30–51.

INDEX